INITIAL BURDEN

An Account of the American and
British Naval Forces Present at the
Outset of the Korean War

Michael Steffan

Copyright © 2012 by Michael Steffan.

All rights reserved.

Made in the USA

Printed by CreateSpace: An Amazon Company

CreateSpace is a DBA of On-Demand Publishing LLC, part of the Amazon group of companies.

ISBN - 10: 1478288640

ISBN - 13: 978-1478288647

Library of Congress Control Number: 2012914255

Cover Photo: USS *Juneau* CLAA-119 anchored at Kagoshima, Japan. Naval Historical Center Photograph #NH 52364.

In memory of my parents

Michael Steffan 1916–1963
(on board USS Juneau 25 June 1950)

Anna Marie (Bucsko) Steffan 1926–1980

CONTENTS

Acknowledgments		ix
Introduction		xi
Prologue	A "Great Monster"	1
1.	Summer Cruise	13
2.	Housekeeping Command	29
3.	"[D]efend us in battle..."	45
4.	Fledgling Navies	57
5.	"[S]moke was observed..."	67
6.	First Things First	77
7.	First Lightning	89
8.	Naval Considerations	99
9.	Hornets' Nest	113
10.	Intel	123
11.	"Bow waves!"	137
12.	Yellow Sea	149
13.	Blockade	163
14.	Sea Control	177
15.	"[N]ecklace of gun flashes..."	189
16.	"[T]he...water had ceased falling"	207

Epilogue 1	Beyond the Nexus	223
Epilogue 2	New Names, New War	233
Postscript	Two Views	243
Bibliography		247
Image Credits		267
Index of Ships		275

ACKNOWLEDGMENTS

I am sincerely grateful to Richard and Michele Gidley for editing this manuscript. Their hard work improved the text immeasurably.

Thanks to William R. Parrett for reading a draft version of this document, challenging certain aspects of it, and offering insightful suggestions. I am also grateful to Dr. Gary Parrett, author of *Teaching the Faith, Forming the Faithful* and other titles, for his wise and sound counsel.

I am indebted to Robert Sitarzewski, owner of Robert's Computer Services (www.RobertsComputerServices.com), for his help with computer hardware and all aspects of the software programs used in relation to this project.

Thanks to Richard Bucsko and Dr. John Atkinson both of whom encouraged me to undertake this project by their thoughtful recognition of a previous biographical effort of mine.

Thanks also to the library staffs at the University of Washington in Seattle and the University of Puget Sound in Tacoma, Washington for their invaluable assistance in finding resources and suggesting others.

Any errors contained in the following narrative are mine alone.

Finally, thanks to my wife Becky and daughter Tori for helping me with this project at every step.

Introduction

The invasion of South Korea on 25 June 1950 came as a complete surprise to the West. The North Koreans attacked without warning and with such ferocity that it was unclear whether the Republic of South Korea would survive. Would the United States and its European and other allies come to the aid of South Korea? Would there still be enough time to affect the outcome if they did? Would the Soviet Union commit its military forces to assist its communist protégé? Had the Soviets already committed forces covertly? Would China become involved in the fighting?

One of the outcomes of the Second World War was the emergence of the "Cold War." By 1950, the Cold War with its confrontation of ideologies between East and West produced a nascent atomic arms race. The advent of the Korean War for the first time raised the specter that nuclear arms might become the weapon of choice. Concomitantly there was a growing realization that the use of atomic weaponry could not be the answer for all, if any, current or future confrontations.

When the conflict erupted, the post World War II navies of the United States and Great Britain had been dramatically reduced in size, strength, and perceived need. The limited U.S. and British naval forces that responded to the onslaught of the communist incursion had no human or signal intel regarding North Korea's war plan or the possible military intentions of the Soviet Union. The crisis was fraught with tension as the first days and weeks of the suddenly hot Cold War unfolded. From atomic considerations, evacuations, air and submarine threats, surface gunnery actions, sea-based airstrikes, shore bombardments, special ops, to amphibious landings and mine warfare, the naval forces present at the start of the war had to do it all in this eye-opening display of the vital importance of sea power.

Korea would be the first, but unfortunately not the last, of many incidents and crises in the last half of the 20th century where naval warships would be first on the scene. In the end, the actions taken by the American and British naval forces in the opening days of the war would prove crucial to South Korea's continued existence.

Lastly, the account is also a tribute and salute to those sailors who served on the ships that "steamed" into harm's way to render service to the cause of freedom at the beginning of the Korean War.

Michael Steffan
Tacoma, Washington
Completed 25 June 2012 — the Sixty-Second Anniversary of the Beginning of the Korean War

Korean Peninsula 1950 [1]

[1] Complete attribution for all images is provided beginning on page 267.

PROLOGUE

A "Great Monster"

Mid Watch 24 June 1950

Tsushima Patrol

A little after midnight, USS *De Haven*, was pushing southeast through the inky darkness, rain, and rising ocean swells in the Tsushima Strait, that runs between the southeastern tip of the Korean peninsula and the southern islands of Japan. *De Haven*, a Sumner class destroyer, had been monitoring the strait for ships attempting to smuggle contraband into Japan from the Asian mainland. This was a routine patrol performed by the U.S. Navy and its allies. It had been a standing operation since the Japanese were defeated in 1945 ending the war in the Pacific.[1]

De Haven was making for the port of Sasebo, Japan on that nation's southern island of Kyushu. The haze-gray American warship was cutting short her assignment because of reports of an approaching typhoon from the west in China's Yellow Sea. The 376-foot vessel was one of 58 Sumner class

---

[1] Tsushima Patrol: USS *De Haven*, War Diary, 24 June 1950, Operational Archives Branch, Naval Historical Center, Washington Navy Yard, DC; USS *De Haven*, "Deck Log," 24 June 1950, Operational Archives Branch, Naval Historical Center, Washington Navy Yard, DC; Geoffrey Hall, "A First Command – III," *The Naval Review,* 82, no. 1 (1994), 59.

destroyers built between 1943 and 1945.[2] *De Haven*, like all of her sister ships of that class, was notoriously top-heavy. This was because of a design that crowded three 50-ton gun mounts, each with twin 5-inch guns, one each fore and aft on her main deck and the third forward on her super structure deck. Mixing that kind of weight with an already heavy superstructure and a relatively narrow beam created a high center of gravity increasing the risk of the vessel "turning turtle" in extreme conditions of wind and sea.[3] The overall weight of the vessel, which varied because of fluctuating amounts of ammunition, fuel, and possible cargo on board at any given time also factored into an assessment regarding high winds and seas. If fuel tanks were emptier than not, then flooding the ballast tanks would be the proper approach to an advancing typhoon. The extra weight would allow the ship to ride much lower in the water protecting the vessel against heavy rolling. To ride out a storm of typhoon magnitude it was also standard practice to head directly into the teeth of the high winds and seas at a reduced speed.

December 1944 Typhoon

De Haven had been in a similar situation late in 1944. Commissioned in January of that year the new destroyer had made her way to the Pacific and a week before Christmas was performing escort duty for three fleet oilers as part of Admiral William Halsey's Third Fleet. A typhoon appeared on 17 December with winds reaching 140 miles

---

[2] General Sumner class destroyer information: "Allen M. Sumner Class," Destroyer History Foundation, http://destroyerhistory.org/ sumner-gearing class/sumnerclass (accessed 13 December 2011).

[3] Characteristics of Sumner class destroyer: James F. Dunnigan and Albert A. Nofi, *Victory at Sea: World War II in the Pacific*, (New York: Quill, William Morrow, 1995), 131.

per hour. Twenty four hours later one destroyer had capsized outright, a second had jammed its rudder and also capsized, while a third pitched to one side so far that she took water down her smoke stacks rendering the engines inoperable leaving the ship to roll over and sink in the extremely heavy seas. *De Haven*, 35 miles from the center of the typhoon, survived. Twenty-eight other warships were heavily damaged and in need of major repairs. Three destroyers sank *Hull*, *Spence*, and *Monaghan* with the loss of over 700 sailors.[4]

However, the seriousness of tangling with a typhoon and the negligible likelihood of smugglers attempting crossings from China to Japan in the severe weather made the decision to end the patrol an uncomplicated one for *De Haven's* commanding officer Oscar B. Lundgren. In *De Haven's* War Diary, the captain simply recorded that he was proceeding to Japan in order to "escape from the path of a typhoon whose predicted path will transverse the Tsushima area."[5] The destroyer continued her passage through heavy seas until well into the morning watch before reaching the channel leading to the relative safety of the harbor at Sasebo.[6]

---

[4] For a detailed description of the December 1944 typhoon see: C. Raymond Calhoun, *Typhoon, the Other Enemy: The Third Fleet and the Pacific Storm of December 1944*, (Annapolis, MD: US Naval Institute Press, 1981). The author, Charles Raymond Calhoun USN (Ret.), was the captain of a destroyer that came close to "turning turtle" during the typhoon.

[5] USS *De Haven*, War Diary, 24 June 1950.

[6] USS *De Haven*, Deck Log, 24 June 1950.

Pro-1 Sumner Class Destroyer in Heavy Seas

Sasebo, Japan

Sasebo's harbor was deep and long, ringed by high hills that afforded some natural protection from possible typhoon force winds. It was a large naval dockyard, the third most important in post-war Japan. The Japanese shipbuilding firm Sasebo Sempaku Kogyo (SSK) now operated the busy harbor, still noticeably scarred with damage from near the end of the Second World War. Sasebo now served as one of the American naval bases in Japan during the post-war occupation of that country. By 0830, *De Haven*, moored to floats in the harbor, was taking on fuel. An hour and a half later, on that threatening Saturday morning, she completed securing for typhoon weather.[7]

---

[7] Description of Sasebo in 1950: GHS, "Naval Operations in Korea," *The Naval Review*, 38, no. 4 (November 1950), 385.

Pro-2 HMS *Triumph* in the Far East 1950

British Carrier in the Sea of Japan

Later that morning two British warships, the light aircraft carrier *Triumph* and destroyer *Cossack*, departed Ominato, on the northern tip of Japan's central island of Honshu. *Triumph*, the centerpiece of the British Far East Fleet, and her escort were making their way south through the Sea of Japan on passage to the crown colony of Hong Kong. The ships' crews were dealing with the same reports of severe weather approaching from the southwest that had chased *De Haven* into port earlier that morning. The British crews labored to secure the ships against the predicted high winds. This effort included the double lashing of the aircraft on *Triumph* firmly to the flight deck.[8]

---

[8]HMS *Triumph* in the Sea of Japan: John R. P. Lansdown, *With the Carriers in Korea: the Fleet Air Arm Story 1950-1953*, (Vilmslow, Cheshire: Crecy Publishing, 1997), 12.

Geography and History of Korea

The peninsula of Korea is composed of mountains and more mountains covering two-thirds of the land. Where it is not outright mountainous, the terrain can otherwise be described as relentlessly hilly with a drab grayish brown hue to it and peculiarly lacking in vegetation and flowers. It is surrounded by over 3,500 small islands primarily along the south and east coasts. Korea is 600 miles long and, on average, about 150 miles wide.

Korea and the West had discovered each other through the shipwreck of a Dutch merchant ship along the Korean coast in the 16th century. Other than Catholic missionaries in the 17th and 18th centuries, Korea was, like Japan, isolationist in nature. It was not until the second half of the 19th century that trading with the West became more or less commonplace. It was in 1910 that the armed forces of the Japanese Empire turned the principally agrarian society of the Korean peninsula upside down. Japan occupied all of Korea until 1945. Japan's intent was to use Korea's land and resources to supply their burgeoning empire and concomitant population growth with food and other essentials. It was during this time that the Japanese, to achieve their ends, laid the foundation for Korea's modern national infrastructure. Japan built this foundation with the express purpose of expanding its economy and especially supplying the needs of its growing military. The Japanese built an extensive railroad system from Pyongyang in the north, the post-World War II capital of North Korea, to the seaport of Pusan on the southeastern tip of the peninsula in what is now South Korea. Additionally, roads and bridges were built linking remote towns and villages, which was no easy feat, given the unremitting up and down of Korea's topography. In particular, the rugged Taebaek Mountains, running north and south along the coastline of the Sea of

Japan, dominate the east coast of Korea. The mountain range literally hugs the shoreline. This forced the Japanese to tunnel through many of the mountainsides that covered the land to the water's edge in order to complete vital rail and road transportation links. Further, Japan improved many of the Korean seaports, especially Pusan, with the idea of shipping raw materials home, while at the same time providing suitable harbors and anchorages for the Imperial Japanese Navy.

The infrastructure allowed Japan to transport the rich harvests of rice, fish, timber, coal, and iron ore from Korea. After the worldwide Great Depression, Japan increased the production of fertilizer, chemicals, steel, and munitions for transport back to the home islands using the subjugated indigenous Korean labor force. Possession of the peninsula with its location and transportation network provided a key geographic advantage by which Japan could move its Army, equipment, and supplies quickly to confront its major mainland rival, China.[9]

Creation of North and South Korea

By 1945, in the closing days of the War in the Pacific, the Japanese Empire was in a total state of collapse. The United States and the Soviet Union, in their new roles as emerging superpowers, bilaterally agreed to split the Korean peninsula in half using the 38th Parallel as a north south divide in order to create two zones of control. The United States would control the southern half and the Soviets the

---

[9] Korean topography and infrastructure: Sandy Sandler, ed., *The Korean War: an Encyclopedia*, (New York: Garland Publishing, 1995), s.v. "Topography and Terrain;" Raymond B. Maurstad, *SOS Korea 1950 Illustrated*, (Edina, MN: Beaver Pond Press, 2003), 4.

northern. This arrangement was for the express purpose of rounding up and accepting the surrender of Japanese Army troops abandoned and thus stranded on the Korean peninsula. The two zones also served to keep the Soviet and American forces at arms lengths even though outwardly allies. As part of the Allied plan for post-war Asia, North and South Korea, creations of this practical expediency, were at the time not intended to remain separated but rather reunited. However, with the onset of the Cold War it became clear that a peaceful re-unification between the rapidly developing communist state in the north and a western-style democracy in the south was not going to occur.

By the time the Soviet Union pulled their military forces out in 1949, North Korea possessed a professionally trained and well-equipped native fighting force of over 100,000 soldiers. The North Koreans also possessed heavy artillery, armor, and an air force with more than 100 combat aircraft at their disposal. The United States Army had also left South Korea in that same year, but its military legacy was a South Korean Army that was smaller in size (eight divisions totaling less than 65,000 men) possessing little heavy artillery, armor, or military aircraft.

Korean born Kim Il-Sung, who had fought against the Japanese during their occupation, both for the Chinese communists and later for the Soviet Union, handpicked by Joseph Stalin, lead the new regime in North Korea known as the Democratic People's Republic of Korea (DPRK). His opposite in the South was Syngman Rhee born in Korea but educated in the United States, receiving a Ph.D. at Princeton. Upon his return to Seoul at the end of the war he entered politics and backed by the United States became head of the South Korean government known as the Republic of Korea (ROK). Both Kim and Rhee quickly became autocrats and did everything they could to eliminate all political opposition in their respective countries. In 1948, Kim Il-Sung began secretly seeking the approval of his communist mentor and ally, Joseph Stalin, for his plan to invade and re-unite North and South Korea on his terms. Stalin rebuffed the North Korean leader more than once. During the same period, the United States denied requests for substantial military weapons and equipment by Syngman Rhee precisely because Washington feared he would use them to attempt to subdue the North. Then in what some have since considered a surprising turn of events, Kim finally secured Stalin's go-ahead for an invasion in April 1950. The North Korean leader promised the Soviet leader that the attack would be swift and lethal and that he would seize the South Korean capital of Seoul in just three days. With the approval for the forced re-unification of North and South Korea in hand, preparations for the invasion began in earnest and with immediacy. The date was set for Sunday, 25 June.[10]

Great Monster of War

The first six months of 1950 had seen an unusually high number of typhoons form in the Yellow and East China Seas. The typhoon designated "Elsie," by western meteorologists, would veer from its projected path during the afternoon of 24 June and end up missing the British warships heading

---

[10] Soviet Union approves North Korean invasion: Richard C. Thornton, *Odd Man Out: Truman, Stalin, Mao, and the Origins of the Korean War*, (Washington DC: Brassey's Inc., 2001), 110; David Rees, "Reckless War-Making: Review of Sergei N. Goncharov et al's Uncertain Partners: Stalin, Mao and he Korean War," *National Interest* (December 1995), http://www.nationalinterest.org/general.aspxid=92&id2=11338 (accessed 11 November 2008).

INITIAL BURDEN

south through the Sea of Japan and the port of Sasebo, due east, where *De Haven* had sought refuge. That caprice of nature would be the last bit of good fortune experienced by American and British naval units in the Far East for a while. Another type of typhoon, a "great monster," as the Greek mythology of the root of the word suggests, was stealthily approaching the Korean peninsula. Ironically, the British, since the 19th century, had referred to Korea as the "Land of Morning Calm."[11]

It was the next day in the early hours of Sunday morning, 25 June 1950 that the North Korean People's Army (NKPA), also known as the "In Min Gun," poured across the 38th parallel border and attacked an unsuspecting South Korean Army. All along the border from the Yellow Sea in the west to the Sea of Japan in the east, the NKPA using surprise, cunning, heavy artillery, armor, and air power smashed headlong into the South Korean defensive formations and positions. The smaller and outmatched ROK units immediately began to reel and fall back at a frightful pace. The mythological hundred-headed fire-breathing "great monster" of war had come to the Korean peninsula that day. Moreover, it would be 1,096 days and an estimated 4 million killed and wounded on both sides (half of them

---

[11] "Land of the Morning Calm": The Chinese since the middle ages have called the Korean peninsula "Joseon" and "Chaohsien" meaning "morning freshness" because of the spectacular natural beauty of the picturesque high mountains. The translation to English most often was rendered as "morning calm."

civilians) until it departed, unsatisfied, with an eye to returning.[12]

---

[12] Total number of soldiers and civilians killed and wounded attributed to the Korean War: *The Unabridged Hutchinson Encyclopedia*. S.v. "Korean War casualties." Retrieved April 5 2012 from http://encyclopedia.farlex.com/Korean+War+casualties (accessed 5 April 2012).

Chapter 1

Summer Cruise

Sunday Evening 25 June

HMS *Belfast*

As was customary on Sunday evenings many of the crew of HMS *Belfast* were relaxing and viewing a movie on board the 613 foot British cruiser as she rode at anchor in northern Japanese waters. As the cinema (as the British called it) rolled on, word was received alerting the ship to the commencement of hostilities on the Korean peninsula.

1-1 HMS *Belfast*

Anchored in the harbor at the port city of Hakodate located in the center of the Kameda peninsula on the Japanese island of Hokkaido, *Belfast* was the flagship for the British Far East fleet. *Belfast's* plan had been to join HMS *Jamaica*, another British cruiser, up the coast in Ominato not far from where they were. The news of the invasion changed everything.

Together the two ships made up the British 5th Cruiser Squadron and their presence in these northern Japanese waters was part of what the Admiralty at Whitehall in London termed their "summer cruise." The summer cruise this particular year was a combination of "showing the flag" and surveying the deep-water bay at Ominato as a possible permanent summer anchorage for the Far East Fleet. The seriousness of the military reports caused *Belfast* to change her plan of rendezvousing with *Jamaica*. She instead weighed anchor a little after midnight and steamed south for Yokosuka, located on the central Japanese island of Honshu.[1]

Laid down in 1937 and launched on St. Patrick's Day the following year, Prime Minister Neville Chamberlain's wife Anne christened the new cruiser *Belfast* after the capital of Northern Ireland. Completed on 3 August 1939, just a month before Great Britain's declaration of war on Germany, she displaced 10,500 tons and carried twelve 6-inch guns mounted in triple-gunned turrets, two forward and two aft.

---

[1] Whereabouts and goings on on board HMS *Belfast* on 25 June 1950 including "summer cruise" and "cinema" references: GHS, "Naval Operations in Korea," 382; Bentley (Pseudonym), "HMS *Belfast* in Korea," *The Naval Review*, Vol. 38, No. 4, November 1950, 374; John Hegarty, "HMS *Jamaica*: Korean War Service 1950," Britains Small Wars, http://www.britains-smallwars.com/Korea/*Jamaica*2.htm (accessed 5 September 2007).

The British cruiser had an inauspicious beginning to her career. *Belfast* and three other cruisers sailed from Rosyth, Scotland through the Firth of Forth, on 21 November 1939 in an endeavor to engage German warships reportedly attempting to move from the Baltic Sea into the Atlantic in order to attack British convoys. However, shortly after her departure she struck a German planted magnetic mine. The ensuing concussion and explosion whipped the ship's keel, essentially breaking her back. Badly crippled, *Belfast* managed to limp back to Rosyth where temporary corrective repairs began. While at Rosyth, further inspection revealed serious structural issues in addition to the obvious extensive hull damage caused by the mine blast. The new but now wounded cruiser would need to be moved to Devonport where in dry-dock her considerable damage could be properly addressed. It took six months to complete even the provisional repairs that allowed the towing of the cruiser to Devonport for what turned out to be a major restoration effort. *Belfast* remained in Devonport for over two years before finally rejoining the fleet in 1942.[2]

HMS *Jamaica*

Belfast notified *Jamaica,* the other member of the British Far East Fleet's 5th Cruiser Squadron, of the invasion. Anchored in Ominato bay, a well-protected deep-water inlet on the northern most point of Mutsu Bay on the island of Hokkaido, *Jamaica* was a British Fiji Class cruiser of 8,500 tons. Constructed between 1939 and 1942, she was the sixth major British warship to carry the name. *Jamaica*,

---

[2] The mining and repair of HMS *Belfast*: Gordon Smith, "HMS *Belfast*," Naval-History.net, http://www.naval-history.net/xGM-Chrono-06CL-*Belfast*.htm, (accessed 23 March 2009).

somewhat smaller than *Belfast,* at 8,500 tons and 555 feet in length, carried nine 6-inch guns (she originally carried twelve 6-inch guns but one of her triple-gunned turrets had been removed late in 1944, replaced with anti-aircraft guns). She made 32 knots carrying a peacetime compliment of 733 officers and sailors that increased to 900 men during time of war.[3]

1-2 HMS *Jamaica* in WW2 Camouflage

Battle of North Cape

Jamaica and *Belfast* had seen action together before. Just as fate brought these ships together in late June 1950 in Korea, they had also crossed paths during 1943 in the frigid waters in the extreme latitudes of the North Atlantic. It occurred in the icy Arctic waters above Norway. Germany, earlier in the war, had overrun Norway and subsequently moved a number of its heavier warships to some of that country's most northern fjords to act as a deterrent to

---

[3] HMS *Jamaica* specifications: S. L. Poole, *Cruiser: a History of British Cruisers from 1889-1960,* (London: Robert Hale, 1970), 195; M. J. Whitely, *Cruisers of World War 2: An International Encyclopedia,* (London: Arms and Armour Press, 1996); Francis E. McMurtrie, and Raymond V. B. Blackman, editors, *Jane's Fighting Ships 1949-1950,* (New York: McGraw Hill, 1949), 30; Hegarty, "HMS *Jamaica,*" n.p.; Smith, "HMS *Jamaica,*" n.p.

British convoys between the United Kingdom and the Soviet Union.

1-3 Altenfjord and North Cape

On 20 December 1943, an Allied convoy of 19 ships sailed from Loch Ewe, Scotland for the Soviet Union's northern port of Murmansk, via the Arctic Ocean route, around the top of Norway. The British battleship *Duke of York* and the cruiser *Jamaica,* along with four destroyers, were providing cover for the convoy. Coming in the opposite direction from Russia was a return Allied convoy of another 19 ships. Three British cruisers *Belfast, Norfolk*, and *Sheffield*, were covering the return convoy. The westbound convoy, like the outbound convoy from Great Britain, in addition to the cruisers had four destroyers also providing cover.

German intelligence not only ascertained the sailing dates of the two convoys but also calculated when and where they would pass each other going in opposite directions. Much to their excitement, they discovered that the convergence point for the two convoys would be extremely close to Altenfjord in the frozen northern reaches of Norway. The German Navy had placed one of their most menacing warships in that anchorage waiting for such an opportunity.

1-4 German Battlecruiser SNS *Scharnhorst* in Action

On Christmas day, the German battlecruiser *Scharnhorst* displacing 32,000 tons and possessing nine powerful 11-inch guns received the order to intercept and destroy the convoys. On Christmas evening at 1900 hours, *Scharnhorst*, accompanied by five destroyers, sortied from Altenfjord.

In the icy fjord, with her mess deck still gaily decorated with traditional German Christmas ornamentation, the powerful warship worked up to speed as she pushed into open seas.

The next morning, Boxing Day in Great Britain, in very poor weather and heavy seas, the German battlecruiser and her attendant destroyers failed to find either the westbound or the eastbound British convoys. At 0730, *Scharnhorst* ordered her destroyers to detach and search further to the west. The destroyers headed out in search of the east bound convoy but once again, they were unable to detect the British. Later that day, the German destroyers would return to their base at Altenfjord, as the weather worsened.

As *Scharnhorst* continued to move north in search of the westbound convoy, *Belfast* and *Norfolk's* radars detected her. She was no longer the hunter, but the hunted. *Belfast* and the other two cruisers were to the northeast of *Scharnhorst's* position. *Belfast*, determining that the German battlecruiser was within range, fired an illumination shell because of the terrible visibility, exposing the German battlecruiser, and allowing *Norfolk* to open fire. The British cruiser's 8-inch shells quickly straddled *Scharnhorst* as they began finding their mark.[4] Stung by the quickness with which the British cruisers had found her range the German warship came about increased speed and began to run to the south. With her 11-inch guns, *Scharnhorst* could easily outrange and hit with more power any one of the three British cruisers. Nevertheless, the three cruisers together posed a problem for the larger German warship. *Scharnhorst* could not take them all on at once without the support of her destroyers who were now far away to the west. At 32 knots, compared to the British cruisers 24 knots,

---

[4] In the process of firing at an enemy ship, when some shell splashes are observed falling just beyond the target and some just short of it the mean point of impact is usually "on" the target and the ship thus "straddled" is being hit.

and in poor sea conditions, *Scharnhorst* was able to move away rapidly from her British pursuers.

Not willing to give up the pursuit, *Belfast* radioed *Duke of York* and *Jamaica*, covering the eastward bound convoy, of *Scharnhorst's* discovery and present course. *Duke of York*, *Jamaica* and their destroyers changed course and moved toward the German battlecruiser from the southwest. Meanwhile back to the northeast, around noon, *Belfast* reacquired radar contact with *Scharnhorst*. This time all three cruisers were in position to fire and did not hesitate. *Scharnhorst* returned fire and hit *Norfolk*. Once again, using her advantage in speed, she managed to move away from her foes retiring again further to the south.

At 1650, as *Scharnhorst* was still attempting to escape, she found herself caught between the *Belfast* force to the northeast and the *Duke of York* and *Jamaica* force coming up from the southwest. The weather continued to deteriorate and night was settling in. Only the weather might still save *Scharnhorst*. In the dark snow filled sky *Belfast*, again using illumination shells, exposed the German battlecruiser. In the ensuing melee, *Scharnhorst,* struck repeatedly and extensively damaged by gunfire from multiple directions, could no longer achieve speeds necessary for a possible escape. The damage received from shellfire slowly reduced her speed to just five knots. *Scharnhorst,* now listing and her guns reduced to wreckage, awaited her fate.

The destroyers moved in to finish her off. At 1930 *Scharnhorst,* riddled with torpedo hits, capsized and slipped beneath the waves. The British destroyers in the extreme wintery conditions were only able to rescue 36 German sailors of a compliment of 1,963. The surface action would go down in history as the Battle of North Cape.[5]

Six and a half years later in the northern waters of Japan, *Belfast* and *Jamaica* found themselves facing a crisis that was completely unforeseen and possibly quite dangerous. Following orders from flagship *Belfast*, *Jamaica* sailed from Ominato to southern Japanese waters early that morning of the 26th.

Royal Navy in Decline

By 1950, British sea power was in serious decline. At the end of the Second World War the British Empire had survived but at a terrible financial and economic cost. Beginning the post-war era Britain confronted the reality that it did not possess anywhere near the revenues necessary to maintain a navy commensurate with British interests around the world. Winston Churchill at the Yalta Conference in 1945, having heard Stalin demand the Kurile Islands located just north of Japan as part of an agreement for the Soviets to enter the war against the Japanese Empire, conceded saying that such matters in the Far East were now, on the whole, "an American affair." He further added that to Great Britain the issue was "remote and secondary."[6] In 1946, the new British Prime Minister,

---

[5] Battle of North Cape: Correlli Barnett, *Engage the Enemy more Closely: The Royal Navy in the Second World War*, (New York: W. W. Norton, 1991), 739-744; British Imperial War Museum, "Battle of the North Cape," in History of HMS *Belfast*, British Imperial War Museum, http://hms*Belfast*.iwa.org.uk, n.p. (accessed 23 March 2009);Gordon Smith, "Battle of North Cape," Naval-History, http://www.naval-history.net/Cr03-56-00NorthCape.htm, n.p. (accessed 23 March 2009).

[6] Churchill quotes "an American affair" and "remote and secondary" are cited in: Paul Johnson, *Modern Times: the World from the Twenties to the Nineties*, (New York: HarperPerennial, 1992), 430.

INITIAL BURDEN

Clement Attlee, said that his country had to recognize that the U.S. Navy was now the dominant naval power in the world. In 1947, a defense paper noted that a major military threat to British interests in the Far East at that time was remote. More importantly, it pointed out that in the event of a crisis the United States, not Great Britain, would have to deal with it. Finally, a British inter-service report in 1949 stated that in the event of a large-scale war, Britain could and would count on the American Navy.[7]

The fact was the Royal Navy in 1950, as one British historian put it, was "no longer permitted by its political masters to even make the pretense of having a role as the world's policeman."[8] Two incidents that occurred in the Far East in 1949 best exemplified the diminished position of British sea power. The first episode involved the British frigate *Amethyst* in China. *Amethyst* received orders to move up the Yangtze River to Nanking. There she was to relieve the destroyer *Consort,* charged with protecting the British Embassy and business community, as the Chinese Civil War between the communists and the nationalists intensified. Before *Amethyst* could reach Nanking, Chinese communist batteries, located about 60 miles downstream from the city, opened fired on her. Under fire, *Amethyst* ran aground with 17 men killed and ten wounded. Upon receiving the news of the attack on *Amethyst*, *Consort* made ready and then proceeded down river from Nanking to rescue the grounded frigate. Upon her arrival at the scene of the attack, she too came under fire killing nine more British sailors. The cruiser

---

[7] Other examples of the decline of British sea power: Eric Grove, *Vanguard to Trident: British Naval Policy since World War II*, (Annapolis, Maryland: U.S. Naval Institute, 1987), 8, 33, 47-48.

[8] Desmond Wettern, *The Decline of British Seapower*, (London: Jane's, 1982), 26.

INITIAL BURDEN

London and frigate *Black Swan* attempted to rescue *Amethyst* the following day but Chinese communist gunfire killed 15 more men and wounded 22 on board the two ships.

Meanwhile, back in London, Clement Attlee, the Prime Minister and Labor Party leader, who had replaced Churchill as the head of the British government, was attempting to convince the Chinese by a speech in Parliament that the Royal Navy's attempt to rescue the stricken frigate was not in any way a "punitive expedition." He further added that the "[British] ships fired only to silence the forces firing against them." Attlee intended to ameliorate the Chinese with the speech. Sadly, the reality was abundantly clear that the mission was non-punitive because it was the British Navy receiving all of the punishment! The British, reduced to this sort of rhetoric, quite simply could not adequately address situations along these lines because of the Royal Navy's diminished naval capacity.[9]

1-5 HMS *Amethyst* in 1949

Aground and pinned down, *Amethyst* finally made a daring escape without help several weeks later in what was indeed

---

[9] Attlee's "punitive expedition" remark: Ibid., 15.

INITIAL BURDEN

an implausible episode in British naval history. Upon reaching the mouth of the Yangtze and then into open water the *Amethyst* famously signaled, "Have rejoined the fleet. No damage or casualties. God save the King."[10] Later, "Yangtze Incident" a major motion picture produced in 1957 told the incredible story to a somewhat shocked British and world audience.[11]

The other episode showing the decline of British naval power also occurred in China and involved the frigate *Black Swan*. While the *Amethyst* affair was still unfolding, Chinese nationalist aircraft bombed the British Blue Funnel cargo ship *Anchises* in the Whang-poo River. Unable to help the cargo ship because she had been ordered not to enter Communist-controlled territorial waters, *Black Swan* instead "*observed* the incident" [emphasis added].[12]

Because of these events in the Far East during 1949, *Jamaica* along with the aircraft carrier *Triumph*, then serving in the Mediterranean, joined the Far East Fleet in that "distant station" of Singapore. Shortly after, another aircraft carrier, *Unicorn*, taken out of reserve, made passage to the Far East to support *Triumph*. This augmentation of

---

[10] *Amethyst's* captain's quote "...God save the King": Ibid., 16.

[11] Information related to the motion picture can be found here: Wikipedia, "Yangtze Incident:" http://en.wikipedia .org/wiki/Yangtse_ Incident_ (1957_film), (accessed 12 December 2010). Interestingly, for the shooting of the film, *Amethyst* was brought out of the reserve to add to the realism. However, by 1957 her main engines were no longer operational. She was used for many scenes, but those involving the ship moving and firing her guns were handled by one of her sister ships, *Magpie*.

[12] The British Blue Funnel cargo ship *Anchises* incident in 1949 and "observed the incident" remark are from: Wettern, *Decline of British Seapower*, 26.

the Far East Fleet came at the expense of the British Mediterranean Fleet, which found itself without the service of an aircraft carrier. In 1947, the Attlee government had inadvertently foreshadowed the move of the British carriers from the Med to the Far East when the Prime Minister informed American President Truman that the Royal Navy could no longer maintain responsibility for the welfare of Greece and Turkey against communist aggression. The United States, in turn, established the Sixth Fleet in the Mediterranean.[13]

The British Navy between 1945 and 1950 had gone from being a navy with an offensive mind-set to one that focused on the defensive. It had forgone developments in amphibious assaults. It now concentrated on keeping the seas open for British trade by defensive anti-submarine warfare advances. It had consciously rejected the idea of using aircraft carriers as an offensive weapon by not supporting fleet or attack aircraft carrier development as it had up until the end of the Second World War. It purposefully now used only "light" carriers with limited offensive capabilities. All of this might have been different had the British not been financially ruined by the world war.

British Far East Fleet

The Royal Navy itself, in the summer of 1950, although materially wanting, still possessed the will and the mettle of its long and storied past. It was simply a matter of whether the navy would ever get a chance to exhibit it again. During

---

[13] Increasing the size of the Far East Fleet at the expense of the Mediterranean Fleet: Daniel Yergin, *Shattered Peace: the Origins of the Cold War and the National Security State*, (Boston: Houghton Mifflin, 1977), 280; Johnson, *Modern Times*, 467.

the Second World War, British naval forces in the Western Pacific, were designated the "Pacific Fleet" and based in Hong Kong. Due to the many serious setbacks the British suffered at the hands of the Japanese during the conflict, it took until 1947 for the Royal Navy to reestablish this distant station. It was then that the Pacific Fleet was renamed the "Far East Fleet" and moved to a new homeport at Singapore.

The British Far East Fleet, at the beginning of the Korean War, totaled 22 Royal Navy warships and auxiliary vessels. The ships were scattered here and there, along the Asian coastline, at the outbreak of the crisis, but the majority of the ships were concentrated in Japanese waters. The main units consisted of the aircraft carrier *Triumph*, cruisers *Belfast* (flag) and *Jamaica*, destroyers *Cossack*, *Consort*, *Comus*, *Cockade*, as well as frigates *Black Swan*, *Alacrity*, and *Hart* (the British referred to them as sloops). *Unicorn*, the second British carrier, played only a supporting role, including ferrying aircraft between Singapore and Japan for *Triumph*. Overall, there were more British warships in close proximity to the Korean peninsula than there were American warships available on 25 June.

It was the beginning of the rainy season and after slogging south through a stormy night *Belfast* arrived at Yokosuka Monday, the 26th. Later that day, the British met with their American counterparts. Upon the conclusion of the meeting with the U.S. Navy, and awaiting further instruction from the Admiralty in London, the British decided to relocate the dispersed elements of the Far East Fleet in Kure, further southwest on Japan's central island. There they would refuel and replenish stores. The purpose was first, to concentrate the fleet in one spot closer to the conflict and second and a bit more ominously, to move further away from Soviet naval and air power less than 600 miles to the northwest across the Sea of Japan at Vladivostok on the Asian mainland.[14]

1-6 Japan

Originally heading south to Hong Kong through the Sea of Japan *Triumph*, the British aircraft carrier, had received orders from the flagship *Belfast* to make for Kure in Japan.

---

[14] General information regarding the "Far East Fleet" and the British decision to move units to Kure, Japan: Grove, *Vanguard to Trident*, 127; Walter Karig, Malcolm W. Cagle, and Frank A. Manson, *Battle Report: the War in Korea*, (New York: Rhinehart, 1952), 35.

Ironically, *Triumph's* movement to Hong Kong was only the first in a series of planned stops on the way back to Great Britain in order to replace the two squadrons of Seafires and Fairley Fireflies on board with more advanced aircraft. Upon notification of the outbreak of hostilities, *Triumph* began maintaining a "flight" of three fully armed Seafires (a carrier-based prop-driven fighter) on her flight deck in order to be ready for any eventuality. Also the British Fireflies on board the light carrier (an older carrier-based prop-driven fighter that doubled as a ground attack aircraft), stepped up their flight drills. While en-route to Kure one of the Fireflies, which were notorious for bouncing upon landing, skipped over the arresting wires on the flight deck and crashed into the plane barrier that protects other planes further forward on the flight deck from runaway landing aircraft. As the different teams on board *Triumph* dealt with the damaged aircraft and the rest of the men on board mused about the news from Korea, one crewman wryly noted to his mates that this was clearly the end of their "summer cruise."[15]

---

[15]*Triumph* ordered to Kure: Tony O'Toole, "The Forgotten Cruise, HMS *Triumph* and the 13th Carrier Air Group, The First Royal Navy Carrier Force in the Korean War, June-September 1950," http://royalnavy researcharchive.org.uk/article_forgotten_cruise.htm, (accessed 31 January 2011); Lansdown, *With the Carriers in Korea*, 12-13.

Chapter 2

Housekeeping Command

USS *Pledge*

USS *Pledge* slowly maneuvered through the inner harbor of the Yokosuka Naval Base. The former Imperial Japanese Naval headquarters now served as the main American naval base in post-war Japan with a group of ships ported there designated U.S. Naval Forces Far East. It was located at the entrance of Tokyo Bay 43 miles south of the heart of Tokyo itself. *Pledge* was a steel-hulled Admirable class minesweeper that weighed 625 tons, operated with twin screws, and had a high bridge with a tall tripod mast. Moreover, although she was 184 feet in length, the class was without a conventional tall funnel, and therefore always looked somewhat smaller than she actually was. After her launch in 1943, she served the last year of the Pacific War in the Japanese theater. Against the backdrop of post-war cutbacks and alternating American naval needs, the minesweeper *Pledge* was commissioned and decommissioned twice, and re-commissioned a third time between the end of the war and June 1950.

The minesweeper had excellent sea-keeping characteristics. These qualities allowed her to maintain station in some of the roughest of seas and weather, an obvious plus for the business of clearing mines.

The pulsing sound of *Pledge*'s engines on Sunday morning 25 June was interrupted momentarily as a solitary puff of white smoke rose from her short stack. The Admirable class sweepers were somewhat prone to this phenomenon and it meant that there was a chance one of the engines would seize, occasionally resulting in serious damage. However, in this instance, *Pledge's* starboard engine was able to re-establish its rhythm as the sweeper continued across the inner harbor to her berth. Because of this mechanical issue, whenever *Pledge* refueled, the crew always made the request to those working on the fuel dock not to pump anything from the bottom of the tank to avoid residue or possible water contamination that might damage these sometimes-troublesome engines.

2-1 Admirable Class Steel-Hulled Minesweeper

Pledge and her crew had returned to Yokosuka that morning after performing check-sweeping operations between Kure and Kobe on the Inland Sea between the big island of Honshu and the southern island of Kyushu. Check-sweeping involved looking for possible moored mines left over from the war missed in previous clearing operations. *Pledge* had once again completed her duties in this regard and now needed to take care of some small maintenance issues. The crew, for their part, was looking forward to some down time and in particular a little shore liberty.[1]

U.S. Navy in Post-war Japan

Following the conclusion of the war in the Pacific, the U.S. Navy's mission changed from defeating the Imperial Japanese Navy to performing duties associated with the formal occupation of that country. The American Navy's role in this effort was quite extensive.

Immediately upon the war's end, the U.S. Navy helped repatriate thousands of Japanese soldiers and dependents by transporting them from the mainland of Asia and countless South Pacific islands back to their homeland. Once that task was completed, the U.S. Navy oversaw the demilitarizing and scrapping of Japanese warships and equipment. After that, there was the monitoring and inspection of Japan's shipbuilding industry to assure that the Japanese could not exploit it for future military purposes.

American minesweepers took on the monumental task of clearing mines laid by the Japanese, especially near the end of the war. The Imperial Japanese Navy had sown upwards

---

[1]Admirable class minesweepers: Malcolm W Cagle and Frank A. Manson, *The Sea War in Korea*, (Annapolis, Maryland: U.S. Naval Institute, 1957), 128; H. T. Lenton, *American Gunboats and Minesweepers*, Series: World War 2 Fact File, (New York: Arco, 1974), 47; Robert Gardiner and Roger Chesneau, *Conway's All the World's Fighting Ships 1922-1946*, (Annapolis, Maryland: U.S. Naval Institute Press, 2001), 151; Tamara Moser Melia, *Damn the Torpedos: A Short History of U.S. Naval Mine Countermeasures, 1777-1991*, Contributions to Naval History, no. 4, (Washington D.C.: Naval Historical Center, Department of the Navy, 1991), 70.

of 10,000 mines in the ocean approaches to Japan and another 55,000 mines in the inland sea between the islands of Honshu and Kyushu. By 1950 the unenviable and dangerous task of sweeping these mines was finally winding down, thus re-opening sea-lanes for commerce.

Now the occupation of Japan had extended into the summer of 1950 and the U.S. Navy had found itself focusing more and more on smuggling operations in and around Japan. Patrolling for pirate and smuggling activity extended as far south as the Ryukyus Islands (Okinawa) to the Tsushima Straits between Japan and Korea as well as in the home waters around the island of Hokkaido.

Another item of business was the continued practice by U.S. Naval Forces Far East of the age-old naval diplomatic tradition of "showing the flag" in Japanese ports. At the same time, American warships in Japan had to participate in annual and special naval training exercises. Regarding South Korea, the U.S. Navy's only task was to provide some logistical support for the small American contingent of advisors to that country.[2]

To accomplish all of this work the U.S. Navy needed working port facilities. Therefore, they turned their efforts to building up and maintaining such former Imperial Japanese naval bases as Yokosuka and Sasebo for their own pressing operational needs.

---

[2] U.S. naval mission in Japan: Ingram, M.D., "U.S. Navy in Japan 1945-1950," United States Naval Institute *Proceedings*. Volume 78, (April 1952) 378-383; Cagle and Manson, *Sea War in Korea*, 31; Karig, Cagle, and Manson, *Battle Report*, 36; Michael T. Isenberg, *Shield of the Republic: In an Era of Cold War and Violent Peace 1945-1962*, (New York: St. Martin's Press, 1993), 179.

Yokosuka Naval Base, the largest in Japan, had been the main facility for supporting the Imperial Japanese Navy throughout the War in the Pacific. In 1950, the base was the main port for U.S. Naval Forces Far East. Soon after the end of the war, many of the victorious Allied countries received much of the machinery and equipment associated with the harbor work as part of post-war reparations. However, the U.S. Navy quickly realized that with their occupation duties in post-war Japan they would need to support their own warships and so began to rebuild and improve the naval base. They constructed repair terminals, machine shops, and quarters for personnel. They repaired some of the larger dry-docks and installed cranes capable of serving the American naval warships. They even constructed a small one hundred-bed hospital.

2-2 Essex Class Carrier at Yokosuka Receiving Aircraft Later in the War with Mount Fuji in the Background

Nevertheless, at the time of the outbreak of the Korean War the base was still wanting in many critical areas. There was no logistical command to speak of, no torpedo shop, and not even an electrical repair shop. The base did have an ordnance depot but with very little ordnance on hand (less than 3,000 tons).[3]

The port of Sasebo, 500 miles to the southwest, was also repaired and upgraded. Sasebo, because of its strategic location, just a couple hundred miles from Pusan, South Korea, became the focal point for the American warships, men, military equipment and supplies during the upcoming struggle on the Korean peninsula.

U.S. Naval Forces Far East

U.S. Naval Forces Far East was the Navy's contribution to the occupation of post-war Japan. Ported at Yokosuka, the American collection of ships, known as a "housekeeping command," because of its small size, also possessed a nominal amount of firepower. Even housekeeping command may have been too strong an appellation as many viewed it as little more than a detachment of the U.S. Seventh Fleet.

The man in charge of U.S. Naval Forces Far East was Vice Admiral Charles Turner Joy. Joy was solid, not flamboyant. He had a quiet demeanor. During the Second World War, he had seen action in multiple naval theaters including the Solomons, Aleutians, Marianas, Philippine Sea, Leyte Gulf, and Okinawa. Joy's foremost overall attribute was his ability to work with others and find accommodation where impasse seemed the only option. This trait served him well in the days and months ahead as his small naval force would grow from around 20 ships to over 150 in the first three months of the war. Joy reported directly to General Douglas

---

[3] Yokosuka naval base background: Isenberg, *Shield of the Republic*, 180; M. D. Ingram, "The United States Navy in Japan," 378-383.

MacArthur who was Supreme Commander of the Allied Powers for the Occupation of Japan after 1945.[4]

For the U.S. Navy, fulfilling all of the obligations it had in Japan became much more of a challenge because of the post-war defense budget cuts. Between the end of the Second World War in 1945 and just five years later in 1950 the U.S. Navy had been reduced in size and budget from thousands of vessels to around five hundred ships and a once $30 billion dollar budget was now barely $4 billion. Additionally, there was a belief in some quarters that held sway with Congress, that the newly created Air Force would play the most important role in any future American conflict. This school of thought viewed naval power as something whose time had come and gone. Furthermore, as the argument went, there were no major post-war surface fleets to threaten the United States. This line of reasoning

---

[4] Information regarding Charles Turner Joy: D. Clayton James, *Refighting the Last War: Command and Crisis in Korea 1950-1953*, (New York: The Free Press, 1993), 80-81, 83.

Turner Joy was born in St. Louis, Missouri, in 1895. He graduated from the U.S. Naval Academy in 1916 and served on the battleship *Pennsylvania* during World War I. Impressed with Joy's leadership in the first year of the Korean War, the Joint Chiefs of Staff in Washington, in July 1951, selected him as the senior UN delegate to the Korean Armistice talks. Ten months later, completely frustrated by the lack of progress in the discussions, he asked to be replaced. A few years later, he published a book *How Communists Negotiate*. In it, he spoke of the North Koreans delaying tactics and their attempts to create propaganda instead of agreement. Admiral Joy contracted leukemia during this time and died 6 June 1956. In 1959, a new Sherman class destroyer, *USS Turner Joy* (DD-951), was commissioned in honor of Admiral Joy. For more Information on Admiral C. Turner Joy: Edward J. Marolda, "Vice Admiral C. Turner Joy, USN," Naval History & Heritage Command website, http://www.history.navy.mil/wars/ korea/joy.htm.

did not however take into consideration the inordinate build-up of Soviet submarines and the new type of threat they would pose. Finally, the military emphasis since 1945 had been on Europe. As part of the North Atlantic Treaty Organization (NATO) formed in 1948 by the Western powers, the United States created the Sixth Fleet, whose station was the Mediterranean Sea. The Pacific Ocean in general and Japan and its surrounding region specifically were bereft of larger American warships.[5]

U.S. Naval Forces Far East's largest fighting ship in Japan was the light cruiser *Juneau*. With the small cruiser was a four-ship destroyer division consisting of *Mansfield*, *De Haven*, *Lyman K. Swenson*, and *Collett*. There was also one submarine, *Remora*, on loan from the Seventh Fleet. Also under this command was a contingent of other auxiliary vessels that included a minesweeping squadron and five amphibious ships for moving men and supplies.

2-3 Wooden-Hulled Minesweeper, USS *Mockingbird*

---

[5]Post-war U.S. Navy: John Kieran, editor, *Information Please Almanac 1951*, (New York: The MacMillan Company, 1950), 287; Dean C. Allard, Chapter 15, "An Era of Transition 1945-1953," In *Peace and War: Interpretations of American Naval History, 1775-1978*, edited by Kenneth J. Hagan, (Westport, Connecticut: Greenwood Press, 1978).

INITIAL BURDEN

The U.S. Seventh Fleet based in the Philippines, over 1,300 miles to the south, was the only other American naval force in the Western Pacific. The Seventh, by American fleet standards was also small with just one aircraft carrier. It was also, at best, three to four days away from Korea under any set of circumstances.

Pledge was one of ten minesweepers that made up the mine squadron of U.S. Naval Forces Far East. The squadron was broken into two divisions. The larger ship division consisted of *Pledge, Mainstay, Incredible,* and *Pirate* all 184 foot steel-hulled Admirable class sweepers. The second division consisted of six smaller 136-foot YMS class sweepers that were of a wooden hull construction. These vessels included *Redhead, Mocking Bird, Osprey, Partridge, Chatterer,* and *Kite*.

Not far from where *Pledge* was maneuvering through the inner harbor, USS *Casinghead*, all 235 feet of her, was temporarily moored to the starboard side of the 311 foot long *Remora*, a Tench Class submarine. *Remora* was the outside vessel in a nest of three ships moored next to each other along with two Sumner class destroyers, *Swenson* and *Collett*. *Swenson*, the inside ship, was secured to the quay wall in the inner harbor. *Casinghead*, a yard oiler, or even less attractively known as a self-propelled fuel barge, was in the process of topping off *Remora's* 100,000-gallon tanks.[6]

---

[6] The "nest" in Yokosuka harbor: USS *Collett* and USS *Swenson, Deck Log*, 25 June 1950, Operational Archives Branch, Naval Historical Center, Washington Navy Yard, DC; Paul R. Yarnell, "USS *Casinghead*," NavSource Naval History, http://navsource.org (accessed 16 March 2008).

2-4 USS *Remora*

Remora was the only American submarine in Japanese waters in late June of 1950. Her express purpose was to assist in anti-submarine warfare (ASW) training exercises for the four destroyers stationed in Japan. Her unexpressed purpose was to provide some surveillance capability across the Sea of Japan around the Soviet naval base at Vladivostok. *Remora* commissioned in 1946 and after only one year in service had undergone extensive modification and equipment upgrades at Mare Island Naval Shipyard at Vallejo, California, before heading for the Far East.[7]

Swenson and *Collett* were both using dockside services provided by the naval facility including steam, electricity, telephone, and fresh water. They, along with *Mansfield* and *De Haven* which were on passage from Yokosuka to Sasebo, had all served at the end of the Pacific War in Japanese waters. *Collett* probably had the best war stories to tell. The first of those stories occurred on 19 November 1944 in the waters of the northern Philippine Islands after the Battle of Leyte Gulf, the four-day battle in late October that had marked the end of Imperial Japanese naval power. On this date, *Collett* was operating as a "picket" ship (a sentinel using its radar and sonar to detect enemy vessels and

---

[7]USS *Remora* history: Yarnall, "*Remora* (SS-487)," http://navsource.org (accessed 16 March 2008).

aircraft) some 15 to 20 miles ahead of U.S. Task Force 38. The American carriers in the task force were in the process of recovering their planes from a raid that had destroyed around 100 Japanese aircraft mostly on the ground in different locations in the northern Philippine Islands. The Japanese reacting to the attack launched 11 separate air raids of between one and five aircraft directed at Task Force 38 and especially its carriers located at the center of the formation. The attacks were unsuccessful but one of the groups of planes found *Collett* and proceeded to engage her. The Japanese air group consisted of four medium-sized bombers known as "Bettys." They initiated a "two-section coordinated attack."[8] *Collett* filled the sky with flak. Maneuvering at 30 knots, she managed to miss a torpedo that the first attacker had launched from only 800 yards distance. The second attacker turned away, possibly damaged by *Collett's* gunfire. The second section of aircraft came in low and one of them managed to drop another torpedo 1500 yards from *Collett* off her stern quarter. Once again, the Sumner class destroyer was able to avoid the torpedo while the fourth and final Betty turned away. Harrowing by any account, she had survived the attack and then went on about her business. Vice Admiral John S. McCain, commander of Task Group 1 of Task Force 38, later wrote in commendation,

---

[8] USS *Collett* under attack in northern Philippine Islands and "two-section coordinated attack" quote found in: Theodore Roscoe, *United States Destroyer Operations in World War II*, (Annapolis, Maryland: United States Naval Institute Press, 1953), 440. Samuel Eliot Morison, *History of United States Naval Operations in World War II, Vol. 12: Leyte, June 1944 - January 1945*, (Urbana and Chicago, Illinois: University of Illinois Press, 2002), 356.

Collett...forcefully demonstrated the invaluable service rendered by...destroyer strike-pickets in disorganizing enemy air attacks threatening the main body of a task force, and in giving early warning of the approach of attacking planes.[9]

Additionally, *Collett* was the first American warship to enter Tokyo Bay after the surrender of Japan. American naval forces had received word that resistance had ceased and it would be all right to enter Tokyo Bay where the surrender would take place. *Collett* drew the duty of finding out whether that information was true. After performing a nervous tour of the harbor to see if the guns surrounding Tokyo Bay would fire upon her or truly be silent in accordance with the surrender negotiations, *Collett* retired to open water. It was only then that the mighty battleship *Missouri* led the rest of the American fleet into the harbor for the formal surrender of Japan.[10]

Built during the late stages of the Second World War, the Sumners represented a response to the larger role of air power that emerged at the beginning of the war. Protecting larger cruisers, battleships and carriers from enemy aircraft was a primary design concern. As such, anti-aircraft weapons were of paramount importance. Each destroyer mounted six 5-inch, twelve 40mm, and eleven 20mm guns

---

[9] Commendation remarks by Vice Admiral McCain "*Collett*...forcefully demonstrated..." Roscoe, *Destroyer Operations*, 440. Vice Admiral McCain was also the grandfather of John S. McCain III Vietnam War hero, Senator, and Presidential Candidate in 2008 from the State of Arizona.

[10] *Collett* and the surrender of Japan: Don Moore, "*Collett* in Tokyo Bay in 1945," USS *Collett*, http//www.uscollett.com/history/d_moore/Don%20Moore%20History.htm (accessed 15 February 2011).

INITIAL BURDEN

for this purpose. As the War in the Pacific progressed, it became apparent that as the speed of aircraft increased, the anti-aircraft weapons were less effective against them. This development rendered the 20mm guns useless for this purpose.[11]

2-5 Sumner Class Destroyer (Far Right) Refueling Underway

At 376 feet in length and a fully loaded displacement of 3,220 tons, the Sumners were the heaviest destroyers ever built until the Soviets built the Kashin class destroyer beginning in 1963. Ten different locations on the ship fed the 5-inch guns what seemed an inexhaustible supply of shells and powder. In fact, there was more space devoted to ammunition on the Sumners than room made available for food to feed a crew of more than 300 officers and sailors. Fortuitously, for these destroyers, the postwar world naval threat turned out to be submarines. The large size of the Sumners allowed for the addition of many more

---

[11] History of Sumner class destroyers: Robert F. Sumrall and Paul Bender, *Sumner Gearing Class Destroyers: Their Design, Weapons, and Equipment*, (Annapolis, Maryland: U.S. Naval Institute Press, 1995), 89.

sophisticated anti-submarine warfare systems. That, with new twin rudders to improve maneuverability, combined to combat the new underwater threat. The size, modifications, and upgrades allowed for a platform in the Sumners that would serve the U.S. Navy and later other navies for decades to come. The post-war destroyers were now the workhorses of the fleet capable of a range of missions.[12]

When word came that afternoon that the North Koreans had invaded South Korea, Admiral Joy assessed the immediate role and actions of U.S. Naval Forces Far East. *Juneau*, the flagship for the command, was in the extreme south of Japan showing the flag and inspecting ships at Kagoshima on the island of Kyushu. As noted, destroyers *De Haven* and *Mansfield* were at Sasebo performing patrol duties in the straits between Japan and Korea, while *Collett* and *Swenson* were at Yokosuka.

Of the four larger minesweepers, only *Pledge* was readily available for active duty. *Mainstay*, *Pirate*, and *Incredible* were in caretaker status, which meant that it would take at least six to eight weeks to repair and make them ready. These three minesweepers also possessed skeleton crews that would need augmentation before active duty was a possibility. Even then, for want of replacement parts,

---

[12] Sumner class specifications: James L. George, *History of Warships: From Ancient Times to the Twenty-First Century*, (Annapolis, Maryland: U.S. Naval Institute Press, 1998), 152; Sumrall, *Sumner Gearing Class Destroyers*, ix; James Edwin Alexander, *Inchon to Wonsan: From the Deck of a Destroyer in the Korean War*, (Annapolis, Maryland: U.S. Naval Institute Press, 1996), 7; NavSource Naval History, "Destroyer Archive Special Feature, Allen M. Sumner Class Destroyers," NavSource Naval History, http://navsource.org/archives/05/interior.htm (accessed 14 January 2011).

Mainstay would not be activated with her sister ships until much later that summer.[13] In addition to her flagship status, *Pledge* served as tender and logistics supply ship for the entire mine squadron. She was ready to lead the smaller "bird" minesweepers, as some preferred to call them, in whatever capacity they were needed.[14]

Besides the engine issues of Admirable class minesweepers, *Pledge* and the other sweepers struggled with communications gear that was extremely out of date. The communications equipment was so old that it did not allow the sweepers to talk to each other on the same radio circuit at the same time. Moreover, since the sweepers often worked in teams, this handicap greatly hindered operations. All of this being said, fate had called upon the American and British warships in the Far East that late June and, ready or not, they were about to taste action.[15]

---

[13] Minesweepers in caretaker status: James A. Field Jr., *History of United States Naval Operations Korea*, (Washington D.C.: U.S. Government Printing Office, 1962), 54, 231.

[14] *Pledge* as flagship and more: Cagle and Manson, *Sea War*, 127.

[15] Minesweepers' communications gear: Ibid., 128-129.

Chapter 3

"[D]efend us in battle..."[1]

25 June 1950, Morning

USS *Juneau*

"St. Michael, the Archangel, defend us in battle..." As a local priest from the Japanese port city of Kagoshima knelt at the foot of the makeshift altar on board the American light cruiser *Juneau*, on that overcast Sunday morning, he listened to the sailors behind him as they recited the last of the prayers that followed the conclusion of the Catholic Mass. The day before, he had graciously accepted the request of *Juneau's* chaplain, a Protestant, to preside at Mass for the contingent of Catholic sailors on board the U.S. warship.

During the homily, the priest, who spoke English well, talked about St. Francis Xavier. Xavier, the great Portuguese Jesuit missionary, who with his arrival in 1650 at this very port city, brought Christianity to the island nation and many of its people. He concluded by reflecting on the connection and continuity of the simple celebration of the Latin liturgy that day with that of St. Xavier's first offering of a Mass in Japan 400 years earlier.

As the men began to rise following the invocation to St. Michael, neither the priest nor the sailors could fully

---

[1] Excerpt from "Prayer to St. Michael" from the Leonine Prayers that were prescribed by successive Popes for recitation after Low Masses in the Catholic Church from 1884 to early 1965.

INITIAL BURDEN

appreciate or grasp the significance of those prayerful words of petition that day.[2]

Juneau rested at anchor in the middle of the harbor in 20 fathoms of water with 120 fathoms of chain paid out to the sandy bottom. The port of Kagoshima is situated on a large bay at the southern-end of the Japanese island of Kyushu, just to the northeast of the volcano Sakurajima. In 1914, a large eruption had covered Kagoshima with ash. The 3,665-foot volcano dominates the skyline and looms over the port city. Kagoshima is also the prefecture, or regional district capital, for the southern area of the island of Kyushu. In 1950, the port city, known worldwide for its exportation of Satsuma earthenware, had a population of over 200,000.

Having arrived two days earlier on the 23rd, *Juneau's* orders were routine. She would show the flag, inspect ships in the harbor for contraband and other illegal activities, and host a reception that Sunday evening for the local officials. Therefore, while a portion of the officers and blue jackets focused their efforts on the two large merchant ships *Takaghisani Maru* and the Panamanian flagged *Orbital* in the harbor at that time, others set about preparing for the reception. Many of the sailors who were not involved with those particular tasks ferried to shore on *Juneau's* launches and enjoyed liberty. Pushed and pulled into position alongside *Juneau's* port quarter, a non-propelled port

---

[2] Sunday morning Mass at Kagashima: T. A. Curtin, "USS *Juneau* (CLAA-119) In the Early Days of the Korean Conflict," Edited transcript of the diary of then Ensign T. A. Curtin, Ammunition Officer on USS *Juneau*, http:// uss*Juneau*.net/CLAA119/index.html, *Juneau* War Diary June-July 1950 (accessed 16 March 2008); T. A. Curtin, "The Galloping Ghost of the Korean Coast, A Memoir," http://uss*Juneau*.net/CLAA119/index.html (accessed March 16, 2008).

garbage lighter performed its mundane task. Thirty minutes later, it had moved on.

The symbolism of a warship "showing the flag" in a foreign port conveys a visual, sometimes visceral, message to the city's inhabitants. First, it literally displays some of the military might of the visiting vessel's country. Second, it makes all who see the ship aware that real power, in this case that of the United States, is not thousands of miles away on the other side of the Pacific, but right there, in their midst, in their harbor. Showing the flag is a subtle and sometimes not so subtle reminder, as it was that Sunday morning in June of 1950 that the United States was still serious about maintaining the post-war peace. *Juneau* was perfectly suited for this role.

Juneau was 541 feet in length with a comparatively slight beam of 53 feet. Twelve 5-inch guns arranged in six twin-barrel mounts equally distributed, three forward and three aft, with another 32 40-millimeter and 16 20-millimeter anti-aircraft guns festooned about her superstructure. From the tip of her high bow through the unbroken sheer-line of her weather deck to her low, unique transom stern, *Juneau* was an exceptional looking naval vessel. The effect was a streamlined and rakish looking warship that bristled with firepower.[3]

---

[3] *Juneau* specifications: Blackman, R.V.B., ed., *Jane's Fighting Ships 1950-51*, (London: Sampson Low, Marston & Co. LTD., 1950), s.v. "United States Anti-Aircraft Cruisers."

INITIAL BURDEN

3-1 USS *Juneau*

Juneau had been in service for only three and a half years, but the genesis for her design, as that of the British cruiser *Jamaica*, dated back 14 years to the Second London Naval Treaty of 1936. It was at this conference when the world's naval powers, but not Japan, agreed to limit construction of new cruiser types to a maximum displacement of 8,000 tons. Although the United States eventually agreed to the provision, it did not sit well with the American Navy. The United States had argued that they needed to build larger cruisers that could carry much more fuel because of the need to operate them in the vastness of the Pacific Ocean.

This need seemed beyond the grasp of many of the participating countries (mostly European). Moreover, for all the rhetoric the United States could muster, none of it created any converts. For the Americans the 8,000-ton limit removed the flexibility, in terms of firepower, size, and armor from future cruiser construction.[4]

Therefore, if the United States could not get the larger multi-mission ship it wanted it opted instead to build a smaller and more focused-role cruiser. *Juneau* and her sisters became "fast sea-going flak [anti-aircraft] batteries."[5] The anti-aircraft aspect of these cruisers required fast firing guns and the most up to date radar available. To achieve the speed necessary to provide protection for aircraft carriers and battleships from enemy warplanes required sacrificing armor. The steel "skin" of this class of ship would measure only 3/4 of an inch, in order to accommodate the number of gun mounts on their decks and the speed that was necessary to keep up with fast carriers and newer battleships. This left them very vulnerable if hit by enemy shells. Additionally, in the planning stage, the design featured larger guns than those eventually fitted. Because of the treaty limitations, and the slower than expected development of a new twin dual-purpose 6-inch gun, the U.S. Navy finally opted to develop a class of cruiser that would displace 6,000 tons, mount 5-inch guns, have a top speed of 32 1/2 knots, and a cruising range of 9,000 miles at 15 knots. In the end, by sacrificing some firepower and

---

[4] Limits on Cruiser development imposed by the Second London Naval Treaty: Norman Friedman, *U.S. Cruisers: an Illustrated Design History*, (Annapolis, Maryland: United States Naval Institute Press, 1984), Chapter 8, "The Second London Treaty."

[5] Preston Cook, "Remembering Those Astounding Atlanta-Class Anti-Aircraft Cruisers of WWII," *Sea Classics*, Vol. 40, No. 4, April 2007, 19.

armor protection the new class of cruiser would achieve the speed and coveted range for duty in the Pacific.

Production of the Atlanta class light cruiser (the class name based on the name of the first ship of the class to be laid down) began in 1940. There eventually would be eleven ships in this class, the last one completed in 1946.[6]

The first two ships of this class, the aforementioned *Atlanta* and the first of what was to eventually be two *Juneau*s, were both lost during the battle for Guadalcanal in the Solomon Islands almost a year after the attack on Pearl Harbor. In a three day slugfest with the Imperial Japanese Navy both *Atlanta* and *Juneau* were sunk on the night of 13 November 1942. *Juneau's* demise was of a spectacular nature and particularly tragic. It had come by way of a single Japanese torpedo that had struck the ship's ammunition magazine, which in turn destroyed the light cruiser in one massive explosion. All but ten of a complement of some 700 officers and sailors either immediately or subsequently perished.[7]

3-2 First *Juneau* CL-52 in Action at Battle of Santa Cruz 17 Days before Her Loss

---

[6] The design considerations for the Atlanta class light cruisers; Cook, "Remembering Those Astounding Atlanta-Class...," 18-25; Dan Kurzman, *Left to Die: The Tragedy of the USS Juneau*, (NY: Pocket Books, 1994), 36.

[7] The first *Juneau's* demise: Samuel Eliot Morison, *History of United States Naval Operations in World War II, Volume 5: The Struggle for Guadalcanal August 1942-February 1943*, (Urbana and Chicago, Illinois: University of Illinois Press), 257; Kurzman, *Left to Die*, 138-147.

3-3 The Sullivan Brothers on Board USS *Juneau*

Among those lost in the sinking of *Juneau* were five Irish-American brothers about whom a motion picture was released in 1944 entitled "The Fighting Sullivans." Due to the publicity generated by the story of the deaths of the Sullivan brothers, the Navy implemented a policy that, going forward, prohibited family members from serving at the same time on the same ship.[8]

The stunning manner of the first *Juneau's* destruction led to the naming of a later Atlanta class cruiser to commemorate the original ship and the sailors who had been lost while serving on her. The second *Juneau's* keel was laid in the fall of 1944. Launched in the summer of 1945, and finally commissioned after the war had ended in the winter of 1946, *Juneau's* role in the post-war American Navy was uncertain.

The Atlanta class cruisers, originally built with the main purpose of defending aircraft carriers and battleships against enemy aircraft, secondarily were tasked with providing protection from possible submarine attack. With the construction of the second *Juneau*, the Navy did not

---

[8] In recent years, the story of the brothers helped inspire the screenplay of the 1998 movie *Saving Private Ryan* that won five academy awards.

waste time installing torpedo tubes and other anti-submarine weapons and systems. Her namesake and other earlier sister ships had proven they were too long to maneuver effectively to hunt for, or defend against, enemy submarines. Destroyers would assume the mantle for the prosecution of submarines. Regarding her primary mission of protecting larger ships from air attacks, *Juneau* was superbly equipped to challenge the propeller driven aircraft of the Second World War. However, by 1950, jet propulsion was coming into its own and *Juneau* was finding it much more difficult to find firing solutions to the speed of such aircraft with her 5-inch guns. If that were not enough, guided missiles were on the horizon. The eventual introduction of guided missile systems on board naval vessels would prove to be the final nail in the coffin for the fine looking class of ships.[9]

Between 1947 and 1949, *Juneau* participated in naval exercises in the Atlantic and deployed on successive tours as part of the newly formed Sixth Fleet in the Mediterranean Sea. In the Mediterranean, she showed the flag extensively, especially in and around Greece, warning the communists there against thoughts of aggression. With the serious budgetary cutbacks the Navy experienced in the late 40s, the smaller and more economical *Juneau* was less expensive to operate than other larger American cruisers and, as a result, was always in demand to fulfill U.S. naval obligations. In March 1949, she and the other surviving members of the Atlanta class were re-designated as anti-aircraft light cruisers. Her alphanumeric designation changed from CL-119 to CLAA-119 (CLAA = cruiser, light, anti-aircraft).

---

[9] Atlanta class cruiser mission: Friedman, *U.S. Cruisers*, Chapter 8, "The Second London Treaty;" Cook, "Remembering Those Astounding Atlanta-Class...," 18-25.

At the beginning of 1950, *Juneau*, now reassigned to the Pacific Fleet, arrived in Bremerton, Washington from the East Coast on 15 January where she underwent an overhaul. After augmenting her crew with some fresh officers and blue jackets, *Juneau* departed Puget Sound and took part in training exercises along the Pacific coast.[10] In late spring, she participated in a joint U.S.-Canadian naval exercise that simulated an attack on the island of Oahu.[11]

In late April 1950, *Juneau* received word that she was to become the flagship for U.S. Naval Forces Far East in what was essentially Army General Douglas MacArthur's "Navy" in the occupation of post-war Japan. She arrived at Yokosuka on 1 June to begin operating in her new capacity. *Juneau* spent her first two weeks there while the crew became acclimated to its new surroundings. On 14 June, she weighed anchor and made a quick visit, in line with her new duties as flagship, to the small port city of Tateyama about 50 miles to the south. After spending the night there, she returned to Yokosuka the following day. A few days later on the 21st *Juneau* stood out of the naval base and headed for the southern Japanese port of Kagoshima to begin her new assignment in earnest.[12]

The backdrop for *Juneau* in Kagoshima on 25 June was breathtaking. A combination of the volcanic soil,

---

[10] It was in Bremerton that the author's father joined the crew of *Juneau*.

[11] Mock attack on the island of Oahu: Associated Press, "U. S., Canada to 'Attack' Oahu, *New York Times*," May 7, 1950. 1.

[12] *Juneau's* duties as flagship: C. F. Hamlin, "Diary 24 April 1950 – 4 October 1950," USS *Juneau.net*, http://ussJuneau.net/CLAA119/marines.html (accessed March 16, 2008).

compliments of Mount Sakurajima, and the sun filtering through the cloud cover gave a reddish hue to the gray American cruiser as it lay at anchor.

3-4 USS *Juneau* at Anchor in Kagoshima Harbor with Mt. Sakurajima in Background

It was shortly after 1500 hours that *Juneau* received a communication from Tokyo that the North Koreans had invaded South Korea. The light cruiser quickly lowered boats into the water to retrieve sailors who were ashore on liberty. By 1700 hours, only eight of the crew were unaccounted for and had not returned to the ship.[13]

The reception for the Japanese local officials that evening, hosted by Rear Admiral John Martin Higgins, would go on as scheduled so as not to contribute to any possible panic among Kagoshima's citizenry. Mr. Yasuoka, the Vice-Governor of the Kagoshima Prefecture and his party, came on board shortly before 1900 hours and departed two and a half hours later. During the visit, the ship's stewards served special appetizers to the Japanese officials and American naval officers, while the flag band played chamber music. All went well. With the visiting officials safely returned to shore, the crew took down the awnings for the event and

---

[13]*Juneau* notified of North Korean invasion: USS *Juneau, Deck Log*, 25 June 1950, Operational Archives Branch, Naval Historical Center, Washington Navy Yard, DC.

INITIAL BURDEN

cleaned up after the reception while *Juneau* returned to the business of preparing to depart.[14]

The next day at 0645, *Juneau's* Inspection Party #2 left the ship in order to carry out one more routine examination of the Japanese steam ship *Nissho Maru #32* that had arrived late the previous evening. Admiral John Higgins, Commander of U.S. Cruiser Division 5, also left the ship late in the morning to fly to Yokosuka for meetings with Naval Forces Far East command. His flag subsequently hauled down and *Juneau's* commission pennant raised for the passage to Sasebo, the admiral would rejoin the warship in a few days.[15]

Juneau was underway by 1300 hours with orders to proceed to Sasebo to fuel and replenish and to await further orders.

---

[14] Reception on board USS *Juneau* the evening of 25 June 1950: Curtin, "The Galloping Ghost," 1.

[15] Admiral Higgins was born in Madison, Wisconsin in 1899. He graduated from the United States Naval Academy in 1922. During Second World War, as commander of Destroyer Division 23, he was on board *USS Gwin* when she was torpedoed at the battle of Kolombangara on 13 July 1943. A Japanese "Long Lance" torpedo struck *Gwin* amidships and exploded in the engine room of the destroyer doing grievous damage. Shortly thereafter, the destroyer was scuttled with the loss of 2 officers and 59 enlisted men. After the war, Higgins commanded the battleship *Wisconsin*. For his service in the first six months of the Korean War, Rear Admiral Higgins would receive the Navy Distinguished Service Medal for "exceptionally meritorious and distinguished service." More information on Rear Admiral John Martin Higgins: Online Library of Selected Images: -- PEOPLE -- UNITED STATES --Rear Admiral John Martin Higgins, USN, (1899-1973), www.history.navy.mil/photos/pers-us/uspers-h/jmhggns.htm (accessed 14 November 2011; John Higgins (admiral), Wikipedia website, http://en.wikipedia.org/wiki/John_ Higgins_ (admiral) (accessed 14 November 2011).

She had been in Japan for less than four weeks. For the crew of the light cruiser all seemed to have been right with the world the previous day. Today a pall descended over them as the warship quietly steamed north that afternoon. No one on board knew quite what to expect next. Questions spawned speculation and, of course, more questions -- and it is just possible that a sailor or two remembered the prayer to St. Michael.[16]

---

[16] Orders for *Juneau* to proceed to Sasebo: Curtin, "Galloping Ghost"; USS *Juneau*, Deck Log, 25-26 June 1950.

Chapter 4

Fledgling Navies

Evacuation of Seoul

Panic was in the air. Cars and buses rumbled out of the city. The concussive sound of artillery fire thundered to the north. The North Korean Army was moving quickly towards the South Korean capital of Seoul that unfortunately, in a military sense, lies just a scant 35 miles south of the 38th parallel border between the two artificial nations. Even though the bulk of the South Korean Army was between Seoul and the invaders, the defenders were unable to mount enough resistance to halt the North Korean offensive in any meaningful way. Almost all of the Americans either had fled Seoul by plane from the capital city's Kimpo airfield, or had made for the port city of Inchon, over an hour's drive away. All foreigners were looking to escape the military action. It was all happening too fast.

North Korean Naval Operations on East Coast

Over on the east coast along the Sea of Japan the North Korean Army quickly faced issues related to the topography of the Korean peninsula. The NKPA 5th Division not only had to contest the South Korean Army in front of them but also the Taebaek mountain range running north and south along the eastern Korean coastline of the Sea of Japan. The mountain range, which has almost no easy passages from east to west, creates two very isolated corridors of operation on either side of the coastal mountain range. The all-important rail line was on the eastern or ocean side of the mountains. In spite of this obstacle, the North Koreans were making great headway, partly due to the use of their naval forces.

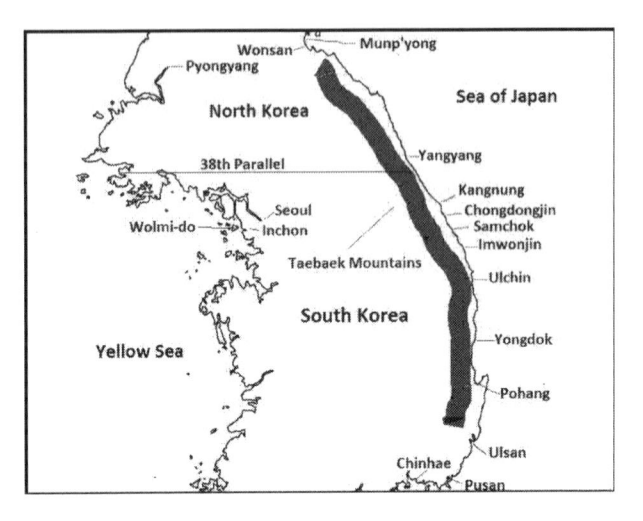

4-1 Taebaek Mountain Range

Like the army and air force, the North Korean Navy patterned itself along the lines of the Soviet naval model. It was also very dependent upon the Soviet Navy. The North Korean Peoples' Navy (NKPN) had its beginnings as a small coastal defense force organized and trained by the Soviet Navy after the war in 1945. By 1950, the North Koreans had organized their naval forces into three sea commands. The Northern Sea Command with the 1st Naval Squadron located at Chongjin, near the Manchurian border, was close to the Soviet port of Vladivostok. The port of Najin, even closer to the Russian base, was the site of a naval training program directly administered and run by the Soviets. Wonsan, on the Sea of Japan, was the naval base and Eastern Sea Command for the 2nd Naval Squadron. The Western Sea Command with the 3rd Naval Squadron called Chinnampo on the Yellow Sea home. Chinnampo was the closest naval base to the North Korean capital of Pyongyang and the site of the North Korean Naval Academy. All three sea commands had garrisons of between 800 and 900 personnel with each base supplemented by a battalion strength 1,800-man naval combat team (marines). These forces along with the personnel it took to operate and maintain the naval vessels constituted the 15,000 man NKPN.

Estimates regarding the number of naval vessels the North Koreans possessed ranged from as few as five to more than two dozen ex-Soviet motor torpedo boats and between three up to as many as twenty ex-Soviet and Japanese minesweepers. Whatever the number, all of the vessels were employed as all-purpose patrol boats. The North Korean Navy may have also possessed three ex-Soviet OD-200 submarine chasers. They also had another six to possibly as many as thirty or so small motor boats of varying displacement and type. Lastly, the NKPN possessed some small former American transport steamers of 1,000 tons that had originally been loaned to the Soviet Union during the Second World War and conveniently never returned.[1]

---

[1] Information regarding the North Korean Navy history and composition is minimal, varied, and sketchy at best. With that said those sources with the most credence are as follows: Joseph S. Bermudez Jr., *North Korean Special Forces*, (Annapolis, MD: Naval Institute Press, 1998), 34-37; Korea Institute of Military History, *The Korean War*, vol. 1, (Lincoln, Nebraska: University of Nebraska Press, 2000), 50; Joseph S. Bermudez Jr., Email to Korean-War-List, Re: North Korean Naval OOB, hosted by the University of Kansas, 19 May 2002, http://www.koreanwar.com /Archives/2002 /05/msg00353. html, (accessed 17 January 2008); Isenberg, *Shield of the Republic*, 1993, 175; Spencer C. Tucker, ed., *Encyclopedia of the Korean War: A Political, Social, and Military History*, (New York: Checkmark Books, 2002), s.v. "Korea, Democratic People's Republic of: Navy (Korean People's Navy [KPN];" Sandler, *Korean War: An Encyclopedia*, s.v. "Korean People's (North Korean) Navy." Information that suggested the lower end of number estimates and that the North Korean Navy possessed three OD-200 type patrol boats can be found here: "History of the Korean People's Navy," which in turn sourced its information to a Russian language book: *War in Korea, 1950-53*, St. Petersburg, 2003,

The Soviet Red Army had played a role in constructing the invasion plan. The North Koreans originally put together the plan the previous year. When Stalin approved the operation in the spring of 1950, his army generals re-wrote parts of the plan more to their liking. The operation called for an all out frontal assault using the North's advantage in manpower, armor, artillery, and aircraft. The only nod to naval strategy called for the NKPN to conduct a few small amphibious operations along the East Coast, landing forces behind the defending South Koreans, to augment the In Min Gun's southern incursion.[2]

Navies take money to construct or purchase and time to train officers and men to properly operate naval vessels. North Korea, not unlike South Korea, possessed no combat craft above the size of patrol vessels. However, the reality of the geography of the peninsula was that South Korea was surrounded on three of four sides by water. The lack of a stronger naval component in the invasion war planning fated North Korea, for the most part, to fighting on land from north to south. The inability of the fledgling North Korean Navy to obtain, operate, and maintain a navy commensurate with the overall mission of defeating South Korea "quickly," severely compromised one of the crucial principles of their war strategy. Much of the blame for this glaring omission of naval power squarely fell on the Soviet Union. With its traditional land-based conception of war,

---

http://en.wikipedia.org/wiki/History_of_the_Korean_People's_Navy (accessed 12 December 2010).

[2] Information regarding the plan for the invasion: "Korean War - June 1950," Global Security, http://www.global security.org/military/ops/korea-2.htm (accessed 14 December 2010).

the Soviets were unable to clearly see the importance of a solid naval component in the Korean theater of action sorely needed to ensure victory for its client state.

Nevertheless, the different elements of the North Korean's naval infantry employed in the amphibious landings assembled at the Naval Base at Wonsan and Munp'yong and also at Yangyang closer to the border. The units included the 766th Independent Unit (equivalent to Army Rangers), 549th Naval Combat Team (equivalent to Marines), and smaller groups such as the Nam Don Ue and the 15th and 27th Guerilla units. These units embarked on board the small, and in some cases, armed transports. The Second Naval Squadron motor torpedo boats (MTBs) out of Wonsan escorted the small invasion flotilla. Regular NKPN personnel manned all the vessels.

The amphibious contingent appeared off the east coast of South Korea at sunrise on the morning of the attack on the 25th. The North Korean amphibious force achieved complete surprise with the local South Korean forces (ROKA) falling back from the coast. The North Korean 549th Naval Combat Team landed at Chongdongjin, near Kangnung, just after 0400. These naval infantry units, disembarked from their transport ships in company-sized units of 80 to 120 men using powerboats and fishing craft that augmented the rag-tag amphibious force. With surprise on their side, some of the transports were able to sail straight into the harbor and the soldiers on board were able to step directly on to the docks and piers. Still other vessels got close enough to the beaches that soldiers were able to wade ashore. Once ashore the North Koreans forced some of the bewildered local village inhabitants to off load ammunition and supplies from the vessels that had docked. Further down the coast, just below the town of Samchok, the North Korean 1st and

2nd battalions of the 766th Independent Unit landed at the village of Imwonjin beginning at 0700.

Both of the landings proceeded virtually unopposed. The North Korean forces were able to form up at their landing sites and then push inland. Once into the mountains they sought out and attacked the retreating ROKA units from the rear. This maneuver added more confusion and panic to the South Korean forces falling back under the furious attack of the NKPA's 5th Division.

Still at sea that morning a solitary North Korean transport continued to move south along the Sea of Japan and the Korean coastline. The weather had not been an issue. The seas were almost flat with just a slight breeze out of the north seemingly encouraging the ship and her most important cargo towards its destination and goal. The only difference between the landings at Kangnung and Imwonjin was that, for whatever reason, no NKPN vessels provided support for the armed transport beyond Samchok. The flotilla of vessels that had participated in the successful landings that morning had retired to the north. Should the armed freighter need protection she possessed a formidable 76-mm gun plus four mounted machine guns. The North Korean 3rd Battalion of the 766th Independent Unit had not landed with the 1st and 2nd battalions that morning at the village of Imwonjin. The lone armed-freighter, carrying the 600-man battalion, continued on its very special mission. [3]

---

[3]North Korean amphibious landings: Roy Edgar Appleman, *South to Naktong, North to the Yalu, June-November 1950*, (Washington: Office of the Chief of Military History, Dept. of the Army, 1961), 27-28, 105; Korea Institute of Military History, *Korean War*, 208-210, 217; Bermudez, *North Korean Special Forces*, 37-39: Joseph S. Bermudez Jr., Email to Korean-War-List, Korean People's Army – 766th Independent Unit – Revision,

INITIAL BURDEN

4-2 Pusan Harbor

Pusan, South Korea

Pusan is South Korea's largest and most important southern port. Strategically Pusan's value is inestimable. As a point of entry to the Korean peninsula, with its location being less than 200 miles from Japan's southern port of Sasebo, Pusan is an absolute necessity. There would be no way for the United States and its allies to sustain a military presence or mount a response to a North Korean invasion of the South without control of this port. Without it, game over.

For centuries, Pusan had been a small trading port. Over time as trade and shipping grew so did Pusan. It was during the Japanese occupation of the Korean peninsula between 1910 and 1945 that the port, with its natural deep harbor and gentle tides, was developed and expanded into a major seaport (many other port locations in Korea are subject to extreme tidal conditions e.g., Inchon). By 1950 there were

---

Hosted by the University of Kansas, 12 March 2000, http://www.koreanwar.com/Archives /2000/03/msg00056 .html (accessed 18 January 2008).

an estimated quarter-million people residing and working in this thriving port city.

South Korean Navy

After the Second World War, the South Koreans set to work developing a naval arm for their military, initially called the National Defense Corps. In terms of officers, seamen, and ships they were starting from scratch. Beginning in August 1946, the foundation for the Republic of Korea Navy (ROKN) made great strides with the help of a select group of U.S. Coast Guard officers and enlisted advisors. By the fall of that year, the new Navy had commissioned eighteen vessels of various types loaned to them by the United States government. These included eleven minesweepers and two mine-planting vessels, all former assets of the Imperial Japanese Navy, and some smaller craft from the Philippines.

4-3 Chinhae, South Korea

The South Koreans did possess some infrastructure that helped in the development of their Navy. During Japan's occupation, in addition to developing the port of Pusan, the Japanese also built a small naval base just thirty miles to the southwest at Chinhae. Chinhae had excellent anchorage, as well as docks, fuel and ammunition storage depots, a radio station, roads, administrative offices, and personnel

INITIAL BURDEN

barracks. There was even a marine railway with tracks extending into the harbor providing a means to haul small naval vessels and other craft out of the water to effect repairs. The South Koreans rehabilitated much of the base and harbor equipment left behind by the Japanese, establishing the site as the first base for their new Navy. It was here at Chinhae that the South Koreans started their Officers Candidate Program with a two-year curriculum to fulfill the pressing need for officers. The newly formed Navy put down their roots at Chinhae.

From these beginnings, the ROKN grew. With the help of the United States, the South Korean Navy implemented a naval radio communications system. After establishing themselves in Chinhae, the Navy built a second base at Inchon close to the capital on the west coast of the Korean peninsula. With the construction of this important base, the South Korean Navy moved its headquarters from Chinhae to Seoul.

By the summer of 1950, the ROKN consisted of 7,000 personnel and 71 naval vessels — mostly ex-American and ex-Japanese ships of varying size and purpose. The disposition of the vessels on the eve of the war was divided into three forces. The 1st Task Force of four minesweepers, two minelayers, and one landing craft was located at Inchon. The largest contingent designated the 2nd Task Force consisted of nine minesweepers, three minelayers, one newly-acquired submarine chaser, four smaller craft, and various training vessels all located at Pusan and Chinhae. Two minesweepers and four minelayers made up the smallest of the groups, the 3rd Task Force, situated at Mukpo along the southwest coast of the Yellow Sea. With the 1st and 3rd Task Forces based on the Yellow Sea, the 2nd Task Force had the charge of defending the entire east coast of the country from its two bases in Pusan and Chinhae.

The ROKN's mission was to protect South Korea's ports and harbors. They could operate in open water if necessary but the size of these ships and patrol craft mandated that they stick close to their shorelines.[4] On the eve of the war, the ROKN was extremely young. For the new Navy there would be much to learn. One of the most important lessons would be establishing sound and reliable communication conventions with the Western navies.[5] Despite these challenges, the ROKN was ready to take the first steps in establishing a solid naval tradition for the future. Their trial by fire would begin immediately.

---

[4] South Korea establishes a naval service: Republic of Korea, *The History of the United Nations Forces in the Korean War,* vol. 1, (Seoul: Republic of Korea. Ministry of National Defense, 1972), 67; Field, *History of the United States Naval Operations,* 51; Gordon L. Rottman, *Korean War Order of Battle United States, United Nations, and Communist Ground, Naval, and Air Forces, 1950-1953,* (Westport, CT: Praeger, 2002), 158-159; Tucker, ed., *Encyclopedia of the Korean War,* s.v. "Republic of: Navy (ROKN);" Duk–Hyun Cho, "Don't Give Up the Ships: United States Naval Operations During the First Year of the Korean War," Thesis (Ph. D.) – Ohio State University, 2002, 2003, 37.

[5] South Korean Navy communication protocol with other navies: Karig, Cagle, and Manson, *Battle Report,* 68.

Chapter 5

"[S]moke was observed..."[1]

Pusan — 25 June

Sunday evening on the first day of the invasion found Pusan a frenzy of activity. United States merchant ships SS *Jesse Lykes* and SS *Pioneer Dale* were dockside and now found themselves with a request from the United States Far East Command in Japan to evacuate the American dependents and others who would be at risk because of the conflict.[2] Somewhat presciently, the U.S. Navy and the U.S. Air Force had created and distributed a plan to evacuate American dependents about a year earlier.[3] U.S. Naval Forces Far East "was to provide the ships and naval escort protection for the water lift; the Far East Air Forces was to provide the

---

[1] The quotation "Smoke was observed..." Karig, Cagle, and Manson, *Battle Report*, 29.

[2] Pusan 25 June, : Appleman, *South to the Naktong*, 39; Karig, Cagle, and Manson, *Battle Report*, 29; The request to the merchant ships to help with the evacuation came from U.S. Army General Walker: Maine Memory Network, *"SS Pioneer Dale,"* Maine Historical Society, "The Voyage Abstract," 20:3, http://www.mainememory.net/bin/Detail?ln=17982 (accessed 19 October 2008).

[3] Appleman, *South to the Naktong*, 39.

planes for the airlift and give fighter cover to both the water and air evacuation."[4]

Some of the American refugees in Pusan did not grasp the seriousness of their plight. The vast majority of the American dependents assumed they were hundreds of miles from where the fighting was taking place and were in no imminent danger. Unfortunately, that was not the case. The North Koreans were pushing hard down the East Coast. Inherent in the NKPA plans was the idea that a quick thrust and capture of Pusan would end the war before the Americans could get involved.

ROKN *Bak du San*

That same Sunday evening the South Korean sub-chaser *Bak du San* led a small patrol force of three ships north out of Pusan. *Bak du San*, the former USS *PC-823,* had picked up the name of "Ensign Whitehead" while serving as a training vessel. Constructed in 1944 by Leatham D. Smith Shipbuilders, in Sturgeon Bay, Wisconsin the ship's design featured the latest technology and weapons systems to perform anti-submarine warfare. *Bak du San* was 173 feet long displacing 400 plus tons. She was very American in her appearance, with a flush deck, where the main or weather deck extends unbroken for the entire length of the ship, plus a prominent sheer, or excess of freeboard, which is the distance from the weather deck to the waterline. Powered by two diesel engines, the Americans had hoped that this class of ship would make 22 knots to give them a ten-knot margin over a typical convoy. That had never worked out; try as they might the naval engineers could never make that

---

[4] Ibid., 39.

happen. *Bak du San* could only make 19 knots. Her antisubmarine capability included two depth charge projectors and ahead-throwing weapons (also known as forward-throwers). *Bak du San's* main battery was one 3-inch/50 caliber gun. This single mount weapon could fire 15 to 20 rounds per minute of 13 lb shells and had a range of about 14,000 feet or over two and a half miles. She could carry a crew of sixty.

5-1 *Bak du San* Receiving Her New 3-inch Gun at Pearl Harbor March 1950

After her commissioning in 1944, the then PC-823 intermittently provided air-sea rescue service in the Western Atlantic for the last two years of the Second World War. She was decommissioned in 1946 and then transferred to the U.S. Merchant Marine Academy at Kings Point, on Long Island in New York, where she served as a training vessel for a few more years. Stricken from the U.S. Navy list in June of 1948 after just four years of limited service, PC-823 found herself a victim of the post-war military cutbacks.

It was about a year later that South Korea purchased PC-823. The purchase price was $18,000 and came from donations made by the personnel of the new Navy. Renamed *Bak du San* and re-designated PC-701 the sub-chaser sailed from New York arriving at Pearl Harbor in January 1950. Over the next two months, the vessel received a new 3-inch/50 caliber gun and six .50 caliber machine guns. Shortly thereafter, she departed the Hawaiian Islands to join the ROKN based at Chinhae. *Bak du San* arrived just weeks before the invasion by North Korea began. South Korea purchased three more American sub chasers like *Bak du San* — all still in transit from Hawaii when the war started.[5]

Accompanying *Bak du San* that evening on the patrol were two former American-built minesweepers YMS-512 and YMS-518. The ROKN had purchased 15 of these minesweepers between 1947 and 1949. These ships were about two thirds the length and displacement of the ex-American sub-chaser. YMS-512 had been renamed *Guwolsan* and YMS-518 *Goseong*. Each ship's compliment was half that of *Bak du San's*. Both vessels mounted one mousetrap anti-submarine throw-ahead system and, like

---

[5] History of PC-701 *Bak du San*: Roger Chesneau, *Conway's All the World's Fighting Ships, 1922-1946.* (London: Conway Maritime Press, 1980), s.v. "Submarine-Chasers;" N. J. M. Campbell, *Naval Weapons of World War Two.* (Annapolis, Maryland: Naval Institute Press, Reprinted 2002), s.vv. "United States of America," "Light Caliber Guns," "Automatic Guns," "Ahead-Throwing Weapons;" Naval History & Heritage Command, "USS PC-823, 1944-1948," Naval History & Heritage Command, http://www.history.navy.mil/photos/sh-usn/usnsh-p/pc823.htm (accessed 17 December 2007); Naval History & Heritage Command, "*Pak Tu San* (Submarine Chaser # PC-701, 1950-1960)," Naval History & Heritage Command, http://www.history.navy.mil/photos/sh-fornv/rok/roksh-mr/paktusn.htm (accessed 17 December 2007).

INITIAL BURDEN

the larger anti-submarine warfare vessel, possessed one 3 inch/50-caliber gun. Their biggest shortcoming was that they could not match even the modest speed of *Bak du San*. The patrol boats could only make 12 knots.[6]

The sub-chasers and minesweepers purchased by the ROKN served but one purpose: to protect South Korea's ports and harbors by seeking out and engaging enemy craft in the littorals of the Korean peninsula south of the 38th parallel.

5-2 YMS Minesweeper

As the final minutes of daylight flickered in the westernmost waters of the Sea of Japan the trio of patrol craft

---

[6]Background on ROKN minesweepers: Chesneau, *Conway's 1922-1946*, s.v. "Submarine Chasers;" Wikipedia, "List of Republic of Korea Navy Ships," "Mine Warfare," "Auxiliary Motor Minesweepers (AMS/YMS)," Wikipedia: the Free Encyclopedia, http://en.wikipedia.org/wiki/List_of_Republic_of_Korea_Navy_ships (accessed 17 December 2007), Wikipedia, "BYMS Class Minesweeper," Wikipedia: the Free Encyclopedia, http://en.wikipedia.org/wiki/BYMS_class_minesweeper (accessed 17 December 2007).

The above Wikipedia "List of Republic of Korea Navy Ships" has surprisingly detailed information on the acquisition, names, and fate of the ROKN minesweepers and ex-Japanese minesweepers and minelayers.

made their way very slowly up the coast. The patrol boats had sortied from Pusan a few hours before upon hearing reports that the North Koreans had undertaken amphibious landings further up the coast near Samchok and Kangnung. There were also some conflicting reports regarding landings even farther to the south. They were making unusually slow progress because *Guwolsan* had begun experiencing mechanical difficulties with one of her 1,000 horsepower diesel engines. Her engine problems had slowed the whole group to just eight knots.

In the gloaming, on board *Bak du San*, "smoke was observed on the horizon"[7] to the north. Because of the difficulties being experienced by *Guwolsan* it was decided that *Bak du San* would leave *Goseong* to look after her ailing sister ship while the former American sub-chaser would detach from the group to investigate the sighting. With agreement from the other vessels, *Bak du San* duly set a course north at flank speed.

At a distance of approximately six miles *Bak du San* challenged the unknown ship by blinker light signal. In the enveloping darkness, it appeared to be a 1,000-ton steamer heading due south. The ship, flying no flags or colors, did not acknowledge *Bak du San's* signal and continued her southerly course unabated at about twelve knots.

In the darkness, *Bak du San* closed quickly and, at a distance of about 600 yards, directed her searchlight on the mysterious ship. What she discovered quickened the hearts of her crew. Visible on her decks were hundreds of soldiers and what looked like stacked boxes of ammunition. The searchlight also revealed that the transport was armed. The

---

[7] "Smoke was observed on the horizon..." The direct quote was taken from Karig, Cagle, and Manson, *Battle Report,* 29.

glare of the light exposed the presence of a 76-mm gun on the forward deck and four heavy machine guns mounted near the stern of the vessel. Switching off her searchlight, she swung away from the armed vessel.

As *Bak du San* circled at a somewhat safer distance, she radioed South Korean Naval Headquarters in Pusan that she had discovered what she believed to be a North Korean attempt to land troops at or near the port city. The small ROKN sub-chaser received almost immediate permission and orders to engage the enemy vessel. The South Korean sub-chaser came about in the darkness, maneuvered into a position opposite the transport, and opened fire. She unleashed about 20 rounds from her sole 3-inch gun. Fired upon, the armed transport returned in kind with the 76-mm gun on her forward deck. A shell from the armed transport tore into *Bak du San's* wheelhouse with deadly force instantly killing the helmsman while seriously wounding the officer of the deck. However, *Bak du San's* gunfire also seemed somewhat successful as it had the effect of slowing the armed transport. In the murky night waters, visibility was extremely difficult. *Bak du San* did not want to turn on her search light for fear of helping the enemy combatant to target her. Therefore, as best she could, *Bak du San* began firing again at the ghost-like ship. However, this time, after firing another 20 rounds, the gun jammed. The former American sub-chaser had only joined the South Korean Navy a few months before. The crew had not had a lot of time to perform gunnery drills and hone their skills with their new weaponry. Greatly diminished in terms of offensive power *Bak du San* turned to her much smaller .50 caliber machine guns. With her wheelhouse in shambles, sailors killed and wounded, would she be struck again? Would she survive another blow?

The only sounds that could be heard were those of the crew of *Bak du San* frantically attempting to un-jam the 3-inch gun. More silence. Realizing that the transport had slowed dramatically and was not returning fire as expected, *Bak du San* again turned on her searchlight and aimed it once more toward the enemy vessel. What the light revealed was exhilarating. The armed transport was listing heavily to starboard. The gun, whose fire had smashed into *Bak du San's* wheelhouse with deadly results, was now tilting at a precarious angle because of transport's list, no longer threatening the South Korean vessel. Enemy troops were going over the side into the water. *Bak du San's* gunfire had in fact been lethal. Some of her 3-inch shells had struck the armed transport below the waterline, quickly filling her with seawater. In short order the North Korean vessel, with the groan of metal straining and twisting, showed her screws and plummeted to the bottom. Many North Korean soldiers, trapped in the hold of the transport, were unable to make their way to the deck in time to go over the side and escape the sinking vessel. There were no recorded survivors. Those who had escaped weighed down by their uniforms, boots, and equipment all drowned.[8]

---

[8] *Bak du San* versus the North Korean armed transport: Karig, Cagle, and Manson, *Battle Report,* 29-30; NavSource Naval History, "Submarine Chaser PC-823," NavSource Naval History, http://www.navsource.org/archives/12 /010823.htm (accessed 18 December 2007); Donald W. Boose, *Over the Beach: U.S. Army Amphibious Operations in the Korean War,* (Fort Leavenworth, Kansas: Combined Studies Institute Press, 2008), 113-114.

I have not been able to secure a copy of the War Diary of the Republic of Korea Navy (Task Group 96.7/95.7). It may provide more detail, or alternatively, it may be closer to the NavSource Naval History narrative cited second above. The NavSource Naval History website purports that their description of the surface action was a translation of a narrative signed by the ROKN CNO on 23 December 1988.

An estimated 600 troops of the 3rd Battalion of the 766th North Korean Independent Unit (regiment) died in the sinking of the armed transport. Had they reached Pusan, their mission was to take the city, destroy the port facilities, and prohibit the United States or any other Western power from landing supplies and reinforcements at this key entry point to South Korea. The 3rd Battalion's orders further stated to hold the port until the North Korean 5th Division and the rest of the 766th Independent Unit could link up with the battalion in Pusan. Those two latter forces were now driving hard down the eastern coast of Korea.

The small but sturdy sub-chaser *Bak du San* had more than rewarded her crew and country for the small investment of $18,000. The deadly encounter between the ROKN patrol craft and the North Korean armed transport was a little known but possibly very significant victory for the young South Korean Navy on that first day of what would soon be called the Korean War.

Chapter 6

First Things First

SS *Pioneer Dale*

On the morning of the invasion, the 459-foot American registered cargo vessel, *Pioneer Dale*, quite unaware of the events unfolding on the Korean peninsula, was steaming across the Sea of Japan in overcast skies from Kobe, Japan heading for Pusan. The good news was that the typhoon that had threatened its schedule the day before had changed course and now no longer posed a problem.

Pioneer Dale had originally sailed from the port of New York two months prior. She had taken on cargo along the East Coast and then transited into the Pacific via the Panama Canal, refueled at San Pedro, California and then sailed to Asia via the Hawaiian Islands. In the Far East *Pioneer Dale* had already made stops in Manila, Hong Kong, Yokohama, and Kobe. She had thirteen more stops to make before a planned return to New York in late August.

Built in August 1945, and originally christened *Resolute* the merchant ship was later renamed *Pioneer Dale* in 1948. The American merchant ship displaced over 10,000 tons when fully loaded with cargo and could make 15 ½ knots. She carried a variety of boxed, crated, bagged and bundled goods. Although she was only five years old, because of new and larger ships under construction in the immediate post-war era, the fiscal pressure of competitive peacetime maritime trade was already putting a strain on her owners.

Pioneer Dale entered the harbor at Pusan and tied up at the head, or seaward end, of Pier #1. Just after beginning the process of off-loading cargo, word reached her of the attack on South Korea. Cargo operations halted and the crew of 51 merchant seamen was ordered to remain on board the ship. The crew waited for some clarification of the state of affairs on shore. Later the U.S. State Department officials conveyed to the crew their wish to confer with them.[1]

It was not the first time *Pioneer Dale* had been involved in a military situation. In September 1948, Chinese Nationalist forces under the leadership of Chiang Kai-shek attacked three American merchant ships, eventually detaining them in the port of Shanghai. This forced the United States to move its shipping operations 350 miles north to the Chinese communist controlled port of Tsingtao on the Yellow Sea. On 27 February 1949 in open water just outside of Tsingtao harbor, military aircraft attacked the merchant ships *Pioneer Dale* and *Flying Clipper*. The crews on both ships would later describe the attack as coming from Chinese Nationalist forces because they recognized the aircraft as P-51s and B-25s. The Chinese Nationalists had purchased these types of aircraft from the United States. The P-51s diving at the merchant ships with impunity strafed and damaged both of the American ships. After the fighters finished their attacks, *Pioneer Dale* and *Flying Clipper* narrowly escaped seven bombs dropped by B-25s. Three days later *Pioneer Dale* docked at Kobe, Japan. The ship

---

[1] Basics on merchant ship *Pioneer Dale*: Miramar Ship Index, "Single Ship Report," "*Pioneer Dale*," Miramar Ship Index. http://miramarshipindex.org.nz (accessed 21 December 2010); United States, *Ships of the American Merchant Marine*, (Washington D.C.: U.S. Government Office, 1950), 10; Maurstad, *SOS Korea 1950*, 247.

showed evidence of the attack with bullet holes from machine gun fire from the fighters having riddled the ship at various locations. The Chinese Nationalists later said the Tsingtao incident, as it was to be remembered, had all been a misunderstanding. *Pioneer Dale's* crew thought otherwise.[2]

U.S. Naval Support for Evacuation of Inchon

Moored to buoys in the middle of Sasebo harbor early Monday morning 26 June, two American destroyers *De Haven* and *Mansfield* each had one boiler steaming to generate electrical power. At 0400, each lit the second of their four boilers and began preparing to get underway. Less than an hour later the sun began to appear in the east over the Sea of Japan. The harbor was glass-like. Around them at Sasebo were merchant ships, naval yard craft, and other small vessels. In another hour, they were ready to stand out of the harbor. By then fog had begun to roll in. Because the temperature had only dropped to 65 degrees during the night, it was already warm in this southern Japanese city. Both warships maneuvered at various speeds and made course changes to conform to the channel leading out of the port. By 0730, they were out to sea and steaming at flank speed of 25 knots.

De Haven and *Mansfield* proceeded toward Inchon along the west coast of Korea on the Yellow Sea as per their orders. They were to provide support and escort for merchant ships ferrying American dependents and others

---

[2]Tsingtao Incident account: *New York Times*, 27 Feb, 2 Mar, 4 Mar, and 17 Mar 1949.

INITIAL BURDEN

fleeing the advance of the North Korean Army that was then bearing down on the capital city of Seoul.

Once out into open water, the two destroyers assumed stations with *De Haven* settling in 2,000 yards on the starboard beam of *Mansfield* while both ships maintained 25 knots. Just after 1000, the pair of destroyers passed a Japanese fishery inspection vessel as the crew on board the inspection boat looked on at the impressive sight of the fast moving warships. Within the next hour, each crew would perform the daily routine of inspecting the magazines and smokeless gunpowder samples on board. By noon, there were only a few clouds in the sky, with the temperature at near 80 degrees, and the wind slight at just six knots. In clear view about 40 miles ahead was Chejo-do. The large island marks the western edge of the East China Sea, where the two destroyers were, and the Yellow Sea to the west, their destination.

The orders from Naval Forces Far East for the two destroyers had come so quickly that the crews had no time to sort out the developing situation. However, their instructions were clear. They were going to support the evacuation of American dependents in harm's way. Whether the United States was going to participate in the conflict had still to be decided. However, as the day progressed, the warships changed their formation to that of a scouting line (a horizontal line) with the ships about 20 miles apart and reduced their overall speed to around 20 knots.

Washington D.C. is fourteen time zones removed from Korea: when *De Haven* and *Mansfield* got underway at 0600 hours on Monday, 26 June, it was 1700 or 5 pm (Eastern Daylight Time) Sunday, 25 June in the U.S. capital. The North Korean invasion had begun while President Harry S. Truman was flying from Baltimore to his home in

Independence, Missouri. The President, ironically, earlier that day, had dedicated the new Friendship National Airport in Baltimore "to the cause of peace in the world." Truman received news of the invasion on Saturday night at his home in Independence. He waited until the next morning to fly back to Washington because of the sketchiness of the initial reports and to avoid arousing the alarm of the press. Once in Washington the president scheduled a meeting for that evening with his aides and the Joint Chiefs to begin constructing a policy to match the events taking place on the other side of the world. By the time the meeting had ended and President Truman had reached some policy decisions, and they had been relayed as orders to American military forces in the Far East, *De Haven* and *Mansfield* had been at sea for six hours.[3] Thankfully, the U.S. armed forces had, much earlier that day, put in motion the plans to support this effort.

Much of the credit for the immediacy of these evacuation orders resulted in large part because of the quick work of the American Ambassador to South Korea, John J. Muccio. The Ambassador, like others present at the beginning of the invasion, thought the attack was a raid, as had frequently occurred in the previous months. His investigations during that first day though had firmly convinced him of the seriousness of the situation. As the possibility of the NKPA overrunning Seoul became more evident, Muccio requested immediate evacuation of Americans. The ambassador was also communicating with the American military in Japan and

---

[3] American destroyers depart from Sasebo on evacuation support operation: *USS De Haven* and *USS Mansfield*, Deck Log, 26 June 1950; WolframAlpha Computational Knowledge Engine, "Weather for Sasebo, Japan, 26 June, 1950," Wolframalpha.com (accessed 12 February 2011).

the State Department officials in Seoul and Pusan. The U.S. military, realizing how fast the situation was deteriorating, put into play evacuation plans in which U.S. Naval Forces Far East and the U.S. Air Force would play vital roles. Muccio directed the evacuation effort. After the evacuation was complete he moved south with the South Korean government when they too abandoned Seoul. Ambassador Muccio eventually received two commendations from the American government for his quick response under extremely difficult circumstances.[4]

M/S Reinholt

The U.S. Air Force flew many Americans out of Seoul's Kimpo Airfield. Those that were not as lucky took to buses, trucks, cars and anything else that would move and headed for Inchon. When all of these vehicles arrived at the port at daybreak, there were two merchant ships, the Norwegian merchant ship *Reinholt* and Panamanian flagged *Norelg*, anchored some distance from the shore in the middle of the bay. The ships were unable to come in any closer because of the severe tides that Inchon experiences. At Inchon, tides rise and fall on average over twenty feet. Even as the evacuees were arriving at the port the crews of both ships were attempting to scrub and clean their holds to remove as much of the remains as possible of the fertilizer cargos they had been carrying.

After inspecting both ships, officials at Inchon made a determination that *Norelg* was too unsanitary to accommodate evacuees.[5] All of the evacuees would have to

---

[4] U.S. Ambassador to South Korea, John J. Muccio: Karig, Cagle, and Manson, *Battle Report*, 20-22.

[5] Maurstad, *SOS Korea 1950*, 211.

make the passage on *Reinholt*. From late morning to mid afternoon small barges full of evacuees were literally "poled" by South Korean personnel out to the Norwegian based cargo ship through muddy shallow tidal conditions.

The U.S. Air Force provided air cover during the day. In the early afternoon two North Korean fighters appeared from out of the clouds over the harbor and attacked a pair of USAF all-weather F-82 fighters. The pilots in the American aircraft were, for whatever reason, unsure as to whether or not to return fire. At least one of the evacuees Dr. Patricia Bartz, writing years later related, "we were poled — slowly-slowly — in barges over the mud flats [and] my barge experienced a few shots from two enemy planes overhead to scare us."[6] Oddly, the USAF fighters "took evasive action."[7] The Communist aircraft hit nothing but the appearance of the North Korean fighters frightened

---

[6] Dr. Bartz remarks: "we were poled — slowly-slowly — in barges..." cited in Boose, *Over the Beach*, 114.

[7] Robert Frank Futrell, *The United States Air Force in Korea 1950-1953*, Revised Edition, (Washington D.C.: Office of Air Force History, United States Air Force, 1983), 9. Edwin P. Hoyt, *The Pusan Perimeter*, New York, Stein and Day Publishers, 1984), 28.

As to the confusion surrounding the North Korean air force attack, Futrell asserts that the U.S. fighter pilots had orders to "shoot in defense of the freighters" and that "the evacuation vessel [*Reinholt*] was not in danger." But what about the evacuees who were incredibly exposed on the barges being manually poled out to *Reinholt*? Without any further explanation Futrell's defense of the American fighters' non-action when they were "bounced" by the North Korean aircraft seems at best a bit thin. It does not really explain the point or value of having between two and four USAF aircraft providing cover for the evacuation effort all day at Inchon if they had no intention of engaging enemy aircraft...even when fired upon.

everyone, especially those mothers attempting to protect their children.[8]

Reinholt operated with a crew of 34 men and had passenger accommodations on board for normally only 12 travelers. Bags of belongings were stored on the deck, but because of rain and squally weather forecast for the next few days, the displaced dependents found accommodations in the four different holds of the ship. Primitive toilet facilities on board necessitated the establishment of a bucket brigade from each of the holds to the railings on the main deck. In all 682 evacuees were on board *Reinholt* when she weighed anchor at around 1600 on 26 June.[9]

Reinholt, a 9,000 gross ton cargo ship had been built in Malmo, Sweden in 1939, and had carried cargo to and from Europe and the United States during the war. In 1942, while carrying a cargo of hides from Santos, Brazil to New York, a German submarine surfaced and began firing. Hit 15 to 20 times *Reinholt* escaped, with one crewmen killed and two injured. The human cargo in her hold on this day however was infinitely more valuable than it had been eight years ago at the height of Second World War.[10]

---

[8] Description of embarkation of evacuees at Inchon: Ibid.; Maurstad, *SOS Korea 1950*, 96-97.

[9] Accommodations on board *Reinholt*: Karig, Cagle, and Manson, *Battle Report*, 27-28.

[10] German submarine attack on *Reinholt* during 1942: Siri Holm Lawson, Warsailors.com website, http://war sailors.com.singleships/reinholt.html (accessed 1 Dec 2008).

Back out in the Yellow Sea, *De Haven* established radio contact with *Reinholt* at 2200. Then just after midnight, *Mansfield's* radar detected a surface contact that turned out to be the Norwegian merchant ship carrying the American dependents. Even at that late hour, the evacuees cheered the news that the destroyers had arrived. The anxiety caused by the quickly unfolding events on the Korean peninsula and the less than adequate conditions on board the ship signaled that not many evacuees were getting much sleep. By 0200, with *De Haven* in the lead and *Reinholt* 2,000 yards astern, the destroyer and merchant ship started on their passage to Japan.[11]

Another merchant ship, the American registered *Marine Snapper*, entered Inchon at about noon on the 27th. As soon as *Marine Snapper* arrived, she took on yet more Americans who had not made it to Inchon in time to board *Reinholt*. After only a few hours in port, she was on her way out to sea where the merchant ship met up with *Mansfield* who had stayed behind to provide her escort. They both then set a course that would take them to Japan.[12]

After completing their escort duties, *De Haven* and *Mansfield* made for Sasebo the next day. Upon arrival, the destroyers made their way to the fuel dock and refilled their tanks. *De Haven* took on 54,451 gallons of what the U.S. Navy called "black fuel oil." Naval vessels, working at a high rate of speed, burn a lot of fuel oil. For the first month of

---

[11] American destroyers and *Reinholt* rendezvous: USS *Mansfield*, Deck Log and War Diary, 27 June 1950; USS *De Haven*, Deck Log and War Diary, 26-27 June 1950.

[12] Evacuation of American dependents from Inchon on *Reinholt*: Maurstad, *SOS Korea, 1950*, 88.

the war, the ships of U.S. Naval Forces Far East would have to make many trips from Korea back to Sasebo to refuel because the United States had no ocean-going oilers in the Japanese and Korean theater. Until those vessels arrived in the following months, it was a back and forth affair for the thirsty warships.

Pusan Evacuation

The other large contingent of American dependents was in Pusan. There, the word had spread that the North Koreans had tried to land troops in or near that port the first night of the invasion. Now, with the capture of Seoul imminent, thoughts turned to evacuating American dependents from this southern most city.

Pusan was the chief port in South Korea. The port facilities themselves were adequate with the piers having rails and cranes to handle heavy cargo. Warehousing was abundant. On the down side, the city's transportation system was rudimentary, with bicycles far exceeding motor vehicles. However, the port boasted a marine radio station, with the eerily appropriate call letters HLP.

Concerns about the value and importance of Pusan in the defense of South Korea were rapidly coming into clear focus. The civilian population and some of the American advisors created round-the-clock guard shifts to help defend the docks, power barge, and marine telegraphy station. Probably the greatest fear was that the North Koreans might attempt to sink a ship at the entrance to the outer harbor at the breakwater. If successful, it would block incoming ships to the harbor and trap ships already there.[13]

---

[13] Some details about Pusan and the evacuation: Maurstad, *SOS Korea 1950*, 52-53, 55, 196, and 200.

On the evening of the 27th, 30 vehicles transported the wives and children of American State Department workers to the docks. The Catholic Bishop of Seoul had made a request to evacuate a group of Maryknoll Sisters that were in Pusan, to which the United States obliged. The dependents and others boarded *Pioneer Dale* and another American cargo ship *Jesse Lykes* that was also in port. With humidity at around 90% and the temperature at 75 degrees both ships were out of the harbor and out to sea by 0300 of the 28th. Only those men who were working for the U.S. State department remained behind.[14]

The advancing North Korean Army and the swirling confusion and alarm associated with the sudden invasion had left little time for those directly involved in the crisis to sort out whether there were larger geo-political forces at work or not and what the implications possibly were. However, that was not the case in the U.S. capital.

---

[14] Evacuation of Maryknoll Sisters: *Maurstad, SOS Korea 1950,* 248, 250-251. The second cargo ship to help in the evacuation from Pusan, *Jesse Lykes*, is cited by Maurstad as *Lyticia Lykes*. All other sources indicate *Jesse Lykes*.

Chapter 7

First Lightning

Semipalatinsk-21

Deep in central Asia in what is today Kazakhstan's arid steppe region at the Semipalatinsk-21 test range, everything was uncertain for Igor Kurchatov and Lavertii Beria. Kurchatov was one of the Soviet Union's finest physicists and technical head of its atomic bomb program. Beria, charged with overall responsibility for that program's success, was Stalin's chief of the Soviet Secret Police (NKVD). Both Kurchatov and Beria were in a bunker well back from the test tower constructed down range on the site. A technician switched a lever to the on position and after a few seconds all present felt a sharp bump in the ground beneath their feet. Then there was an unnerving moment of stillness as the two solitary figures standing next to each other unconsciously stopped breathing. After what seemed to both men like an eternity. A.I. Ioirysh, a Russian writer, describes what happened next.

> At the top of the tower an unbearably bright light flared up. For an instant it weakened and then began to grow quickly with new strength. The fiery white sphere swallowed the tower and structure and, rapidly expanding, changing color, strove upwards.[1]

---

[1] A. I. Ioirysh, cited in: Michael D. Gordin, *Red Cloud at Dawn: Truman, Stalin and the End of the Atomic Monopoly*, (New York: Farrar, Straus and Giroux, 2009), 174.

When the two men finally witnessed the poisonous mushroom-like cloud, both exhaled and Kurchatov burst out "It works! It works!" Beria, for his part, in an expressive act completely out of character, impulsively grabbed and hugged the Russian physicist.

At the test site, in addition to detonating the nuclear device, the Soviets had built a variety of structures to test the impact of the explosion. These constructs included buildings, houses, a railroad bridge complete with rail cars, and even a subway. To measure the blast's effects, scientists placed cars, trucks, and military equipment of all kinds at varying distances from ground zero.

To gain information concerning the effects of radiation, scientists further placed 1,000 animals of different types in preselected positions around the test site with varying degrees of protection. This was all new. The Soviets knew the American bomb had been extraordinarily powerful. Yet, for most, there was still a lack of appreciation for just how destructive atomic power could be. The heat alone generated by the blast incinerated fully a quarter of the test animals. The Soviet Union had successfully exploded its first atomic bomb. The date was 29 August 1949.

How important was the success of the test? Beria is purported to have told Kurchatov that had the test been a failure Stalin would have certainly had both of them shot. In fact, about a year before the test took place, Beria asked another Soviet physicist, A. I. Alikhanov, to become Kurchatov's assistant. In attempting to make the assistant position more acceptable to him, Beria intimated that should the first test fail Kurchatov would be shot and Alikhanov would succeed him as head of the project. Alikhanov discreetly declined the position.

The 22 kiloton explosion, equivalent to the American Nagasaki bomb of 1945, now leveled the military playing field between the Soviets and the Americans. The Americans named their original atomic bomb test "Trinity." The Soviets named their test blast *"Pervaia Molniia"* (First Lightning). Each side now possessed in their military arsenals what many would have described as the next major weapon with which to prosecute future wars.[2]

A little over three weeks after the Soviet test, President Truman announced to the nation that the Soviets had indeed exploded a nuclear device. After Truman's announcement the *Bulletin of American Scientists,* an academic journal that had been regularly featuring a doomsday clock on its front page, changed the time left from eight minutes to just three minutes remaining before the clock would strike 12.[3]

On 31 January 1950, President Truman directed the Atomic Energy Commission (AEC) to pursue the development of the hydrogen bomb or as it was commonly then referred to — the "super bomb." Truman said, "[I]t is my responsibility as Commander-in-Chief to see that our country is able to defend itself against any possible aggressor."[4]

---

[2] Soviet atomic bomb test: Gordin, *Red Cloud at Dawn*, 167-68, 171, 173; Robert Service, *Stalin: A Biography*. (Cambridge, MA: Harvard University Press, 2005), 508; Thomas Ott, Writer, Producer, Director, "Race for the Super Bomb," From the television series American Experience, Public Broadcasting System (PBS), Originally aired 1999.

[3] Nuclear weapons development: Lisle A. Rose, *The Cold War Comes to Main Street: America in 1950*, (Lawrence, Kansas: University Press of Kansas, 1999), 99.

[4] Truman remarks regarding the hydrogen bomb cited in: Edward Teller and Judith Schoolery, *Memoirs: a Twentieth Century Journey in Science and Politics*, (Cambridge Massachusetts: Persus, 2001), 289.

Both the United States and Soviet Union were now firmly committed to the further development of nuclear arms. The world at the beginning of the second half of the 20th century seemed less safe than ever.

American culture began to reflect a growing consciousness of the destructive power of nuclear weapons and their possible use. In 1948, W. H. Auden authored a Pulitzer Prize winning poem and the following year conductor Leonard Bernstein composed a symphony. Each titled their work *Age of Anxiety*.[5]

U.S. Foreign Policy

By the time President Truman had returned to Washington from Independence it was clear to him that he was going to do whatever might be necessary to save South Korea. Moreover, Truman in a less nuanced manner was saying the United States, from this point forward, would stand up to any possible Soviet sponsored aggression anywhere in the world. Truman saw the developing situation on the Korean peninsula, as a means of clearly signaling this intention to Stalin. Moreover, the president was not alone in this thinking. Almost all voices in Washington and for that matter Western Europe felt the Korean crisis was a direct result of Soviet global designs. They believed that the invasion of South Korea might be a stratagem before an attack by the Soviets on Western Europe. The communist thrust had to end here. Though it was not the location of

---

[5] American culture in the late 1940s: Bernard Grun, *The Timetables of History: A Horizontal Linkage of People and Events*. (New York: Simon and Schuster, 1982), 528-29.

INITIAL BURDEN

their choosing, President Truman and the United States would make their stand in South Korea.[6]

Also on that Sunday, the United Nations Security Council met and adopted Resolution #82 that called for the "immediate cessation of hostilities." Two days later the United Nations would publish a follow-up resolution recommending that member states assist the South Koreans. The speed and purposefulness with which the UN acted was not due to that body's willingness to come together during a crisis and take firm action. It happened because the Soviet Union was, at that time, boycotting the United Nations for recognizing the Chinese Nationalists on Formosa (Taiwan) as the sole government of China, and refusing to recognize the Chinese Communists on the mainland. Had the Soviets not been protesting the Security Council they would have certainly vetoed at least the second of the resolutions calling for the support and defense of South Korea if not both.

In its first edition following the invasion, The *New York Times* called North Korea a Soviet "puppet regime" and stated that the attack was "obviously Soviet-authorized." Though the intentions of the Soviet Union were still foggy to the signers of the United Nations resolution, it was clear

---

[6] Blair House meeting 25 June and Soviet threat: Robert J. Donovan, *Tumultuous Years: the Presidency of Harry S. Truman 1949-1953*. (New York: W. W. Norton, 1982), 196-197; Richard Whelan, *Drawing the Line: The Korean War*, 1950-1953, (Boston, Massachusetts: Little, Brown), 1990, 119-120; Sean M. Maloney, *Securing Command of the Sea: NATO Naval Planning 1948-1954*, (Annapolis, Maryland: U.S. Naval Institute Press, 1995), 100.

that the North Korean military was a product of the Soviet Union and completely dependent upon them.[7]

The Soviet Union saw the world differently than the Western powers did at the end of the Second World War. The Soviets, through intimidation and force, had begun to take control of most of Eastern and Central Europe. Countries that the Soviet Union had liberated while fighting the Germans, such as Poland, Romania, Hungary, Bulgaria, and Albania, succumbed swiftly to internal communist movements controlled by Moscow.

The United States, somewhat naively in the beginning, had begun searching for a foreign policy that was appropriate to the new Soviet threat. In February 1946, George Kennan, an American diplomat to the Soviet Union, sent to the State Department a communiqué later to be known as the "Long Telegram" (because of its overall length of 8,000 words). The document contained the seeds from which grew the United States' policy of "Containment" of the Soviet Union. Kennan stated that Soviet pressure should "be contained by the adroit and vigilant application of counter-force at a series of constantly shifting geographical and political points."[8] From this start, President Truman, in March 1947, announced a policy, which incorporated much of Kennan's thought, specifically promising economic and military aid to

---

[7] Soviet aggression and state sponsorship: John Lewis Gaddis, *Strategies of Containment: a Critical Appraisal of Postwar American National Security Policy*. (New York: Oxford University Press, 1982), 110; Glenn Paige, *1950: Truman's Decision: The United States Enters the Korean War*. (New York: Chelsea House Publications, 1970), 54, 66-67.

[8] Kennan's remarks regarding Soviet containment "...adroit and vigilant application of counterforce..." cited in: Gary B. Nash, *The American People: Creating a Nation and a Society*, 6th ed., Combined Volume, Chapters 1-31, (New York: Pearson Education, 2008), 825.

Greece and Turkey for fighting aggression by armed minorities and outside pressures. From the tenets of this policy speech, the Truman Doctrine emerged. Greece was embroiled in a Civil War, while the Soviet Union directly pressured Turkey for control of the Dardanelles Straits and territory in eastern Asia Minor. In its inchoate state, the Policy of Containment focused on using economic, diplomatic, and other means hopefully short of military action to reign in Soviet expansion. A year after the brutish takeover of Czechoslovakia by communists under the direction of Moscow in 1948, President Truman and the Western allies created the North American Treaty Organization (NATO) to rebuff Soviet advances. As part of this strategy, the United States created the Sixth Fleet for the Eastern Mediterranean, adding many larger warships to what had previously been a much smaller command known as Naval Forces Mediterranean.

The Korean crisis was the event that forced Truman and his aides to confront the Soviet threat and develop a strategy that was more realistic and less theoretical. Truman had decided to take a stand. However, there was a catch. How would he do it with the American armed forces eviscerated in so many ways over the previous five years? For example, the post-war conventional military cutbacks had reduced the active number of U.S. aircraft carriers from over 100 (including light carriers) to a mere 5 at the beginning of 1950. Further, there had been a serious shift in emphasis to nuclear weaponry and away from conventional warfare in the late 1940s American defense budgets. After the Second World War, as sole possessor of this destructive technology, (until the *Pervaia Molniia* test explosion in late 1949) the United States had built its military strategy around twin pillars: atomic strength and the creation of the United Nations to moderate disputes.[9]

Historically, military leaders have been ready to fight the next conflict with the previous war's weapons, tactics, and assumptions. However, between 1946 and 1950, the American military instead embraced the idea of prosecuting future wars, in general, using either tactical or strategic nuclear weaponry. Shifting one third of the defense budget to its newly created (1947) independent Air Force, the United States envisioned battles fought with massive air strikes using atomic weapons to win wars for the foreseeable future. As for the United Nations resolving disputes, even by 1950 the limitations of this idealistic approach were becoming increasingly apparent.[10]

The successful Soviet atomic bomb test finally changed the global geopolitical landscape. The Soviet achievement seemed to galvanize American strategic thinking. It was the beginning in earnest of the Cold War. Now the Pentagon realized that any war that involved the Soviet Union could involve the widespread, at not just one-sided, use of atomic weapons. A new perspective on the basic Containment policy was set forth in a U.S. National Security Council memorandum known as NSC-68. The memorandum argued

---

[9] Post-war American military strategy: E. B. Potter, and Chester W. Nimitz, editors, *Sea Power: A Naval History*. (Englewood Cliffs, NJ: Prentice Hall, 1960), 842-43; Steven T. Ross, *American War Plans 1945-1950*. (London: Frank Cass, 1996), 17.

[10] Acceptance of new technology: Max Boot, *War Made New: Technology, Warfare, and the Course of History, 1500 to Today*. (New York: Gotham Books, 2006), 308; Ronald H. Spector, *At War at Sea: Sailors and Naval Combat in the Twentieth Century*. (New York: Penguin Books, 2002), 319.

that the United States should increase defense spending on conventional military forces as a way of countering incremental and ongoing Soviet challenges. This idea slowly began to crystallize for Truman and his cabinet with the invasion of South Korea. Once the Soviets had the atomic bomb, the United States bit by bit began to realize that its air power and atomic weapons strategy might not be the best course, and possibly a disastrous course, in any future conflict scenario.

However at the outbreak of the Korean War, such precision regarding the possible outcomes for those involved were murky at best. North Korea was clear as to its intentions. The goal was to re-unite North and South Korea under communist rule. The Soviet Union's intentions as the sponsor, chief military advisor, and supplier of weaponry to the North Koreans seemed to be clear but historical analysis today presents an uneven picture of assumptions made by the Western powers of that era. For the West, total victory, which was the military policy of the two previous world wars, could no longer be the only option.[11] Rather, "limited war," that is one in which the objective is of smaller scope than total military defeat of the enemy, would become the new maxim. The Truman administration and the U.S. military had not yet sorted out the implications of a limited war. This lack of interpretation and discernment would haunt the President in the coming months.

---

[11] Soviet Union atomic bomb test as a turning point for American war fighting strategy: Gordin, *Red Cloud at Dawn*, 283; John R. Schindler, "A Dangerous Business: The U.S. Navy and National Reconnaissance During the Cold War" (Brochure), (Fort George G. Meade, Maryland: Center for Cryptologic History, National Security Agency, no date) 4.

Chapter 8

Naval Considerations

Blair House — Initial Orders

At 8pm on 25 June, President Truman sat down for a late dinner with his top aides and military advisors at Blair House in Washington to discuss the crisis unfolding on the Korean peninsula.[1]

As the light meal was finished and the room cleared, President Truman and his aides got down to business. The President asked Air Force General Hoyt S. Vandenberg if the United States could knock out Soviet air bases in the region. The general replied that with the use of atomic weapons the bases could be destroyed but that it would take some time. Truman then directed that the Air Force, "should prepare plans to *wipe out* [emphasis added] all Soviet air bases in the Far East." Indeed The President's instruction to the Air Force also noted, "This was not an order for action but an order to make the plans."[2] Nevertheless, it is clear that Truman, in the first blush of the crisis, was thinking

---

[1] Truman was temporarily residing at Blair House while the White House was undergoing some renovations.

[2] The remarks are taken from Phillip C. Jessup's summary of conversation as recorded in his notes taken during the 1st Blair House Meeting. Jessup was present at the meeting as a member of the State Department staff for then Secretary of State, Dean Acheson.   Phillip C. Jessup, "Memorandum of Conversation, 25 June 1950," From the Papers of Dean Acheson, President Harry S. Truman Library, http//www.trumanlibrary.org/korea (accessed 25 February 2010).

more along the lines of the American military strategy that was more theoretical and less realistic than the more conventional approach suggested by NSC-68.

The discussion then shifted to the Navy. The President asked specifically about the strength of the Soviet naval forces in the Far East. The suggestion surfaced that American naval forces could be of great help in stemming possible further amphibious operations on the east coast of Korea. He also requested more information regarding a report received of forces landing in the southeastern Korean port of Pohang. The President was adamant about the need to obtain more intelligence about what the next move might be by the Soviets.

The result of the meeting was that Truman authorized General MacArthur, to send any ammunition and equipment the general deemed necessary to help the South Koreans. The President also notified MacArthur that he had ordered the Seventh Fleet to move north from Subic Bay in the Philippines to Sasebo in Japan joining U.S. Naval Forces Far East under the direct control of Admiral Joy.[3]

Douglas MacArthur was arguably one of the finest military minds the United States has ever produced. He graduated first in his class at West Point. Decorated nine times for heroism as a colonel and then as a brigadier general in France during the First World War, MacArthur became Army Chief of Staff in the 1930s. Recalled to duty in 1941, he was to lead all U.S. armies in the Southwest Pacific

---

[3] Blair House Meeting 26 June 1950: Phillip C. Jessup, "Memorandum of Conversation, 26 June 1950," From the Papers of Dean Acheson, President Harry S. Truman Library, http//www.trumanlibrary.org/korea (accessed 25 February 2010).

during the Second World War. Awarded the Congressional Medal of Honor for his efforts, the now five-star general had accepted the surrender of Japan for the United States on the battleship *Missouri* in Tokyo Bay. After the war, MacArthur became Supreme Commander of the Allied Powers in post-war Japan. It was during this tenure that the crisis in Korea presented the old general (he was now 70 years of age) with his third major conflict. Asked to take responsibility and control of all U.S. military operations concerning Korea, MacArthur accepted the challenge one last time.

Finally, yet importantly, Washington also ordered the air force and Navy to provide support in the evacuation of all American dependents and other U.S. non-combatants from South Korea.[4] As noted earlier, Truman upon returning from Missouri on that Sunday afternoon did not immediately meet with his advisors. He even waited until after he and his advisors had finished a light dinner. It was nearly 1300 on Monday afternoon of the 26th in Korea, by the time the Navy and Air Force in Japan received the orders to evacuate all U.S. dependents. That is why it was critical that in the early evening, before the supper at Blair House and the following wide-ranging discussion between the President, the cabinet, and military leaders, the Joint Chiefs had contacted General MacArthur by teletype. During this teletype exchange, MacArthur was apprised of the tentative plans to be proposed to the President by Defense and State officials for evacuating the dependents as well as military

---

[4] Orders for the evacuation of American dependents from South Korea: U.S. Military Officials, "Teletype Conference, 25 June 1950," from the Papers of Harry S. Truman: Naval Aide Files, President Harry S. Truman Library, http://trumanlibrary.org/Korea (accessed 12 Feb 2009).

and naval strategies.⁵ The early "heads up" allowed for MacArthur and Admiral Joy to jump-start the evacuation effort.

Blair House — Orders Altered

The next evening the President and his top aides met once again as the crisis in the Far East deepened. At the conclusion of this second meeting, Truman, via teletype conference from his Joint Chiefs to MacArthur in Tokyo, authorized the use of American naval and air forces to defend South Korea, as opposed to providing only ammunition and other military related equipment. He did temper the order by restricting U.S. forces to operating only south of the dividing 38th parallel.

As they had the previous evening, the President and the Joints Chiefs of Staff sought more intelligence regarding Soviet intentions. Asked what he believed the Soviets would do in light of the new orders from the President committing American naval and air forces to the defense of South Korea, MacArthur, in a teletype reply stated "[I]t is believed *most probably* [emphasis added] that retaliatory Soviet action may be taken against Japan or South Korea."[6]

---

[5] Preliminary teletype conference between the Joint Chiefs and MacArthur: James F. Schnabel, *Policy and Direction: the First Year*, (Washington D.C.: Center of Military History United States Army, 1992 Reprint), 67.

[6] MacArthur's quote "...retaliatory Soviet action may be taken...": U.S. Military Officials, "Teletype Conference between Pentagon and General Douglas MacArthur 26 June 1950," Papers of Harry S. Truman: Naval Aide Files, http//www.trumanlibrary.org /korea (accessed 25 February 2010).

Washington also changed an order that it had issued the previous day. Ordered to Sasebo 24 hours earlier, the Seventh Fleet now set a new course for the Formosa Strait. Truman, who's administration had heavily supported Chang Kai-shek's Nationalists, now decided he would insert the naval group between the Communist and Nationalist factions in order to bar either side from attacking the other while the United States was elsewhere occupied dealing with the Korean situation. The President and his administration had decided to use the United States' naval power, as represented by the U.S. Seventh Fleet, in a direct attempt to control the volatile circumstances regarding China.

There was a larger issue surrounding the order to neutralize the Formosa Strait. The problem was that with this directive the United States had unthinkingly provided the Chinese Communists a military gift by, in essence, providing protection for the mainland. As a staff aide of MacArthur's at that time, Major General Courtney Whitney, later stated in his biography of the Five Star General:

> Here for the first time and in a form that seemed harmless to all but a few farsighted military strategists, was the odd concept that was later to so cripple MacArthur in Korea — sanctuary for the enemy. Thus protected from any harassment from Formosa, the Red Chinese leaders moved two of their best field armies from their coastal defenses opposite Formosa to the staging areas north of the Yalu [river] [the border between North Korea and China].[7]

---

[7] Major General Courtney Whitney quotation: Courtney Whitney, *MacArthur: His Rendezvous with History*. (NY: Alfred A. Knoph, 1956), 370.

INITIAL BURDEN

8-1 East Asia

Before the teletype exchange ended, MacArthur and Joy asked that the Seventh Fleet currently heading for the Formosa Strait, instead steam for Buckner Bay in Okinawa.

First, both General MacArthur and Admiral Joy believed that preventing the two Chinese factions from attacking each other could be accomplished using destroyers and military aircraft patrolling the strait between the two belligerents. Second, and more importantly, the Navy did not want the Seventh Fleet at Sasebo either because they were uncertain as to the Soviet Union's intentions regarding the Korean crisis.[8] They did not want to expose the U.S. Seventh Fleet, especially *Valley Forge,* (the fleet's only aircraft carrier) to a possible Soviet attack. After the war with Japan had ended, the American military had estimated that if a war began in Korea the Soviets could easily attack bases, installations, and airfields in Japan at night with up to 200 medium range bombers.[9] Buckner Bay in Okinawa was 400 miles farther south than Sasebo and thus provided more warning and some added assurance of protecting the fleet. That same military study had suggested that if the Soviets gained control of Pusan, they could extend their air attacks as far as Okinawa.[10] The U.S. Air Force in Japan had responsibility for air defense for both Japan and Okinawa. Yet the Air Force

---

[8] If the Soviets wanted to attack Japanese ports with air power the precedent had already been established. During 1945, United States Army Air Force B29's on 30 March had mined the approach to Sasebo. On 28 June, an incendiary strike against Sasebo destroyed half the city. In addition, during July and August the U.S. 7th Air Force's 41st Bombardment Group employed experimental "glide torpedoes" that targeted the harbor of Sasebo. All of the attacks were flown from bases on the Asian mainland. Wesley Frank Craven and James Lea Cate, *The Army Air Forces in World War II: The Pacific: Matterhorn to Nagasaki June 1944 to August 1945*, Volume 5, (Chicago, Illinois: University of Chicago, 1953), 668, 674, and 697.

[9] Possible Soviet air attacks on Japan: Jeffrey G. Barlow, *Revolt of the Admirals: the Fight for Naval Aviation, 1945-1950*, (Washington D.C.: Brassey's, 1998), 83.

[10] Ibid.

lacked sufficient aircraft to meet this mission. As one example, its standard F-80 jet fighter had a combat radius of only 100 miles.[11] As Admiral Joy stated regarding the change in orders to the Seventh Fleet: "I wanted to avoid another Pearl Harbor."[12] Later he would explain, "I thought the Russians intended to start World War Three."[13] Because of this threat, all U.S. naval heavy units (especially *Valley Forge*) and her accompanying support ships replenished at Buckner Bay. In fact, it was not until August that the United States judged Sasebo to be in less danger from the threat of Soviet air attack. It would be only then that the southern Japanese port would become the major staging area for American forces.

U.S. Seventh Fleet

Far to the south, the American Seventh Fleet was at anchor in Subic Bay, the American naval base near Manila, in the Philippine Islands. *Valley Forge* was the only U.S. carrier in the Western Pacific. She was the platform around which the Seventh Fleet's only carrier group was constructed. She had been transiting from Hong Kong to the Philippines when the invasion began, reaching Subic Bay just before 0900 on Monday the 26th. *Valley Forge* spent the day taking on over 400,000 gallons of fuel oil and 140,000 gallons of aviation gasoline.

---

[11] U.S. Air Force air defense capability in the Far East: Ibid., 232.

[12] Joy's quote "I wanted to avoid another Pearl Harbor" cited in Thomas B. Buell, *Naval Leadership in Korea: The First Six Months*, (Washington D.C.: Naval Historical Center, Department of the Navy, 2002), 13-14.

[13] Ibid., 13-14.

The Seventh Fleet was a subset of the U.S. Pacific Fleet. The Pacific Fleet, known for being somewhat less formal than its counterpart in the Atlantic, also exhibited a bit more "swagger". This overall difference in operations between the two major American fleets was due in part to the way the U.S. Navy fought and achieved success in the vastness of the Pacific Ocean during the Second World War. For the most part the Pacific and Atlantic fleets operated independently of each other and only rarely did ships shift between fleets, *Juneau* was one such exception.[14]

The U.S. Seventh Fleet traced its origins to the Second World War. Formed in 1943 the fleet operated out of Brisbane, Australia. While under the command of Admiral Thomas C. Kincaid, the Seventh Fleet made up the bulk of the American ships that participated in the Battle of Leyte Gulf, considered the largest sea engagement in history. After the war, the Seventh Fleet moved its headquarters to Qingdao, China. In 1948, it moved again to Subic Bay, in the Philippines, after the construction of new facilities there and the building of a new airfield at nearby Sangley Point. Today, in 2012, the Seventh Fleet is based at Yokosuka, Japan in close proximity to the Korean peninsula.

Five months before the outbreak of war in Korea, on 2 February 1950, Chief of Naval Operations, Admiral Forrest Sherman, told reporters in Tokyo, that he was proposing to add another aircraft carrier to the Seventh Fleet. In short order USS *Boxer*, a long hull Essex class aircraft carrier (named after a British frigate captured by the U.S. Navy in

---

[14] Pacific Fleet versus Atlantic Fleet: Charles F. Cole, *Korea Remembered: Enough of a War, the U.S.S. Ozbourne's First Tour 1950-1951,* (La Cruces, New Mexico: Yucca Tree Press), 6-7.

the War of 1812), left Alameda, California in order to show the flag in the Western Pacific. She made well-publicized calls to Hong Kong, ports in French Indo-China, Tokyo, and Inchon. *Boxer* was not assigned to the Seventh Fleet. She arrived back at San Diego, ironically on 25 June, where just a day earlier the invasion of South Korea had begun.

Built at the Philadelphia Naval Shipyard and commissioned in 1946, *Valley Forge* CV-45, was an Essex class aircraft carrier. After her shakedown cruise, she joined the Pacific Fleet in San Diego in 1947 using the Panama Canal (the largest ship to have ever done so up to that time). Showing the flag at ports around the world beginning the following year, she joined the Seventh Fleet on 1 May 1950.

As the Seventh Fleet began to move north that Tuesday morning, first toward Sasebo, then in the direction of the Formosa Strait, and finally to Okinawa's Buckner Bay, the countermanding of orders seemed to set the tone for the decidedly unclear beginning to this international crisis. The Seventh Fleet's battle group consisted of the aircraft carrier *Valley Forge*, heavy cruiser *Rochester*, destroyers *Shelton*, *Eversole*, *Fletcher*, *Radford*, *Maddox*, *Samuel L. Moore*, *Brush*, and *Tausig*. The attendant submarines attached to the fleet included *Catfish*, *Segundo*, and *Cabezon*.[15]

British Foreign Policy

After the outbreak of hostilities in Korea, the British Cabinet, led by Prime Minister Clement Attlee, had also

---

[15] History of Seventh Fleet and its composition: Frank A. Manson, "60th Anniversary of the Korean War," *Sea Classics*, June 2010; Field, *U.S. Naval Operations*, 48; U.S. Military Officials, "Teletype Conference, 25 June, 1950," n.p.; Karig, *Battle Report*, 18.

been meeting to discuss policy as it pertained to the North Korean invasion. The British government officials in London, like their American counterparts in Washington, believed that the Soviets were pulling the strings in Asia. In Attlee's government, there was also great fear that if left unchecked the Soviets would foment trouble in places like the Middle East or worse threaten war in Europe.

However, Korea was anywhere from not very, to not at all important, within the framework of the larger picture of British interests. Great Britain had recognized the Communist Chinese government in January of that year, while the U.S. had not. This had happened because the British economic interests with regard to the Chinese mainland and surrounding areas e.g., Hong Kong, Singapore, and the Malay Peninsula, were just too strong. The United States had yet to recognize the Chinese Communist victory in that country's civil war that drove Chang Kai-shek's failed Nationalists to the island of Formosa. Still heavily invested in the Nationalists, the Truman administration had not yet come to terms with the reality of the situation.

Nevertheless, the largest post-war interest of the British government had been to nurture the "special relationship" between herself and the United States. Economically, strategically, and militarily the British now looked to the U.S. as their most important and vital world partner. On Tuesday 27 June, the British Cabinet, based on their assumptions regarding the Soviet Union's role in the invasion and responding to the United States' position of the previous day, gave their full support to the defense of

South Korea.[16] Attlee summed up British policy: "We'll have to support the Yanks".[17]

The day after the invasion had begun, British Rear Admiral William Gerrard "Bill" Andrewes, second in command of the Far East station, with his flag on *Belfast* arrived at Yokosuka at the head of Tokyo bay.[18] The British flagship had slogged her way through heavy seas from Hakodate the previous night. The admiral had a lot on his mind, and once *Belfast* had anchored, made his way ashore and met with American Vice Admiral C. Turner Joy who was responsible for Naval Forces Far East (and shortly would be in charge of the Seventh Fleet and all other American ships in the Korean theater). After exchanging information, they decided that

---

[16] British policy regarding the North Korean invasion: Seow Hwye Min, "British Interests in the Korean War (1950-53)", *Pointer, Journal of the Singapore Armed Forces*, Volume 25, Number 3, July-September 1999.

[17] British decision to support the U.S.: Kenneth Harris, *Attlee*, (London: Wiedenfeld & Nicholson, 1982), p. 454. Cited in Seow Hwye Min, "British Interests in the Korean War (1950-53)", *Pointer, Journal of the Singapore Armed Forces*, Volume 25, Number 3, July-September 1999.

[18] Born in 1899 at St Giles Hill in Winchester, Hampshire, Admiral Andrewes was the second son of the Reverend Canon Gerard Thomas Andrewes. He entered the Royal Naval College at Osborne at the age of 13. In August 1915, he was assigned to the battleship *Canada* that then saw action at the battle of Jutland the following May. He commanded the cruiser *Uganda* for much of the Second World War and then two aircraft carriers in the late 40s. He would go on to command all British and Commonwealth forces in Korea. For his service in the Korean War, he was awarded a Silver Star by the United States and received the Knight Commander of the Order of the British Empire (KBE). Sir William Andrewes would eventually reach the rank of full Admiral retiring in 1957. For more information about Rear Admiral Andrewes see: Wikipedia, "William Andrewes;" Royal Navy Officers (RN) 1935-1945 website, http:// www.unithistories.com/officers/RN_officersA5.html

until more substantive orders were forthcoming, the British fleet would coalesce around the southern Japanese port of Kure. The orders for the British Far East Fleet to support the Americans would come from London within 24 hours.

The naval base at Kure was just 18 miles southeast of Hiroshima. It had been a major base for the Japanese during the Second World War. Since 1946, Kure had served as a naval dockyard for the British Commonwealth Occupation Forces.[19] During the next few days, the British warships and their attendant support vessels moved to the port where they fueled and replenished. The aircraft carrier *Triumph* arrived on Wednesday 28 June. While in port *Triumph* had four Seafire and two Firefly aircraft removed from the ship, all in varying states of disrepair. The disembarkation of the half dozen aircraft freed up some badly needed space on the hangar deck of the light carrier and by Wednesday, the British fleet was ready for action.[20]

U.S. Naval Forces Far East

Meanwhile, as the Royal Navy's Far Eastern Fleet was gathering at Kure and the U.S. Navy's Seventh Fleet was now steaming for Okinawa, ships of U.S. Naval Forces Far East began heading for Korea. The protection from a possible Soviet air attack afforded the Seventh Fleet by diverting it to Okinawa did not extend to the ships of U.S. Naval Forces Far East. Those warships were now commencing operations along the coastline of Korea. For the sailors on those American ships, if the danger from above was not enough to get their blood pumping there

---

[19] British and American admirals meet at Yokosuka: GHS, "Naval Operations in Korea," 382

[20] HMS *Triumph* at Kure 28 June: Lansdown, *With the Carriers in Korea*, 13.

was always the looming menace of the peril from beneath to quicken their hearts.[21]

---

[21] Seventh Fleet's second set of orders: Cagle and Manson, *Sea War*, 34; Karig, *Battle Report*, 43; Field, *U.S. Naval Ops, Korea*, 54; Cole, *Korea Remembered*, 6.

Chapter 9

Hornets' Nest

Soviet Submarine Development

The Soviet Navy had developed sturdy classes of submarines before and during the Second World War. Its employment of them against Nazi Germany had met with much success, particularly in the Baltic Sea.

On the evening of 30 January 1945, the German ocean liner *Wilhelm Gustloff* was well out into the Baltic Sea. She was heading west making her way through the cold and snow some eight hours after her departure from the Polish port of Gotenhofen (now Gdynia). Since the beginning of the war, she had operated as a hospital ship for the Third Reich. With a designed maximum capacity of around 2,000 passengers and crew she, in fact, had on board over 6,000 soldiers and German refugees fleeing Poland from the advancing Soviet Red Army.

In the bitter cold and darkness the Soviet submarine *S-13* fired a spread of three torpedoes that all struck home on the port side of the almost 26,000-ton liner. *Wilhelm Gustloff* shuddered and then, ever so slowly, rolled over and sank.

Over 5,000 souls perished that night. It was the largest loss of life involving one ship in history — twice that of *Titanic* and *Lusitania* combined. The same Soviet submarine just eleven days later sank the 14,000-ton German transport *Steuben*, with loss of life exceeding 3,000. In the battle against Nazi Germany in 1945, the Soviet Navy was taking charge in the Baltic.[1]

In spite of the exploits of the Soviet submarine *S-13* and some others, the Soviet Union has always been a land power. The Navy, especially under Soviet control, has always acted as a seaward extension of the vaunted Red Army. By 1950, the Soviet Navy had made strides in developing a surface fleet, but it was by no means ready to challenge its American counterpart. There were surface ships in Vladivostok that could challenge *Juneau,* but overall the surface fleet of the United States was simply much stronger.[2]

As it proved to the Germans in the Second World War, the Soviet Navy did pose an underwater warfare threat to the U.S. Navy. The Soviets, between 1945 and 1950, had made many advances in the construction of new submarines.[3]

After the war, the Soviets followed two tracks in submarine development. Both paths caught the attention of the

---

[1] The sinking of the *Wilhelm Gustloff*: Brayton Harris and Walter J. Boyne, *the Navy Times Book of Submarines: A Political, Social, and Military History*, (NY: Berkely Books, 1997) 339. The death toll due to the loss of the *Wilhelm Gustloff* has been challenged recently. Heinz Schon has argued that more than 9,000 Germans lost their lives in the sinking. See Robert M. Wise, and James Younger, Directors, "Wilhelm Gustloff," *Unsolved History*, Discovery Channel, 2003.

[2] The Soviet Union as a land power: Jurgen Rohwer, and Mikhail S. Monakov, *Stalin's Ocean-Going Fleet: Soviet Naval Strategy and Shipbuilding Programmes 1935-1953*, (NY: Frank Cass, 2006), 187.

[3] Soviet naval strengths: Jakub, J. Grygiel, "The Dilemmas of U.S. Maritime Supremacy in the Early Cold War," *Journal of Strategic Studies* 28, no. 2: 187-216.

American and British navies. First, the Soviets continued to produce advanced versions of their wartime submarines such as the Stalinet class *S-13* that had sunk *Wilhelm Gustloff*. In all, the Soviets built 62 more submarines based on this track into the early 1950s. The second track involved the amount of attention and effort the Soviets put into the study and development of German submarine technology that they had acquired by either war reparations or capture in 1945 as the Red Army advanced on Berlin. These German U-boats, specifically Type XXI and XXIII versions, launched very near the end of the war, were far in advance of American and British submarines. This was particularly evident in their superior submerged speed, diving capability, endurance, and torpedo reloading technology.

9-1 German U-boat Type XXI

Soviet adaptation and learned expertise of the German submarine technology lagged after the war because of the steep learning curve it presented. Every aspect of the German U-boats provided new insights including: battery life for staying submerged, new steel types, advanced electrical welding techniques, and an anechoic coating on the submarines used to deaden sound and thus help evade detection. The Soviets even had to build a completely new research center in Leningrad that specifically dealt with the development of a propulsion system based on the German design.[4]

The Soviets eventually gained the necessary knowledge to produce advanced submarines but not without some trial and error. In one case during 1946, the Soviets tested a German Type XXIII u-boat in the Caspian Sea. The boat submerged and never resurfaced.[5]

Soviet sonar development came courtesy of the British upon acquisition of radar-equipped Royal Navy surface warships in 1944. In 1948 Raymond Spruance, U.S. Pacific Fleet Commander, stated that the greatest threat to the freedom of the seas was the "high submerged speed and great underwater endurance"[6] of the Soviet Union's submarine force.[7]

The United States' estimate that the Soviets were completing 20 and possibly as many as 30 submarines per month beginning in 1949 turned out to be high. In fact, the numbers were much smaller due to the incredible damage suffered by Soviet ship yards during the Second World War and the lack of technological expertise needed to produce such numbers. Yet the Soviets persisted: for example, M-

---

[4] Soviet submarines and German technology: Norman Polmar, *Soviet Naval Power: Challenge for the 70s,* Revised Edition, (NY: Crane, Russack, 1974), 25. Norman Polmar and K. J. Moore, *Cold War Submarines: The Design and Construction of U.S. and Soviet Submarines*, (Washington D.C.: Potomac Books, 2004), 23.

[5] Caspian Sea incident: Maloney, *Securing Command of the Sea*, 206.

[6] Raymond Spruance quote cited in Kenneth J. Hagan, *This People's Navy: the Making of American Sea Power*, (NY: The Free Press, 1992), 348.

[7] Post-war Soviet submarine development: Polmar, *Cold War Submarines*, 23-24; Allard, *In Peace and War*, 63.

class submarine production shifted from the coastal shipyards to Krasnoye Sormovo Shipyard in Nizhniy Novgorod. Located in the heart of the Soviet Union the smaller shipyard remained undamaged during the war. Here, because of the yard size limitations, the underwater boats were produced in sections and then transported by rail or barge to various shipyards along the coasts for assembly. Thus on the eve of the Korean War, despite the incorrect estimates by the United States, the Soviet Navy still had twice as many boats as the Americans.[8]

Vladivostok Naval Base

Just 500 miles north of Pusan is the Soviet port city of Vladivostok. In 1950, it was home to the 5th and 7th Fleets of the Soviet Navy. During the Second World War Vladivostok's then named Pacific Fleet had been the only Soviet naval force to survive intact and, in only one week of naval operations in 1945, had secured for the Soviet Union the Kurile Islands from the Japanese.

From its geographic location, Vladivostok dominates the Sea of Japan. What is striking about the port is that it looks so much like a city plucked out of the heart of Europe and deposited on the Asian coast in the heart of the Far East. Because of its importance as a year round warm water port on the Pacific Ocean and the construction of the Trans-Siberian Railroad in 1891, Vladivostok sprang to life and flourished until the end of the Bolshevik Revolution. By 1917, because of its activity as a major port and its

---

[8] Soviet submarine production: Norman Polmar, and Jurrien Noot, *Submarines of the Russian and Soviet Navies 1718-1990*, (Annapolis, MD: U.S. Naval Institute, 1991), 138, 327, 331; Spector, *At War, at Sea,* 317; Hagan, *This People's Navy*, 346.

connection to the rest of Russia via the rail system, Vladivostok had become an industrial, cultural, and even a scientific center with the construction of the Oriental Institute. It was from this port city, just 300 miles from the 38th Parallel, that the Soviet Union maintained its largest threat to the course of the Korean War.[9]

Intelligence sources estimated that the Soviets had about 70 submarines at Vladivostok at the beginning of the conflict. Applying the usual naval rule of thumb, approximately one-third of the boats would be available for operations at any given time. Therefore, the assumption was that between the two fleets based there the Soviets had about two dozen submarines that were active to deploy should they wish. Maintained at a high state of operational readiness, these submarines were clearly the greatest threat to the Western navies and merchant shipping.[10]

The U.S. Navy had definite ideas as how to confront the danger of Soviet submarines. During the Great War (1914-1918), President Wilson proffered some advice to U.S. Navy officers about the Royal Navy operating in the Atlantic against German submarines during World War I. In essence, he stressed the importance of attacking German U-boats in their bases, otherwise, as Wilson put it, "[W]e are hunting

---

[9] Vladivostok and the Soviet Navy: Rohwer, *Stalin's Ocean-Going Fleet*, 190; Frank Uhlig, "The Threat of the Soviet Navy," *Foreign Affairs*, Vol. 30, no. 1, (October 1951), 444-454; Eric Morris, *the Russian Navy: Myth and Reality*, (Briar Cliff Manor, NY: Stein and Day, 1977), 118.

[10] Active Soviet submarines in the Pacific at the outbreak of hostilities: Maloney, *Securing Command of the Seas*, 206; Natalia I. Yegorova, "Stalin's Conception of Maritime Power: Revelations from the Russian Archives," *Journal of Strategic Studies* 28, no. 2: 157-186.

hornets all over the farm."[11] He argued that instead of chasing submarines all over the Atlantic; why not destroy them in their homeports? Of course, air power was not that technologically advanced at that time, but it foreshadowed ideas and events to come. At about the time of the Korean conflict U.S. Chief of Naval Operations, Admiral Forrest P. Sherman, had proposed that American naval strategy ought to be, if necessary, attacking the naval base at Vladivostok, and using naval air power to destroy the submarines in their pens (this is before submarine pens were hardened). Therefore, at the beginning of the Korean War the American naval strategy for fighting the Soviet Union was not to focus on escorting convoys and using anti-submarine warfare techniques but rather to hit and destroy the enemy at its source.[12]

There were, of course, a couple of problems with this approach. If there ever was a war with the Soviets, the U.S. Navy wanted to bomb Vladivostok using naval air power from the decks of carriers, while American war fighting strategy at the time was to use the U.S. Air Force with nuclear weapons. The other and immediate problem was that the United States and the Soviet Union were not at war. Korea became the beginning of the Cold War dance that the United States and Soviet Union would engage in for the next forty years.

---

[11] Woodrow Wilson quote cited in George W. Baer, *One Hundred Years of Sea Power: The U.S. Navy 1890-1990,* (Stanford, CA: Stanford University Press, 1994), 72.

[12] American naval strategy for fighting the Soviet Union: Baer, *One Hundred Years*, 289; Spector, *At War at Sea*, 317; Grygiel, "Dilemmas of U.S. Maritime Supremacy," 204-205.

The intelligence the United States possessed regarding the Soviet Navy was unclear and conflicting. However, reported submarine sightings already pointed to the possibility of Russian submarines participating in the growing conflict.

Submarine Tactics

The Americans and British both believed the Soviets might very well join the fray. Submarines in general are known for their stealth and sudden destructive power. For the Western navies this "silent service" was their greatest fear. After all, just one day after the Korean War began the United States had convincing reports of a submarine presence in Korean waters. Tactically, the greatest concern of the Western navies was the speed of the newer Soviet submarines. The current British frigates, such as *Black Swan* and *Alacrity*, both on station in Japan, slow by any standard struggled mightily with this large Russian advantage. Anti-submarine warfare had changed in just the five years since the end of the Second World War. Back in 1943, *Black Swan* performed the duty of protecting convoys between the United Kingdom and Freeport, South Africa. On 2 April 1943, convoy OS45 was west northwest of Lisbon, Portugal when *Black Swan*, along with a British corvette *Stone Crop*, sank the German u-boat *U-124* using depth charges. *U-124* had notoriously sunk 46 merchant vessels and a British light cruiser *Dunedin* before meeting her end. Since then submarines had gotten much faster and frigates like *Black Swan* seemed to have gotten much slower. When in 1950, the representative for the Admiralty and Royal Navy explained and described to the British House of Commons the new technology known as "homing," that is air, surface, and underwater launched torpedoes with the ability to track down their targets, the House members looked dubiously at the speaker and then broke into "incredulous laughter." [13]

9-2 HMS *Black Swan*

Tactically, submarines usually detect surface ships long before they are themselves detected. However, for a submarine to attack a surface ship it has to move into that vessel's sonar detection range. Once the sonar of the surface ship detects a submarine, the assumption is the underwater boat is closing in with hostile intent. At that point, the surface ship will attempt to engage the submarine with anti-submarine weapons. For the crews of the British and American ships on the scene at the beginning of the Korean War nothing focused a sailor's

---

[13] Torpedo homing technology: Wettern, *The Decline of British Seapower*, 31-32.

mind quite like the sound of general quarters signaling a possible imminent submarine attack.

Strategically, the Soviet Navy's submarines posed the most ominous threat to the U.S. and British ships in the Korean theater. If the Soviet boats were lying in wait in the Korean littorals, U.S. Naval Forces Far East, the Seventh Fleet, and the British Far East Fleet would have their hands full.

Chapter 10

Intel

Naval Orders

Juneau arrived at Sasebo at 0600 on the morning of Tuesday 27 June, 17 hours after departing Kagoshima. By 0700, two naval tugs had come alongside *Juneau's* starboard bow and quarter respectively and were easing her into position at the port's fuel dock. She took on 75,000 gallons in less than two hours. In the late afternoon, as *Juneau* prepared to get underway she received the unusual cargo of six cases of hand grenades. A little later that evening, the lean anti-aircraft light cruiser was steaming alone toward the Korean peninsula.

On the night of 26 June, after the second Blair House meeting between President Truman and his top aides, General MacArthur received orders to support South Korea in its defense against the invasion. The orders were received midday on the 27th in Japan. That evening, Admiral Turner Joy issued Naval Operation Order 5-50. U.S. Naval Forces Far East was to patrol South Korean coastal waters, oppose hostile landings, destroy vessels engaged in aggression, provide fire support for friendly forces, and escort ships carrying supplies. The order specified two geographic areas of concern. The first was located in the southeastern corner of the peninsula south and north of Pusan from Tongyong up to Ulsan. The second area was much further to the north around Samchok and Kangnung where the North Koreans had made their amphibious landings a few days before. However, the order specifically stated that American warships were not to venture into North Korean waters above the 38th parallel. At this point, Truman and his top aides were not at all convinced the North Korean invasion was not a diversion for a larger Soviet plan in Europe. Because of this fear the President would end up sending a second carrier group to the Mediterranean.[1] The fact remained that there was no way to divine Soviet intentions.

Lack of Intelligence

The United States had little or no military intelligence regarding North Korea. At the outbreak of the war the Armed Forces Security Agency (AFSA), the forerunner to today's National Security Agency (NSA), had just two part-time cryptanalysts and one linguist dedicated to providing analysis of signal intelligence emanating from North Korea. There was no reading or analysis of signal intelligence intercepts on a daily basis. In fact, daily reading of intercepts did not begin until 29 June; four days after the war had begun. The U.S. Army controlled all captured intelligence documents during the war and was less than forthcoming in providing information to the Navy — even documents with an apparent naval interest.[2]

---

[1] Korea as a Soviet diversion: Paolo E. Coletta, *The United States Navy and Defense Unification*, (Newark, New Jersey, University of Delaware Press, 1981), 238.

[2] State of American military intelligence at the beginning of the war: David A. Hatch with Robert Louis Benson, "The Korean War: The SIGINT Background," http://www.nsa.gov/about/cryptologic_heritage/center_crypt_history/publications/koreanwar_sigint_bkg.shtml#8, (Accessed 3 March 2011); John Keegan, *Intelligence in War: Knowledge of the Enemy from Napoleon to Al-Qaida*, (New York: Alfred A. Knopf, 2003), 323, and Chapter 1; Wyman H. Packard, *A Century of U.S. Naval Intelligence*, (Washington D.C.: Office of Naval Intelligence, 1996), 138; Paul M. Edwards, *Small United States and United Nations Warships in the Korean War*, (Jefferson, North Carolina: McFarland, 2008), 224.

Military intelligence is part science, part art, and often a best guess as to an enemy's capabilities, intentions, and immediate plan of action. The United States had little if any information regarding events unfolding on the Korean peninsula. In the theater itself, the American naval intelligence section in Japan at the outbreak of the war consisted of one officer. He became so overworked at the beginning of the war, not sleeping for days, that he broke his leg after falling asleep while driving a jeep to a meeting. There simply was no intel.[3]

North Korean Resupply Convoy

That same evening, as *Juneau* was standing out to sea from Sasebo, there was naval activity in the North Korean port of Wonsan. The light slowly faded, as the sky, streaked with high clouds, began to darken. Engines on board four motor torpedo boats of the North Korean Eastern Sea Command were sputtering to life. Motor Torpedo Boat Squadron 2, normally consisting of five boats, found itself reduced to four with the decision to leave boat *#25* behind because of engine trouble. Boats *#21* through *#24* eased away from the dock and one by one began to form up in the middle of the harbor. Their orders were to make passage south to Suk Cho, a small port just north of the 38th parallel. There, ten small freighters were waiting for escort to Chumunjin on the South Korean coast. Each of the transports carried food and ammunition. The cargo would help resupply the North Korean 5th Division that was engaged in offensive combat operations along the eastern coast as it moved south with the objective of taking Pusan. After a few more minutes the squadron slowly swung out of the harbor in single file and

---

[3]; Karig, Cagle, and Manson, *Battle Report*, 37.

headed south with additional orders to engage any and all enemy vessels.[4]

Searching for the Enemy

During the night of the 27th/28th *Juneau* crossed the Tsushima and Korea Straits from Japan to the island of Kojedo about 25 miles southwest of Pusan. The solitary cruiser did not have with her any of the four Sumner class destroyers to provide support and cover against underwater threats, with *De Haven* and *Mansfield* still supporting the evacuation of American dependents from Inchon, and *Swenson* and *Collett* on their way to Sasebo from Yokosuka.

As *Juneau* approached the Korean peninsula, reports of enemy naval activity flooded her radio room. U.S. Air Force pilots had sighted multiple submarines and two destroyers painted black with double gun mounts forward. Another report spoke of three enemy warships shooting at a local fishing fleet. In addition, the South Korean Armed Forces reported a North Korean destroyer and three minelayers heading south toward Pusan. These reports, and others like them, led the United States to believe that more amphibious landings had taken place, were in progress, or were imminent along the East Coast, leaving Pusan in jeopardy again. In the end, *Juneau's* Admiral Higgins and Captain J. C. Sowell had to sort out the conflicting reports, establish an intelligence baseline, and then find and attack the enemy.

---

[4] North Korean Motor Torpedo Squadron 2: Robert Leckie, *Conflict: The History of the Korean War 1950-53*, (NY: G.P. Putnam's Sons, 1962), 64; Karig, Cagle, and Manson, *Battle Report*, 57.

Juneau, with ammunition now at all gun mounts, arrived at the island of Koje-do before dawn. Reports indicated the presence of North Korean forces on the island. The weather was rainy and miserable. She slid into the first available bay on the island large enough to allow her entry, anchored in 12 fathoms of water, and proceeded to lower two whaleboats for landing and reconnaissance purposes.

The naval officer in charge of the landing party along with a detachment of marines (now the delivery of hand grenades made more sense) made their way ashore. After some difficulty with basic communication between the landing party and some of the island residents it was determined there was no enemy activity in the area. The eleven sailors and eight marines returned to *Juneau* late that morning. The men came on board, the whaleboats were hoisted, and the light cruiser weighed anchor and began to make her way out to sea.

Juneau received orders to investigate possible enemy activity in and around Urusan Bay near Pohang to the north. The cruiser headed in that direction at 20 knots. The previous day military officials in Washington had asked for information about the present location and direction of movement of enemy forces landed in the Pohang area. General MacArthur on the 27th had sent a message to the members of the U.S. State Department that had remained behind in Pusan asking them to confirm a report that 1,000 North Korean soldiers had landed in that area. The landing could not be confirmed. *Juneau* arrived at Urusan Bay in the early afternoon. After anchoring in 11 fathoms of water, another landing party made their way to shore. Again, the native residents were unable to confirm any enemy activity — although the locals had heard rumors of the enemy being active elsewhere. While waiting for the second landing party to return, *Juneau* went to general quarters because her radar had picked up suspicious air contacts. The aircraft turned out to be some U.S. Air Force planes operating in the area. *Juneau's* search for the enemy was becoming a bit nerve-wracking.[5]

A little after 1800 on the evening of the 28th, *Juneau*, with orders from Admiral Joy of Naval Forces Far East, headed north to the Samchok and Kangnung area between the 37th and 38th parallels. The focus now shifted to the original orders to help defend South Korea which made infinitely more sense than scouting around small islands looking for intel. Amid the confusion surrounding enemy intelligence, Higgins and Sowell were still more concerned with the possibility of Soviet naval participation in defense of its client state North Korea. As *Juneau* began steaming north toward Samchok, she still did not have a destroyer screen.

Barrier Patrol — Yellow Sea

That evening, two of the U.S. Naval Forces Far East destroyers Juneau desired received orders to proceed to the Inchon area along South Korea's west coast to establish a barrier patrol. At 2030, *Mansfield* stood out of Sasebo. The next morning *Mansfield's* sister ship, *Swenson,* followed. On the 29th, both destroyers made their way to "Point Apple," the designated rendezvous destination in the Yellow Sea northwest of Inchon. On board *Swenson,* two steering casualty drills proceeded with hypothetical steering

---

[5] Information regarding the recon efforts at Koje-do and Urusan Bay as well as the confusion surrounding the enemy's movements and intentions: *Juneau*, Deck Log, 27-28 June, 1950; *Juneau*, Action Report, "Personnel Participating in the Landings of Foreign Territory," 14 July 1950; Cagle, *Sea War*, 285-286; Curtin, "Early Days," 27th and 28th; Curtin, "Galloping Ghost;" U.S. Military Officials, "Teletype Conference 25 June 1950, np;" Field, *History of Naval Operations*, 51; Karig, *Battle Report*, 56; Maurstad, *SOS Korea*, 171-172.

maladies occurring and the crew teams responding. Over on *Mansfield* investigations of several sampans proceeded with no issues. Later she test fired 14 rounds of 5-inch Anti-Aircraft Common (AAC) shells and exercised the 40 and 20-millimeter guns. Used against aircraft and lightly armored ships, the AAC projectile consisted of a medium penetrating shell with a mechanical time fuse that exploded 25 milliseconds after contact. At 2000, *Swenson* identified the Panamanian flagged freighter *Unita* and one hour later passed two South Korean patrol craft out of Mukpo on the southwest coast of the peninsula.

The destroyers finally met up at the prearranged location at 0530 the next morning. The two ships promptly set up their barrier patrol along the seaward extension of the military demarcation line between North and South Korea. *Swenson* began patrolling between points "Mike" and "Nan" on an east west axis with *Mansfield* employing the same tactic further to the east. A barrier patrol's purpose is quite simple. *Swenson* and *Mansfield's* task was to distinguish and take action against passage of any North Korean vessels. The two destroyers using radar and good old-fashioned lookouts spent the next couple of days identifying and then investigating junks, sampans, and other watercraft that were heading south from North Korean waters. No North Korean naval vessels attempted to pass. Each of the ships kept their sonar equipment working and each was prepared to use their anti-submarine weapons against any attacking Soviet submarine.[6]

---

[6]West Coast barrier patrol: *Swenson*, Deck Log and War Diary, 28-30 June 1950; *Mansfield*, Deck Log and War Diary, 28-30 June 1950.

Contact?

Would Soviet aircraft or submarines attack American warships? *Juneau* was ever ready for an aircraft threat (after all, she was not known as a "flak battery" for nothing). It was the Soviet submarines that gave *Juneau* pause. The cruiser, built without anti-submarine weaponry, relied on destroyers to perform that sort of work.

Juneau still had no escorts. There were no aircraft available to fly anti-submarine patrols in the area of the cruiser. As *Juneau* continued north toward the 38th parallel, she resorted to using the only tactic she had available to avoid a torpedo attack...zigzagging to present less of a target.[7]

Later that evening *Juneau* began patrolling between Samchok and Kangnung. At 0145 on 29 June, the sound of general quarters sent the crew scrambling to their battle stations. *Juneau's* radar was picking up surface contacts moving south close to the shore. During the next hour, she changed course three times and speed twice trying to sort out the activity on the radar screens. *Juneau* received word that the North Koreans were landing troops along the South Korean coast. The light cruiser, now about 38 miles north of the 37th parallel off Bokuko Ko, opened fire at a range of almost seven miles. The salvos leapt into the night sky. Later information would prove the shellfire to be accurate and deadly.[8]

---

[7] Soviet submarine threat: Paul M. Edwards, *Small...Warships in the Korean War*, 63; Alexander, *Inchon to Wonsan*, 184.

[8] Night action: *Juneau*, Deck Log, 29 June 1950.

British Fleet at Sea

Back in southern Japanese waters, official word came from London that the British Far East Fleet was going to join with the U.S. Navy against North Korea. The British reasoned that a good result in Korea would strengthen their positions and interests in Malaya and Hong Kong. The United Nations Security Council passed a second resolution, No. 83, on 27 June calling in part for member nations to "furnish such assistance to the Republic of Korea as may be necessary to repel the armed attack and to restore international peace and security in the area."[9]

The Royal Navy's orders were to put their ships at the service of the U.S. naval commander for Korean Operations in support of the UN Security resolution. The British fleet would operate with the U.S. Navy under the aegis of the United Nations, which had rebuked North Korea for starting the war and demanded that it return to pre-war positions immediately. It would be the first time a UN led naval force would participate in a shooting conflict.

The aircraft carrier *Triumph* and a destroyer *Cossack* sailed from Kure at dawn on the morning of the 29th. The two vessels would rendezvous with heavy cruiser *Belfast*, light cruiser, *Jamaica*, and the destroyer *Consort* in the afternoon for their passage to Buckner Bay to link up with the U.S. Seventh Fleet. There was only one problem: the British did not know where Buckner Bay was located. During the American assault and battle for the island of Okinawa, in the war against Japan in 1945, American Lieutenant General

---

[9] British naval policy in Korea: Grove, *Vanguard to Trident*, 137; UN Security Council, *Resolution 83* S/RES/83 (1950), available at: http://www.unhcr.org/refworld/docid/3b00f20a2c.html [accessed 1 June 2012].

Simon Bolivar Buckner was killed in action by fragments from a Japanese artillery shell. The American Marines under his command later nicknamed the bay after him and it had stuck — at least on the American charts. A quick chat between the parties resolved the issue. With the matter finally cleared up, the British Far East Fleet made for Nagagusuki Wan on the southern tip of the island of Okinawa, a spot clearly identified on their charts.[10]

As the British fleet made the passage to Okinawa, there were rumors of air attacks. *Triumph* maintained combat air patrols and conducted precautionary anti-submarine patrols with Fireflies.[11] The British Far East fleet had not gotten far when the light cruiser *Jamaica* received updated orders directing her to join *Juneau* on the east coast of South Korea. *Jamaica* detached from the main group and began retracing her course north toward South Korea.[12]

The Sinking of *Daegu*

De Haven, with her support of the evacuation of American dependents from Seoul now complete, proceeded north to rendezvous with *Juneau*. As the sun came up that morning of the 29th, *De Haven* sighted two ships along the Korean coast, one of them on fire. The ship was the ROKN patrol craft *Daegu*. She was sitting low in the water and had

---

[10] Royal Navy joins UN naval force: Lansdown, *With the Carriers*, 14; GHS, "Naval Ops in Korea," 383; Bentley; "HMS Belfast in Korea," 374-375.

[11] British fleet rumors about Soviet air and submarine threats: Lansdown, *With the Carriers*, 14.

[12] *Jamaica* ordered to join *Juneau* on east coast of Korea: Bentley, "HMS Belfast in Korea, 374;" GHS, Naval Ops in Korea, 383.

obviously been on fire for quite some time. The other ship was the *Ozungzu*, a small freighter that had happened by and was just finishing the process of transferring *Daegu's* crewmen off the stricken vessel. Through an interpreter, *Daegu's* captain reported that she and another South Korean patrol boat, *Dumangang*, had come under attack during the night. *Dumangang*, had been sunk with eight crewmembers killed and another four wounded. Upon further inquiry, the South Koreans reported an attack at about 0300 by what was believed to be a "USSR destroyer."[13]

After this encounter, *De Haven* continued to steam north finally joining up with *Juneau*. *De Haven,* after reporting the facts about the attack on the South Korean naval vessels to *Juneau,* received direction from the cruiser to return to the site of the shelling to see if the *Daegu* could be saved. After returning and re-inspecting the former minesweeper, *De Haven* reported to *Juneau* that *Daegu's* bridge had collapsed and the vessel had been "holed at the water line"[14] amidships leaving her unsalvageable. It was now quite apparent a tragic error had occurred the night before: *Juneau* had mistakenly engaged the South Korean vessels that had been patrolling the eastern shoreline north of the 37th parallel. *Juneau's* shellfire had sunk *Dumangang* with devastating hits to her engine room and bridge, while Daegu had been set ablaze. Three factors had played heavily in the tragedy. First, the intelligence received by *Juneau* indicated that enemy landings were taking place along the South Korean coastline. Second, *Juneau* had been

---

[13] *De Haven*, War Diary, 29 June 1950.

[14] Ibid., 29 June 1950.

informed that all South Korean naval activity had been moved south of the 37th parallel; thus, any activity by its Navy should have been at least 40 miles to the south of where the patrol craft actually were. Lastly, in the opening days of the conflict, there were no recognition or identification protocols in place between the South Korean and American navies. This last issue was quickly remedied.[15]

One former crewmen of *Juneau* has made available an edited transcript of his personal diary while on board during this incident. He described the attack as a "needless error." He asserted that the contacts appeared as "large and frequent" spots on the radar screen in the plot room and thus were not reliable. However, at that time, after almost an hour of evaluation, they had been judged enemy landing craft and subjected to fire. *Juneau's* radar had clearly detected the two ships off Bokuko Ko. With the information *Juneau* possessed at that moment, her orders, and intelligence of North Korean landings in this area, it was logical to engage the targets. Unfortunately and regrettably, "friendly fire" incidents are a fact of every war.[16]

Heading North toward the Parallel

For the crews of *Juneau* and *De Haven,* confusion, apprehension, and frustration were the orders of the day.

---

[15]Information regarding the friendly fire incident: *Juneau*, Deck Log, 29 June 1950, very interestingly, *Juneau*'s Deck Log goes into much detail on the radar contacts and her engagement of them. On the other hand *Juneau*'s War Diary for that date makes no mention of the incident; *De Haven*, Deck Log and War Diary, 29 June 1950; Fields, *History of U.S. Naval Operations*, 53; Karig, *Battle Report*, 56-57, 65; *Juneau*, Action Report: North Korea, 3 August 1950, 14; Curtin, "Galloping Ghost," 2-3.

[16] For a point of view that argues the accidental attack could possibly have been avoided see, Curtin, Diary, 29 June 1950.

At this point, the intelligence received by *Juneau* had been unreliable. There had been no landings on islands in the Pusan area to the south. There had been many false reports and false sightings of enemy activity along the eastern coastline of South Korea. Uneasiness ran high as to whether the Soviets might enter the conflict. Since the beginning of hostilities, there had been no fewer than eight reported submarine sightings by American aircraft and ships. Now there was the tragedy of the friendly fire incident. Uncertainty increased and best described the mood of the crews of the American vessels. To add to their frustration, they lacked rather basic geographic information concerning the Korean coastline. They had detailed charts for the Japanese islands but nothing to help them with the Korean littorals along the peninsula. It would be three full months before American warships acquired aerial photographs of the contours of the shoreline. Those photographs were extremely valuable with later bombardments.[17] In addition, there was no air cover, reconnaissance, or anti-submarine patrols because of the lack of air assets. *Juneau's* captain and crew however, were thankful that *De Haven* had arrived on scene and would now provide anti-submarine screening capability for both of the ships.

While the U.S. Seventh Fleet made passage to Okinawa and the British Far East Fleet moved into southern Japanese waters, both initially because of the fear of Soviet air attacks, elements of U.S. Naval Forces Far East steamed directly into harm's way. As the slight naval force of *Juneau*

---

[17] Lack of charts and "radar photography" for the coastline of the Korean peninsula: *Juneau*, Action report, Report of operations - 24 June1950 to 6 July 1950, dated 3 August 1950, 13.

and *De Haven* made its way further north along the coastline everyone knew something would have to give.[18]

---

[18] Summation of intelligence and operational issues in the first days of the crisis: First Endorsement on *Juneau*, "Report on Operations - 24 June 1950 to 6 July 1950," 1(b), 2(d).

Chapter 11

"Bow waves!"

Bombardment at Mukho

By mid afternoon on Thursday 29 June, *Juneau* and *De Haven* had begun a barrier patrol to detect and take action against North Korean ships that might attempt to cross the 38th parallel from the north. Shortly after the patrol got underway, general quarters sounded on both ships because of unidentified aircraft in the area. They turned out to be American. There was a tendency, especially early in the conflict, for U.S. Air Force aircraft not to observe the usual precautions in identifying themselves when approaching naval units.[1]

During the day, the two-ship force received new orders, expanding their mission. The new instructions extended the patrol's operations north of the 38th parallel for purely military targets. The directive finished by noting that the decision to engage North Korean forces on their own soil, air, and water did not constitute a decision to start a war with the Soviet Union. The order stated that should the Soviets actively oppose American operations they were to defend themselves. However, the orders explicitly stated that the American forces were not to take any actions that

---

[1] Lack of communications between services: First Endorsement on *Juneau*, "Report of Operations - 24 June to 6 July 1950," dated 3 August 1950, 2(j).

might aggravate the situation. As always, military orders tinged with political policy are more vague and ambiguous than one would want. It is left to the captain of a warship to think through as thoroughly as possible the circumstances his vessel is in and then attempt to take the appropriate action. Such is the unpredictability of war. [2]

The invasion was now four and a half days old. The crews of *Juneau* and *De Haven* were coming to terms with their situation. The confusion of the preceding days was clearing up. The previous day *Juneau* had been attempting to gather intelligence — not the optimal use of a mid-20th century cruiser. The two American warships now had orders that made sense: disrupt the advancing North Koreans along the East Coast, sink any North Korean vessels, and if possible, avoid a confrontation with Soviet naval forces. However if push came to shove they would be ready to take them on also. Maybe the crews preferred to be dockside at Yokosuka but they were ready to see action rather than continue with the current tedium. The warships of U.S. Naval Forces Far East were the tip of the sword of American policy. They were ready to bear the "initial burden" of a conflict far from American soil.

At 2130, *De Haven* began to investigate yet another possible submarine contact. The anti-submarine warfare team scrambled to action and the captain, Commander O. B. Lundgren, personally took control of the ship. He maneuvered *De Haven* as the ASW team, and especially the

---

[2] Order to extend the war north of the 38th parallel: U.S. Joint Chiefs of Staff "Directive to Douglas MacArthur, 29 June 1950. Harry S. Truman Administration File, Elsey Papers. President Harry S. Truman Library, http://www.trumanlibrary.org/korea (accessed 12 February 2009).

Sonar Officer, strained to identify a possible underwater intruder. Depending upon water depth, temperature, distance from shore, other sources of sounds, and most importantly, how a ship's sonar was tuned, the equipment on board *De Haven* could detect a submarine out to roughly 2,000 yards. Twenty minutes later *De Haven* secured her ASW team, confident there was no threat, and rejoined *Juneau* in formation. As soon as the matter was resolved, *Juneau* moved in toward the shoreline. The crew went to general quarters and the light cruiser began a shore bombardment against North Korean troops located near a cove in the Mukho area of Kangnung and Samchok. *Juneau* illuminated the beach with her searchlight and commenced the barrage with her 5-inch guns. *Juneau's* shelling drew counter battery fire from the beach. She took evasive action and began shelling the source of the returned fire. In all, *Juneau* expended forty-three rounds of 5-inch shells on the enemy. The U.S. Navy had joined the war.[3]

United Nations Surface Group

The forces were gathering. It was Friday afternoon, 30 June, and *Jamaica*, which had left the British Far East Fleet the previous day in southern Japanese waters, was now struggling to find *Juneau* and *De Haven*. Large amounts of high-precedence radio traffic clogging the airwaves among the allied forces hampered *Jamaica's* efforts. *Collett* also had been steaming north along the Korean coast. In the late afternoon, the Sumner class destroyer sighted *Jamaica* about 13 miles to her northwest. After signaling each other,

---

[3] Possible submarine contact and bombardment in Mukho area: Cole, *Korea Remembered*, 55; *De Haven*, Deck Log, 29 June 1950; *Juneau*, Deck Log, 29 June 1950; Appleman, *South to Naktong*, 52.

the two ships proceeded in tandem in their search for the American light cruiser and destroyer. Shortly after 2100 hours that evening *Collett* made radar contact with *Juneau* and *De Haven*. Within two hours, she and *Jamaica* joined the group. The first United Nations surface group was now ready for action.

The 1st of July was rainy and uneventful except for the increase and then reduction in size of the newly formed UN surface group. *Alacrity* and *Black Swan*, two small British frigates, joined the force that morning raising the number in the surface group to six. However, no sooner had this occurred than *Alacrity* was detached from the group with orders to proceed to the Yellow Sea to spell the American destroyer *Mansfield*. A little later *De Haven* and *Collett* were also detached to return to Sasebo for refueling, reducing the surface group to three vessels. The officers from the two cruisers met on *Jamaica* to discuss orders and protocols. *Jamaica* lowered and used a pulling whaleboat with six oarsmen to fetch and return the officers from *Juneau*. As the British sailors completed the transfer many of the crew on board *Juneau* commented on how crisp and smart they had looked while rowing. The Americans, of course, used powered whaleboats.[4]

Surface Action off Chumunjin

The three-ship United Nations' surface group consisting of *Juneau*, *Jamaica*, and *Black Swan* spent a rather quiet night performing patrol duties. The surface group was just a little over six miles off shore. At 0615 the next morning, word

---

[4]HMS *Jamaica* and USS *Juneau* rendezvous along the east coast of Korea: *Juneau*, *Collett*, and *De Haven*, Deck Logs, 30 June 1950; Karig, Cagle, and Manson, Battle Report, 58; Field, *History of Naval Ops*, 60-61; Curtin, "Early Days," np.

came down from a lookout on *Juneau* — "Bow waves!" The sighting was just off the beam along the shoreline a little over six miles away near Chumunjin. General Quarters sounded. The compact UN surface force in column formation, performing a long box patrol off the coastline just below the 38th parallel, had just turned toward shore. The lookout on *Juneau* had detected four motor torpedo boats (MTBs) and two other smaller motor gunboats heading north close in to the shore. The different radar sets on board the three ships in which both the American and British navies had invested countless millions had failed to detect the enemy craft. The smaller size of the watercraft and their close proximity to the shore had interfered with the radar return impulses and signals. *Jamaica* and *Black Swan* were quickly informed. The enemy force was the squadron of MTBs and motor gunboats that had left Wonsan a few days earlier with the mission of protecting vessels attempting to resupply the advancing North Korean Army along the South Korean coast. The squadron also had orders to engage any enemy warships. The North Korean naval units immediately turned toward the surface group and attacked at great speed.[5]

The MTBs were the mainstay of the North Korean Navy. These boats were of the G5 class. The Soviets had built nearly 300 of them during the 1930s and 1940s. They were 62.5 feet long with an 11-foot beam. They weighed 16 tons and were capable of speeds of at least 30 knots, and in some cases, as much as 45 knots. Each boat carried two torpedoes and a heavy machine gun mounted amidships. The G5s were equipped with two SAET-50 Soviet built

---

[5] Detection of the North Korean MTBs by USS *Juneau*: USS *Juneau*, Deck Log, 2 July 1950; Karig, Cagle, and Manson, *Battle Report*, 58; Field, *History of U.S. Naval Ops*, 61; Cagle, *Sea War in Korea*, 282; Curtin, "Early Days of the Korean War," np.

homing acoustic electronic-powered torpedoes (in Russian the importance and need for the acronym SAET becomes abundantly clear — *samonavodiashaiasia akusticheskaia elektricheskaia torpeda*. Each torpedo weighed 3,600 lbs, had a range of 4,400 yards, and could run at 23 knots. The boats were of a bluish aluminum construction and designed by a team under the guidance of the famed Russian aircraft builder A. N. Tupolev. The Soviets had used the fast boats extensively during the Second World War. In the late 1940s, the Soviet Pacific Fleet at Vladivostok transferred several of the vessels to the North Korean Navy.[6]

The four MTBs came straight at the UN force in line abreast formation at well over 30 knots. Motor torpedo boat doctrine was to concentrate your forces, use speed and maneuverability, and most of all surprise your enemy. The element of surprise had now been lost. The G5s sped straight at the two cruisers with the hope of getting within firing range of their torpedoes. If they could obtain just one hit, it would be a glorious victory for the fledgling communist navy.[7]

Juneau opened fire at a range of 11,000 yards. Ships, like *Juneau* and *Jamaica*, with 5 and 6-inch guns respectively, open fire as soon as the enemy can be seen 10,000 to

---

[6] Information regarding the G5 motor torpedo boats: Chris Bishop, Editor, *Encyclopedia of Weapons of World War II*, s.v. "G5"; Jurg Meister, *Soviet Warships of the Second World War*, (NY: Arco, 1977), 236; Tony Digiulian, "Russia/USSR Post-World War II Torpedoes," Naval Weapons, http://www.navweaps.com (accessed 31 January 2009).

[7] Motor Torpedo Boat doctrine: Dave Schueler, Bill Madison, Chris Carlson, and Larry Bond, *Mighty Midgets: Scenarios and Rules for Small Craft in WWII*, (Phoenixville, PA: Clash of Arms, 2002), 4.

12,000 yards on a clear day. The effective range is less. Open fire range is used to get the warship's guns operating and trained so when an enemy ship reaches effective range (usually a little more than half the distance) the gunnery system is actively engaged with the target. *Juneau*'s 5-inch shells each weighed 54 lbs. Each of the twin-gun mounts took 27 crewmen to operate with nine in the mount itself and 18 more down the stalk below deck in the handling room and then lower yet in the magazine to do the heavy lifting. *Jamaica* then joined in with her 6-inch guns. Geysers of spray rose out of the water as the variable time (VT) shells from the two cruisers splashed closer and closer to the MTBs. The terminology to describe the shells as "variable time" or VT came from an attempt by the U.S. Navy during World War II to keep secret the actual term "proximity" which, of course, perfectly describes how the then new technology worked. A very small radar fuse is contained in the nose of the shell. When the shell is fired, the tiny radar on board senses the distance or proximity and detonates the shell when it reaches a point about 70 feet from the target - in this case the MTBs.[8]

The charging MTBs had closed the distance between the cruisers and themselves to a little over 4,000 yards when the first of the Soviet built craft *(#22)* was struck by an incoming shell, immediately setting her afire. Moments later a second well-placed salvo shattered and sank MTB *(#24)*. The brutal quickness of the destruction of the first two MTBs took all of the fight out of the remaining two G5s and the two other smaller motor gunboats. As *Juneau's* Action Report later noted the motor torpedo boats "were

---

[8] For a further explanation of VT fusing: R. W. King, *Naval Engineering and American Sea Power*, (Baltimore, MD: Nautical & Aviation, 1989), 226-227.

demoralized by heavy fire and broke off the attack."[9] One of the remaining MTBs (*#23*) and the two motor gunboats wheeled about and headed directly for the shore. The last of the G5s (*#21*) broke away laterally and managed to slip between the beach and *Black Swan* into open water. *Black Swan* dutifully gave chase but was not fast enough to maintain pursuit of the fleeing enemy vessel. The boats that had turned back toward the shore had all managed to beach themselves: their crews jumping out and running for cover. *Juneau* and *Jamaica* continued to blaze away at the beached vessels hitting them and setting them on fire.[10]

As both of the light cruisers continued firing on the beached North Korean boats, North Korean shore batteries of field artillery caliber opened fire. *Juneau*, which seemed to be the main recipient of the enemy fire was straddled three times but luckily not hit. One NKPA shell had splashed extremely and dangerously close to her port quarter. Despite this narrow escape, both cruisers managed to move back out of range and then proceeded to fire a few more

---

[9] *USS Juneau*, Action Report, 3 August 1950, 9.

[10] Details regarding the surface action of 2 July 1950 including general narrative, VT fuses, and who fired first? General Narrative: *USS Juneau*, Deck Log, 2 July 1950, War Diary, 2 July 1950; Field, *History of Naval Ops*, 61; Karig, Cagle, and Manson, *Battle Report*, 59; Alexander, *Inchon to Wonsan*, 31-32; Curtin, "Early Days," np; Alexander, *Inchon to Wonsan*, 123. For those who might have thought *Jamaica* fired first I have information to the contrary. Able seaman Walter Hughes, serving on *Jamaica* at the time in a memoir states "[A]s I ran out to open deck...*Juneau* was already firing." Walter Hughes, "E-Boat Action off the Korean Coast: *HMS Jamaica*, 1950," Britain's Small Wars 1945-2005, http://www.britains-smaillwars.com/korea/walter/photos.htm (accessed 5 March 2009).

INITIAL BURDEN

rounds from about 14,000 yards at the batteries.[11] Then it was over. *Juneau's* Ensign T. A. Curtin describes what happened next:

> [B]y dawn's early light we were again policing up the brass [shell casings] scattered about the decks around the 5-inch mounts... As Ammunition Officer, I was amazed at how many hundred rounds we'd expended in these first actions... We had a few 20mm mounts on the 01 deck, which, in the heat of battle, had not had their crews secured. A couple of those poor gunners had had the shirts blown off their backs, and their ear drums ruptured by the muzzle blasts of the 5-inch blazing away beside them.[12]

Could the North Korean MTBs actually have sunk or damaged either cruiser that day? The traditional view is that the North Korean vessels needed to close to about 4,000 yards before they would be able to fire their torpedoes. The Motor Torpedo Boats were just not able to get that close before the barrage of fire from the cruisers demolished two of them. The remaining MTBs and gunboats, shaken by the ferocity and precision of the gunfire, chose discretion over valor. In recent years, a revisionist view of the North Korean use of torpedoes has arisen. It holds that the MTBs were not carrying torpedoes at the time of the engagement. One author claims North Korean survivors hauled from the water by *Jamaica* told a South Korean officer (who was on board as a translator) that the Soviets had not yet instructed them on the use of the weapons. Another author suggests that

---

[11] Shore batteries engage cruisers: *USS Juneau*, Deck Log, 2 July 1950; Karig, Cagle, and Manson, *Battle Report*, 59; Cagle *and Manson, Sea War*, 282.

[12] Curtin, Galloping Ghost," 2 July 1950.

the torpedo launchers themselves were "quite likely"[13] removed from the boats in order to carry troops or supplies, thus effectively turning them into large gunboats. However, both of these arguments assume the MTBs would charge at high-speed directly toward the two cruisers with nothing but a 12.5-mm gun each. This would have been foolhardy and reckless to say the least. On the other hand, closing enough to launch a torpedo that might damage or sink an American or British cruiser may have been seen as worth the risk and possible success.[14]

The UN surface group surmised that the MTBs must have been providing cover for North Korean transports and supply vessels when discovered. Later that morning *Black Swan* attempted some reconnaissance around Chumunjin harbor in search of the suspected vessels the MTBs had been escorting. *Black Swan* sighted at least three 200-ton supply ships in the harbor. Respecting the possible counter-battery fire in and around the harbor, *Black Swan* opened fire with her 4-inch guns at some distance producing what was described in a later report as "uncertain results."[15] When she returned to the two cruisers that afternoon with the news that a number of supply vessels were in Chumunjin harbor, *Jamaica* was in the process of detaching from the surface group and heading for Sasebo to refuel.

The following morning, 3 July, *Juneau* maneuvered as close as she could to Chumunjin harbor to bombard the supply

---

[13] Grove, *Vanguard to Trident*, 138.

[14] Arguments that propose the North Korean MTBs were not carrying torpedoes: Michael Hickey, *The Korean War: the West Confronts Communism*, (Woodstock, NY: Overlook, 2000), 62; Grove, Eric, *Vanguard to Trident*, 138; Cagle and Manson, *Sea War*, 282.

[15] *HMS Black Swan*,"Report of Proceedings 28 June to 7 July 1950," 2 July.

ships *Black Swan* had discovered the previous day. *Juneau* expended 174 rounds of 5-inch shells from her main batteries. The results were direct hits on supply ships #9, #10, #11, and #14 that set them all on fire. In addition, as *Juneau's* war diary recorded, she "rendered useless one large fuel storage tank north of the harbor."[16] As *Juneau* drew away from Chumujin, three more loud explosions were heard and observed.

That evening two North Korean aircraft swept in from the west through a hazy sky and attacked *Black Swan*. They raked her upper deck with cannon and machine gun fire. *Black Swan* returned anti-aircraft fire. *Juneau*, who was some distance to seaward, increased speed to come to her assistance. However, the attack was over in less than five minutes. The British frigate suffered splinter damage above the waterline but was otherwise intact. Rattled a bit, the crew of *Black Swan* remained at general quarters until after sundown.[17]

The talk on board *Juneau* since the surface action the previous day centered on the seaman who had spotted the torpedo squadron. What if he had not sighted the motor torpedo boat squadron when he did? Had that happened it was certainly possible that either of the cruisers could have

---

[16] *USS Juneau*, Deck Log, 3 July 1950.

[17] Post Action Reports and general descriptions regarding *Black Swan* and *Juneau* firing on supply ships in Chumunjin harbor and later, *Black Swan* being attacked by North Korean aircraft: HMS *Black Swan*, "Report of Proceedings 28 June to 7 July 1950," 2-3 July; Grove, *Vanguard to Trident*, 138; South Korea, *The History of the United Nations Forces in the Korean War*, Vol. 2, (Seoul: Ministry of National Defense, Republic of Korea, 1972), 666. *USS Juneau*, Deck Log, 2-3 July 1950; Field, *History of Naval Ops*, 61-62.

INITIAL BURDEN

been hit by a torpedo. The crew reflected on how just the week before they had been visiting ports in Japan, showing the flag and enjoying the early summer in the Far East — now this. For once there was no scuttlebutt answering the questions what would happen next and how long might this go on? All on board now knew this was no drill: it was deadly serious.[18]

---

[18] Seaman Paul J. Smith was the spotter on the *Juneau* that morning of the attack. His action may have saved many lives: P. J. Smith, "History of USS *Juneau* CLAA-119," ussJuneau.net/CLAA119/jun2hist.html, (accessed 7 June 2010).

Chapter 12

Yellow Sea

Combined Carrier Operations

While *Juneau* and her British allies were patrolling the east coast of Korea near the 38th parallel, the U.S. Seventh Fleet and most of the British Far East Fleet were preparing for a carrier-based air strike. On 30 June, orders went out to both fleets charging them with a combined air strike against airfields, railroad yards, and bridges over the Taedong River around the North Korean capital of Pyongyang. Working together in the Korean theater they would be designated Task Force 77. The American fleet arrived at Buckner Bay in Okinawa at around 2000 hours that evening. The focal point of the fleet, *Valley Forge,* began taking on fuel from one of the fleet oilers *Navasota.* In just over an hour, the American carrier had taken on almost 160,000 gallons of fuel and over 10,000 gallons of aviation gasoline.

The following day the American warships took on provisions and began preparations for the air strike. Radars were checked. Charts were updated. New frequencies were set up and recognition signals prepared for working with their British allies. The destroyers checked their sonar and depth charges and loaded 5-inch shells for their multi-purpose anti-aircraft guns. Heavy cruiser *Rochester,* by contrast, took on 220 lb 8-inch shells for her main batteries. *Valley Forge* loaded rockets and bombs for her air squadrons. The rockets were unguided High Velocity Aircraft Rockets (HVARs) nicknamed "Holy Moses," because of their speed. The bombs were of the 500-pound general-purpose variety with "daisy cutter" fuses to trigger the bomb before it buries itself in the ground thus producing greater destruction over the surrounding terrain. Maintenance work proceeded on the aircraft and their engines. Guns and bomb releases were greased. Shackles, the encoding system used with voice radio communications, were tested. These tasks and countless others were performed as the American fleet hurried to complete its preparations.

The Royal Navy's Far East Fleet, with aircraft carrier *Triumph*, arrived at Buckner Bay during the morning of the same day. British officers met with their American counterparts, planning suitable targets for the different types of aircraft on each of the carriers. The fleet had provisioned and fueled at Kure in southern Japan a few days earlier and was ready to begin the operation. At 1700, the British fleet departed Buckner Bay for the Yellow Sea and west coast of Korea. A little over an hour later, the American fleet followed. In all, the combined strike force included two aircraft carriers, *Valley Forge* and *Triumph*, two cruisers, *Rochester* and *Belfast*, U.S. destroyers *Radford*, *Fletcher*, *Shelton*, *Eversole*, *Maddox*, *S.N. Moore*, and *Taussig*, Royal Navy destroyers *Cossack* and *Consort*, Australian destroyer *Bataan*, and three U.S. submarines, *Catfish*, *Cabezon*, and *Segundo*. It was time to take the war to the enemy.[1]

Shortly after 1100 hours the morning of 2 July, just five hours after the surface engagement at Chumunjin on the east coast of Korea, the British Far East Fleet and the

---

[1] The gathering of the U.S. 7th Fleet and the British Far East Fleet at Buckner Bay in Okinawa: USS *Valley Forge*, *Deck Log* 30 June - 1 July 1950; Field, *History of Naval Ops*, 60; Karig, Cagle, and Manson, *Battle Report*, 38, 44, 60, 62; Bentley, "HMS Belfast in Korea," 374-375; Lansdowne, *With the Carriers*, 15.

American Seventh Fleet linked up at the southeastern entrance to the Yellow Sea. Task Force 77 began working out the coordination that would be necessary for operations between the two carriers. Thankfully, because the navies had recently held joint maneuvers, they understood each other's way of doing things. First things first, they calculated the task force's speed since *Valley Forge* was capable of an extra eight to ten knots over *Triumph*. They considered how wide and long the destroyer screening force would need to be, how the combat air patrol would be structured over the carriers, where the launch points would be for each of the carriers' targets, preparation for an enemy air attack, and the planning necessary to deal with the possibility of a submarine attack.

American helicopters facilitated the joint planning as they flew from ship-to-ship carrying staff and orders. The British were quite impressed with this application of aviation technology.

There was a problem with the appearance of the British aircraft. The American pilots thought the British fighters looked a lot like some of the communist aircraft they might have to face. In an attempt to avoid having their aircraft mistaken for the enemy, *Triumph* launched a Sea Fire and a Firefly. The piston engine planes then circled around the U.S. warships to familiarize the Americans with the British fighters to minimize the possibility of a mistake in identification.

Task Force 77 was on a wartime mission. Not knowing what to expect, they did not use wireless communication during their passage through the Yellow Sea and darkened the ships at night. The North Koreans were the known combatants in this conflict and they did possess air assets. The Soviets had an airbase at Port Arthur about 220 miles to the north, which of course, if used, constituted a lethal threat to the naval group. The Soviets also had submarines available in the region. The two aircraft carriers had the services of the three American submarines, as well as destroyers that together could screen the task force and prosecute hostile underwater threats. Only time would tell if the Soviets would join the fighting with an air assault or covertly attempt to influence the fighting with a submarine attack. Many of those on board *Belfast* were reminded of the last war. They discussed that in such a short space of time (five years) they "stood a very good chance of having to go through the whole business again." [2]

Valley Forge was an Essex class aircraft carrier, one of 26 constructed between 1943 and 1946. This class of American carrier had been the backbone of the U.S. Navy the last two years of the Second World War and now the first five years of the post-war period. She displaced over 27,000 tons and fully loaded that number jumped to almost 35,000 tons. She headed into the Yellow Sea with 1,479 crewmen on board. This number represented several hundred sailors less than a normal peacetime compliment and only half of what was required during wartime operations. In addition, because of Congressional cutbacks in the naval budget it meant that the carrier had only half the normal compliment of fighter

---

[2] Quotation from Bentley, "HMS *Belfast* in Korea," 375. The creation of the joint strike force, Task Force 77, in the Yellow Sea: USS *Valley Forge*, Deck Log, 2 July 1950; Field, *History of Naval Ops*, 60; Karig, Cagle, and Manson, *Battle Report*, 61-62; Lansdowne, *With the Carriers*, 15; Randal Gray, *Conway's All the World's Fighting Ships 1947-1982. Part 2., the Warsaw Pact and Non-Aligned Nations*, (Annapolis, MD: U.S. Naval Institute, 1983; Norman Polmar, "The Navy's Frontline in Korea," *Naval History*, Historic Aircraft, (April 2008), 14-15.

pilots. *Valley Forge* was particularly short of ordinance men to help load bombs onto the aircraft. As it stood, most crewmembers had to do two jobs. This resulted in very little sleep. In spite of these issues, her crew still affectionately called the Essex class carrier "Happy Valley".

12-1 USS *Valley Forge* (late 1940s)

For this strike, *Valley Forge* carried 86 aircraft. The aircraft were broken into two jet fighter squadrons each with 15 F9F-2 Panthers; two piston engine fighter squadrons each with 15 World War II vintage Vought F4U-4B Corsairs; one piston engine attack squadron of 14 AD4 Skyraiders, and a dozen other aircraft, mostly Skyraiders, that were specially equipped and configured for photographic, night, and radar missions.[3]

---

[3] Information regarding USS *Valley Forge*: Karig, Cagle, and Manson, *Battle Report*, 60-61; Lisle A. Rose, *Power at Sea: Volume 3, A Violent Peace, 1946-2006*, (Columbia, Missouri: University of Missouri, 2007), 41; Field, *History of Naval Ops*, 48-49.

INITIAL BURDEN

12-2 F9F-2 Panther Jet

12-3 F4U-4 Corsair

12-4 AD4 Skyraider

Triumph was a light fleet carrier. At 630 ft in length, she was noticeably shorter (200 feet) than *Valley Forge*. *Triumph* displaced 18,000 tons fully loaded — half that of the American carrier. As such, she carried only 37 aircraft.

Of that number, *Triumph* carried only a dozen serviceable piston engine Seafire fighters with the rest being Fairey Fireflies. 800 Naval Squadron flew the Seafires. The aircraft, originally designed as a short-range land-based interceptor, and only later conceived as a carrier-based fighter, suffered in this role because of frequent structural damage caused by heavy landings on carrier decks. The World War II aircraft would be replaced by the new Sea Fury beginning in 1951.

12-5 Supermarine Seafire 47

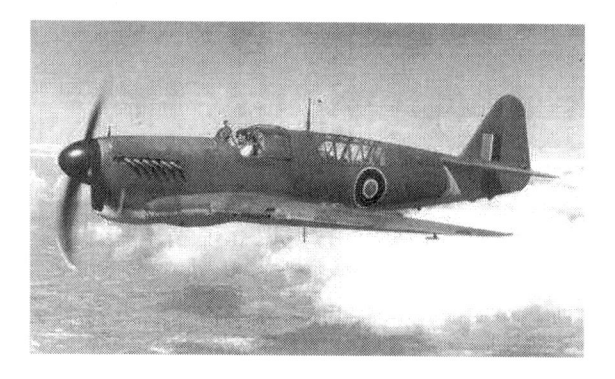

12-6 Fairey Firefly Mk. 1

INITIAL BURDEN

The Fairey Fireflies were flown and maintained by 827 Naval Air Squadron. The Fireflies could achieve speeds of over 380 mph and carried an observer. As described earlier the Fireflies had a tendency to bounce upon landing to such a degree that the plane's tail hook would on occasion miss the arresting wire used to stop the aircraft. When this occurred, the plane would crash into a barrier erected to stop runaway aircraft. The Royal Navy had a term for this phenomenon — "barrier engagement."[4]

Task Force 77's two aircraft carriers were not the best that either country had to offer. Better compartmentalization and armored flight decks were lessons learned during the Second World War. Both navies had learned about better compartmentalization the hard way. In addition, the British had proven that armored flight decks were superior to the American wooden decks during the War in the Pacific with their Illustrious class carriers. The Japanese kamikaze aircraft would tend to crumple upon striking British armored flight decks. However, *Triumph* was not an Illustrious class carrier. She was a light carrier having a wooden flight deck like *Valley Forge*. *Valley Forge* was an Essex class carrier. It was not until the next generation of U.S. carriers, the Midway class, that the Americans would include armored flight decks in their design. Neither of the newer Midway class carriers the United States possessed during the Korean War was ever to serve in the Korean theater, both serving in the Mediterranean with the Sixth Fleet.

---

[4] Information regarding HMS *Triumph*: Gardiner, *Conway's 1922-1946*, 22; Lansdown, *With the Carriers*, 485, 497; Paul & Spirit, Britain's Small Wars, Britains-smallwars.com, "*Triumph*"; Grove, *Vanguard to Trident*, 139.

Another major issue in both post-war navies was adapting to the advent of jet-engine aircraft. The speed at which jets landed combined with a "lag in throttle response" created high-speed landings with less control than desired. A related issue was the manner in which aircraft landed on carriers. Aircraft would approach a carrier from the stern and land moving directly towards the bow of the ship. However, aircraft were getting heavier and faster increasing the likelihood of overshooting the flight deck runway (not just bouncing over the arresting wires) and crashing into the barrier protecting planes parked forward on the bow. The solution, attributed to a British captain, was to create a runway; using striping that was "angled to port about 10 degrees relative to the ship's center-line."[5] The angle created a space on the forward flight deck where planes could be parked safely away from the danger of landing aircraft. It also allowed landing aircraft that were going too fast to pull the throttle back, regain airspeed — and take off again. They could then circle back around for another landing attempt. The solution was surprisingly simple. However, it did not become a reality until the U.S. Navy conducted tests based on the idea in 1952. Once the concept was proven, all new carrier construction included a "true" angled deck. Until then, as they had since the beginning of naval aviation, some thirty plus years before, aircraft continued to suffer "barrier engagements."[6]

---

[5] Brian Johnson, *Fly Navy: the History of Maritime Aviation*, (London: David & Charles, 1981), 350.

[6] Aircraft Carrier evolution from World War II to the Korean War: Ibid., 346-352.

Pyongyang Airstrikes

Early in the predawn light of 3 July, the carriers put up their combat air patrols over the task force and launched their anti-submarine patrols. The strike force had reached the first of its launching points. Earlier, the destroyers *Swenson* and *Mansfield* moved from where they had been performing barrier patrol duties the last few days to a position between the aircraft carrier strike force and the North Korean mainland. Arriving at their individual "lifeguard stations" each of the vessels, as *Swenson's* deck log records, "commenced boxing counter clockwise four miles to the side."[7] This would position the destroyers for rescuing any pilots forced to ditch should they be unable to reach their respective carriers upon completion of their missions.[8]

The airstrike operation began precisely at 0545 when *Triumph* launched 12 Fireflies and nine rocket-loaded Seafires for their raid on Haeju Airfield south of Pyongyang. Fifteen minutes later *Valley Forge* launched 16 Corsairs, each with eight 5-inch HVAR rockets and 12 Skyraiders with 1,600 lb bomb loads against the North Korean capital's Pyongyang Airfield. Still later *Valley Forge* catapulted eight Panther jets into the sky. Once aloft all of the aircraft faced poor weather conditions between the carriers and the target area. The American jets launched last, because with their greater speed of up to 575 mph, they would catch up to the rest of the attack aircraft and actually be the first to arrive on the scene at the large airfield at Pyongyang. The

---

[7] USS *Swenson*, Deck Log, 3 July 1950.

[8] USS *Swenson*, War Diary, 3 July 1950 and Deck Log, 3 July 1950.

American Grumman-constructed Panther fighters swept in over the field and destroyed eight aircraft on the ground. They further scored kills on two North Korean Soviet-built Yak 9 aircraft that had managed to get airborne. Those two Yak 9s represented the first kills ever by American Navy jet fighters. The Panthers also strafed a transport plane on the ground and set it afire. The Skyraiders and Corsairs then arrived to begin their attack. They scored a direct hit on the airfield's fuel storage farm and heavily damaged all three of the airfield's hangers. The Skyraiders also cratered two of the runways with their half-ton bombs. There was very little anti-aircraft fire because the naval air attack had caught the North Koreans completely by surprise.

12-7 Pyongyang Airstrike

About 60 miles to the south, the British aircraft were coming in low towards their target, Heiju Airfield, attempting to evade radar detection. However, the low clouds and fog forced them to climb above some of the worst of the weather. In spite of having to expose themselves to enemy radar, they seemed to achieve surprise and, as a bonus, the skies cleared upon arrival over the airfield. With no enemy planes in sight, the British aircraft swooped down on the airfield and fired their rockets. The hangers and other buildings in the area suffered extensive damage. A few of the attacking aircraft sustained superficial damage from debris caused by the rockets' impact and subsequent explosions. However, one of the Seafires struck by debris did suffer some major damage to its engine and would not be available for further duty.

Upon the completion of the attacks both strike groups headed back out to sea in search of the combined fleets. An hour later they were all back on the decks of their respective carriers. All of the strike aircraft returned safely. However, a Corsair from *Valley Forge*, while flying combat air patrol over the carriers while the attacks were in progress, experienced an engine fire and ditched into the sea. The pilot was safely pulled from the water.

Each of the carrier's crews worked feverishly to refuel and load out each aircraft for a second attack. With the primary targets being the Pyongyang railroad and the bridges across the Taedong River, the second raid launched in the early afternoon and proved successful destroying 15 locomotives and damaging ten others.

The next day, 4 July, One last air strike was launched. The result: a span of the main bridge of the Taedong River crashed broken into the water. However, the North Korean anti-aircraft fire was getting better and four of the Skyraiders sustained damage from enemy 37-mm cannons. All four of the damaged aircraft managed to make it out to sea and find their way back to *Valley Forge*.

The North Koreans had not been able to shoot down any of the American or British planes during the two days of attack but the joint task force's luck ran out at the very end of the operation. The last plane attempting to land on *Valley Forge*, having sustained hydraulics damage from anti-aircraft fire while over the target area, came in too fast in its approach overshooting the arresting gear altogether, bounding off the deck and over the protective barrier, crashing into the aircraft parked quite tightly forward on the flight deck. In the aftermath, one Skyraider and two Corsairs were destroyed while one Panther jet and three more Skyraiders were damaged. That was not the end of the bad luck. The strike force suffered another loss when one of *Valley Forge's* Sikorsky S-51 helicopters, aloft during recovery operations, had to ditch when it experienced engine failure. Nevertheless, even with these mishaps, the American and British navies gained confidence working together and the overall operation was deemed a great success.[9] The joint operations provided a template and a model of cooperation, which the U.S. Navy and other allied countries would use repeatedly in responding to incidents and crises around the world in the second half of the 20th century.[10]

---

[9] Task Force 77 air strikes of 3-4 July: Richard P. Hallion, *The Naval Air War in Korea,* (NY: Kensington, 1988), 60-62; David Hobbs, "British Commonwealth Carrier Operations in the Korean War," *Air &Space Power Journal*, 18, no. 4 (Winter 2004), 62-71; Field, *History of Naval Ops,* 62, 65; Cagle and Manson, *Sea War,* 37-38; Lansdown, *With the Carriers,* 15; Bentley, "HMS *Belfast* in Korea," 375; Brian Catchpole, *The Korean War, 1950-1953,* (London: Magpie Books, 2010), 183; O'Toole, "The Forgotten Cruise," Royal Navy Research Archive http://www.royalnavyresearch archive.org.uk/Article_Forgotten_Cruise.htm (accessed 24 February 2011).

[10] U.S. Navy first response capability with carrier groups: Spector, *At War at Sea,* 315.

Chapter 13

Blockade

Implications for Naval Forces

After the surface action on the East Coast and the air strikes at Pyongyang, the American and British naval forces threw themselves headlong into slowing down the North Korean advance toward Pusan. President Truman declared a naval blockade on 1 July. His order as relayed to MacArthur by the Joint Chiefs of Staff stated:

> In keeping with the United Nations Security Council's request for support to the Republic of Korea in repelling the Northern Korean invaders and restoring peace in Korea the President announced that he had ordered a Naval blockade of the entire Korean coast.[1]

However, it was not until 4 July that the actual orders made their way to the ships. The blockade consisted of interdicting enemy supply lines, bombarding military targets, and providing gunfire support to ongoing land operations.

The Soviets responded to the American proclamation. Their response said in part:

---

[1] Joint Chiefs of Staff message to MacArthur: JCS, "Army Department Message, Joint Chiefs of Staff to Douglas MacArthur, July 1, 1950." From the papers of George M. Elsey, http://www.trumanlibrary.org/ whistle stop/study_collections/koreanwar/documents/index.php?documentdat= 1950-07-01&documentid=ki-5-6&pagenumber=1, (accessed 1 February 2012).

The blockade of Korea represents a new act of aggression. This blockade is just as incompatible with the principles of [the] U.N. as is entire armed intervention of [the] United States in Korea. As a consequence of what is set forth above [the] Soviet Government will consider [the] government of U.S.A. responsible for all consequences of this act and for entire damage which may be caused to the interests of the Soviet Union in connection with the conduct of the blockade mentioned.[2]

Direct Soviet intervention was still a clear and present danger.

How did the new blockade orders affect ships going in and out of North Korean ports especially along the East Coast? Five days after implementation of the blockade, the U.S. Chief of Naval Operations made the proclamation more specific. He sent instructions that the UN forces would strictly abide by international law. This actually created some danger to the American and British warships. Entry into North Korean ports, such as Wonsan and Najin, would be granted to "all warships not under United Nations' command."[3] This would allow for the ingress and egress of Soviet warships. However, entry would be denied to all other shipping including Soviet armed and unarmed non-warships, merchant or otherwise. This posed a risk, or as the British would say, created a "dodgy" business. The UN Naval forces had to cut off the North Koreans from incoming supplies but at the same time avoid a provocation

---

[2] Bentley, "HMS *Belfast* in Korea," *The Naval Review*, 38, No. 4, 377.

[3] Karig, Cagle, and Manson, *Battle Report*, 64.

that might bring the Soviets into the conflict. The warships walked a tightrope that did not have a safety net beneath it. Luckily, during the first month of the implementation of the blockade, the small UN surface force had their hands full with events happening below the 38th parallel where the North Koreans were making great headway in their drive south.[4]

Implementation of Blockade Orders

During the first three weeks of July the American and British warships including the cruisers *Juneau*, *Jamaica*, and *Belfast*, as well as destroyers and frigates from both navies, plied the western and eastern coasts of the Korean peninsula enforcing the blockade. The seaborne logistical supply that the North Koreans were providing to their attacking 5th Division along the East Coast had been stopped cold by the surface action involving *Juneau*, *Jamaica* and the North Korean motor torpedo boats the week before. As one sailor on board *Juneau* put it, "we sank their whole navy."[5] If they did not, at least the NKPN's remaining vessels were not venturing outside of their home bases after the mauling at Chumunjin.

Following the implementation of the blockade, two patrols were established, one in the Yellow Sea and one on the East Coast. On the West Coast, *Belfast* and a two ship screening force of destroyers *Cossack* and *Consort* established a patrol within a week of the blockade orders. Day and night, the

---

[4] Blockade on east coast and its implications: Appleman, *South to Naktong*, 52; Karig, Cagle, and Manson, *Battle Report*, 64.

[5] Correspondence concerning surface action of 2 July: Allyn Thompson, Crewmember USS *Juneau*, email message to author, 28 February 2006.

ships would monitor and be ready to intercept any attempts to run the blockade in the Yellow Sea shipping lanes between the ports in Manchukuo and North China to the North Korean port of Chinnampo, as well as the captured South Korean ports of Kunsan, and Inchon.[6]

After the surface action at Chumunjin on 2 July, *Jamaica* had returned to Japan to take on fuel and provisions. Before noon on 5 July, she had rejoined *Juneau* and *Black Swan* on the east coast of Korea. The weather was clear but showing signs of worsening as the day went on. In the evening, it began to rain. On board *Jamaica,* the conditions were described as "wet and thickish."[7] During the night, headlights from a small convoy of vehicles were observed ashore. However, *Jamaica* did not fire to avoid frightening off what the British termed as "somewhat larger fry,"[8] (North Korean shipping) that she was hoping to encounter.

At dawn on the morning of the 6th, *Jamaica* and *Black Swan* investigated the harbor at Chumunjin again to look for enemy shipping. None was found. *Black Swan* commenced a bombardment at some oil tanks and a bridge at the southern end of the town. Her log recorded three direct hits on the oil tanks.[9] The shelling of the bridge brought return

---

[6] British west coast patrol: Bentley, "HMS *Belfast* in Korea," *The Naval Review*, 38, No. 4, 377-78.

[7] HMS *Jamaica*, "Report of Proceedings for Period 4th-9th July 1950," Paragraph 6.

[8] Ibid., Paragraph 5.

[9] *Black Swan* bombarding oil tank and bridge: HMS *Black Swan*, Report of Proceedings 28th June to 7th July 1950," 0600 6 July.

fire from NKPA elements ashore with an anti-tank weapon. Some of the shells came close to hitting *Black Swan* so she forced to withdraw to seaward. *Jamaica* then fired three 6-inch salvos that ended the contest. That night *Black Swan* moved in as close as she could get to the shoreline in order to engage any vehicular convoys using the coastal road. Unlike the previous evening, when *Jamaica* chose not to engage the procession of headlights moving south, *Black Swan* this time assailed the military jeeps and trucks on the road, halting and scattering the convoy.

On the 7th, *Black Swan* returned to Japan. In her place, the British frigate *Hart* and the American destroyer *Swenson* joined *Jamaica*. While steaming north the three ships received battery fire from around the city of Samchok, one of the sites of the North Korean amphibious landings the first morning of the invasion. However, the shells from the two separate batteries fell well short of the British and American ships and then stopped. *Jamaica's* report surmised that the North Koreans had "evidently decided to waste no more ammunition."[10] A fuel storage tank and some cliff roads became the next targets for the UN surface force as they worked their way along the shoreline. That evening, *Jamaica* shelled a power station near Yangyang with plenty of electrical sparking showering down on and around the site. *Hart* detached later in the evening and headed back to Sasebo.

On Saturday the 8th, intelligence reported that North Korean forces had moved as far south as Ulchin at about 37 degrees latitude along the East Coast. At that point, the South Korean Army had forced them inland off the coastal road, at least temporarily. *Jamaica* received orders to

---

[10] HMS *Jamaica*, "Report of Proceedings for Period 4th-9th July 1950," Paragraph 17.

attempt to destroy the main coastal road to impede the North Koreans moving south. This required the destruction of the bridges along the highway. The problems were twofold: first, most of the bridges were just enough inland to be invisible from the sea. The second was that summer is the dry season. The reality of the situation was that destruction of most of the targeted bridges would cause the enemy little delay. During this time of the year, the rivers beneath many of the bridges slowed to trickles leaving them easily fordable. One bridge, near the South Korean naval outpost at Mokpo, spanned a river that was much too wide and deep to be crossed year round. However, *Jamaica's* captain J. S. C. Salter decided that because of the close proximity of the bridge to the Mokpo naval outpost that a South Korean combat team from there could destroy it when the time was right.[11]

As the East Coast blockade progressed, *Jamaica* and *Juneau* devised a plan to help with hampering southbound highway traffic. The ships of the East Coast blockade would use their main batteries to shell cliffs that overhung the main coastal road, creating landslides. They would use this tactic to loosen hundreds of tons of earth and rock that would tumble down the sides of the hills that made up the leading edges of the Taebaek Mountains, blocking the road below for days at a time.[12]

Later that day on 8 June, *Jamaica* and *Swenson* bombarded the coastal road itself. They were patrolling in column formation 3,000 yards off shore between the villages of

---

[11] *Jamaica* and *Swenson* reconnoitering bridges for possible bombardment along South Korean coast: Ibid., Paragraph 30.

[12] Blocking coastal roads with cruiser gunfire: Karig, Cagle, and Manson, *Battle Report*, 65.

Ulchin and Samchok with *Jamaica* leading and *Swenson* 1,000 yards astern. The two ships were making only about 6 knots when what was probably a 75-mm NKPA mobile battery, hidden from sight, opened fire on them from just beyond the shore. Each ship took evasive action and increased its speed to 20 knots. As the two ships turned to seaward, *Jamaica* found herself bracketed by the gunfire. Then one of the shells struck the starboard tripod of *Jamaica's* mainmast and exploded, sending a shower of fragments down onto the after gun deck killing two crew members outright and wounding a number of others. *Swenson* promptly began to return fire. For her efforts, the destroyer received much unwanted attention as the shore battery shifted its focus to her. *Swenson* suffered no hits, and the exchange continued until the fire coming from the gun emplacement ceased.

The final count of casualties on board *Jamaica* was six killed and six wounded. Only one of the dead was an able seaman. The other five were British soldiers from Hong Kong who had embarked on board *Jamaica* for the "Summer Cruise" and had volunteered to pass ammunition to the secondary guns. As *Jamaica* would not return to port in the next few days and the weather was hot, burial of the six dead would take place the following morning at sea. The on board chaplain conducted the service with the ship's officers turned out in their summer white shorts and knee high stockings and the Royal Marines on board providing the Guard of Honor. The partial reporting of the incident in Great Britain the following day caused much public disquiet.[13]

---

[13] *Jamaica* and *Swenson* versus mobile shore battery: HMS *Jamaica*, "Report of Proceedings for Period 4th-9th July 1950," Paragraphs 32-44; *Lyman K. Swenson*, Deck Log, 8 July 1950; Lansdown, *With the Carriers*, 17-18; Cocker, *West Coast Support Group*, 22-23.

Special Ops

The Soviets, for their part, continued to send supplies south from Vladivostok via the North Korean Han-Kyung railroad in support of the communist offensive. To impede the resupply of the North Korean advance along the East Coast, *Juneau* and one of the Sumner class destroyers, *Mansfield*, undertook a mission that would take them above the 40th parallel along the North Korean coast and dangerously close to Soviet and Chinese borders.

After working their way up the coastline on the night of 11 July, the two ships slowed to begin an interdiction operation. *Juneau* maneuvered toward *Mansfield* as the destroyer completely throttled back her engines. It took about fifteen minutes to transfer a team of skilled explosives experts from *Juneau* to *Mansfield*. It was now 2000 hours. The two ships then fell into column formation

---

On Sunday, 9 July, the BBC in London reported that a British ship had been hit while in action off the Korean coast without identifying the vessel. Since there were two dozen British warships in the Korean theater at the time the message, lacking the name of the ship, led to complaints and worry.

The Royal Navy had, in fact, notified the families of those killed and wounded before the BBC broadcast, but the incompleteness of the radio broadcast had caused undue anxiety for families and friends of all the British sailors serving in the Korean theater. Future BBC broadcasts did not make that mistake again. Interestingly, just a few short years before this episode, during the Second World War, broadcasting war related information in any sort of detail e.g., names of ships, would have been classified and not put on the air fearing it would provide comfort and intelligence for the enemy. HMS *Jamaica*, "Report of Proceedings for Period 4th-9th July 1950," subsequent messages attached to report.

and headed further north with *Mansfield* taking the point and *Juneau* positioned 2,500 yards astern.

For the next four hours, the two ships made their way still further up the North Korean coastline at a speed of 20 knots. At midnight, they arrived at Onshuntoku San, a deserted beach about 100 miles south of the Soviet border near Vladivostok. With both vessels darkened, the crews went quietly to general quarters. The American warships were four miles from the shoreline. Independently, *Mansfield* maneuvered to within a quarter mile of the beach.

The all-volunteer demolition team consisting of two officers, four marines, and two blue jackets pushed off in a whaleboat heading toward shore. The weather was chilly with a low hanging cloud cover that revealed no stars. Upon nearing the breaker line, where the water turns to waves, a light passed over their craft. The team realized it was the light of a locomotive as a train passed by just above and back a little from the shoreline. They attempted to set the stern anchor but the line became fouled in the screw. With the anchor line cut, the team paddled the boat the remaining thirty yards to the beach. Once on shore the party, save the two blue jackets left to tend to the boat, made their way up the beach and then through some waist-high grass before finding the northern entrance to the rail tunnel. The team carried back packs with detonating cord, rubber-covered conductors, time fuses, weather proof lighter fuses, electric blasting caps, demolition blocks, shaped charges, fuse cutters, and blocks of demolition TNT.

The Han-Kyung Line railroad tunnel had been constructed by controlled blasts through the solid rock and was only a little over a quarter of a mile long. The group proceeded some distance into the tunnel and dug a trench crosswise about one foot deep from one rail bed under the tracks to the rail bed on the other side. Team members placed the TNT charges in the trench. They then connected the TNT charges with primer cord to create a single explosion and then mounted detonator caps to the rails for the next train to set off the charges. The team then re-emerged from the tunnel and retraced their steps back down to the beach where the whaleboat was waiting. While the Marines had been planting the charges the two sailors remaining with the boat had managed to clear the screw of what was left of the tangled anchor line. The group pushed the whaleboat out into the surf and headed back out towards *Mansfield*.

At 0300 hours, the American destroyer hoisted back on board the demolition team. Quietly, *Mansfield* maneuvered to deeper water. A half hour later, both ships headed south again. Crewmen from the sterns of both ships witnessed a train headlight disappear into the northern end of the tunnel and not reappear at the southern end. The crew heard no explosion. This was in part due to the placement of the explosives in the middle of the tunnel and that the retreating warships moved quickly down the coast into a strong breeze out of the south

Two days later U.S. Air Force photos showed the destruction of the train with some of the rolling stock still extending out the northern end of the tunnel. This was the first attack by U.S. ground units on North Korean soil. More commando raids of this type followed, destroying and damaging other train line tunnels and trestles along the North Korean coast.[14]

---

[14] Train demolition raid in North Korea: USS *Juneau*, Deck Log, 11-12 July 1950; USS *Mansfield*, Deck Log, 11-12 July 1950; Wilson Fielder, "Last Train from Vladivostok," *Time Magazine*, 24 July 1950; Cagle and Manson, *Sea War in Korea*, 290-91: Curtain, "Galloping Ghost," n.p..

Bombardment at Yongdok

In the third week of July, with the NKPA desperately trying to finish their drive down the peninsula to Pusan, the ever-shrinking perimeter around the seaport became the sight of fierce combat. *Juneau, De Haven, Swenson, Mansfield* and *Belfast* received orders to proceed to the eastern coastal village of Yongdok located 25 miles north of Pohang and 90 miles north of Pusan. There on 18 July, multiple North Korean divisions were driving back the South Korean Army's 3rd Division. At this point also, elements of the U.S. Eighth Army that had arrived, via Pusan, from Japan and were now attempting to help the South Koreans on the front lines. Communication between the ships and the American Army units on shore was almost non-existent. *Juneau* and *Belfast* landed a couple of their gunnery officers by whaleboat near the fighting in the Yongdok area. There they talked to some of the American combatants. While ashore, the naval gunnery officers supplied their army counterparts with two naval wireless sets and in return received two army wireless sets. The arrangement allowed for direct communications between the two cruisers and the American forces ashore.

The next evening, at 1900 hours, with U.S. Army soldiers on shore providing target information for the cruisers, *Juneau* and *Belfast* opened fire on NKPA gun emplacements, road intersections, and troop formations in and around the village of Yongdok. During the bombardment, a gun on one of *Juneau's* stern mounts failed to fire. This is a dangerous situation as it is possible for the heat of the gun to "cook off" the live ammunition in the gun barrel, which in turn can result in a terrible explosion. *Juneau's* gun crew checked and discovered the powder case that sits behind the shell had not fired. Placing a short charge casing of powder directly behind the original one the gun fired successfully, clearing the live round from the gun barrel.[15] Even with the misfire, *Juneau* fired over 100 rounds of 5-inch shells while *Belfast* managed to fire 192 6-inch shells during the bombardment. The attendant American destroyers provided illumination shellfire for the cruisers. For four days they fired together expending thousands of shells. The targets in and around the village were decimated. A U.S. Army observer ashore stated "this coordination and use of naval gunfire caused the largest proportion of the 5th North Korean Division casualties..."[16] On the 21st, *Juneau* alone was credited with killing an estimated 400 North Korean soldiers. American naval reports stated,

> [O]ur ships have broken up enemy attacks, silenced enemy batteries, destroyed their observation posts, interdicted their traffic and troop concentrations, and made Yongdok untenable for their forces with heavy personnel losses.[17]

The initial phase of the conflict in Korea was winding down. The war itself was gaining a new intensity. The naval blockade was being effectively enforced. Swept from the sea were the North Korean naval units visible in the opening

---

[15] An explanation of a misfire and a short charge can be found in: The Master Chief's Lair, "Short Charge," http://www.silverfoxnavy.blogspot.com /2010/05/short-charge.html, (Accessed 6 August 2011).

[16] U.S. Army Colonel Rollins S. Emmerich quote regarding bombardment: Karig, Cagle, and Manson, *Battle Report*, 101.

[17] Gun fire support against North Korean Army at Yongdok: Karig, Cagle, and Manson, *Battle Report*, 101; USS *Juneau*, Deck Log, 19-20 July 1950; Appleman, *South to Naktong*, 184-85; Bentley, "HMS Belfast in Korea, 379; Quote from Rear Admiral Higgins' report to Vice Admiral Joy: Cagle and Manson, *Sea War in Korea*, 287-88,

days of the war. Waterborne resupply efforts had been stopped cold. Interdiction through bombardment of the troops, equipment, and supplies of the In Min Gun's southward advance along the shores of the Sea of Japan was ongoing day and night.

One author described the small UN naval contingent of ships there at the beginning of hostilities in this manner:

> For one entire month, until the arrival in the area of [reinforcements] the original ships of [U.S. Naval Forces] Far East [and the ships of the British Far East Fleet]...like hungry dogs in an unattended butcher shop had more than they could handle.[18]

---

[18] Bombardment of Yongdok: Cagle and Manson, *Sea War in Korea*, 286-88; USS *Juneau*, Deck Log, 18-22 July 1950.

Chapter 14

Sea Control

Assumptions

The North Korean plan for the invasion of South Korea called for using their superiority in troops, armor, artillery, and air assets to overwhelm the defending forces. The plan incorporated the assumption that it would take three to four days to capture Seoul. The premise was that once the fighting began a guerilla style uprising of thousands would ensue in the South led by well-trained bands of armed fighters from North Korea leading to a quick end of the fighting and total victory.[1] The planning also assumed the non-participation of the United States in this "civil war," for the most part based on a speech given by Secretary of State Dean Acheson earlier in the year. In the speech, Acheson strongly implied the United States would not defend the interests of the Republic of South Korea. He rhetorically asked and responded to the following question.

---

[1] Invasion plan assumptions: David Rees, "Reckless War-Making; Review of Sergei N. Goncharov et al's *Uncertain Partners: Stalin, Mao, and the Korean War*;" Geoffrey Perrett, *Commander in Chief: How Truman, Johnson, and Bush Turned a Presidential Power into a Threat to America's Future*, (NY: Farrar, Straus and Giroux, 2007), 143; Kathryn Weathersby, "Soviet Aims in Korea and the Origins of the Korean War, 1945-1950: New Evidence from Russian Archives," (Washington D.C.: Cold War International History Project, Woodrow Wilson International Center for Scholars, 1993), Florida State University, Working Paper No. 8.

What is the situation in regard to the military security of the Pacific area, and what is our policy in regard to it?

The [U.S.] defensive perimeter runs along the Aleutians to Japan and then goes to the Ryukyus....[and then] to the Philippine Islands....*So far as the military security of other areas in the Pacific is concerned, it must be clear that no person can guarantee these areas against military attack.* [emphasis in original] But it must also be clear that such a guarantee is hardly sensible or necessary within the realm of practical relationship.[2]

For all of the plans and assumptions of the Soviets and North Koreans, they utterly failed to grasp the strategic importance of quickly capturing Pusan. The feeble attempt to take the port city with a small and unsupported amphibious landing was a disaster with the loss of an estimated 600 North Korean soldiers. It was a crucial opportunity lost. Not sending more troops and particularly not providing naval cover directly contributed to the failure of this most important objective. Allowing the United States and Great Britain to control the coastlines with small numbers of warships in those critical first weeks of the conflict proved crucial to the early allied response and eventual success of the United Nations' forces.[3]

By 6 July, Pusan had received 15,000 U.S. Army troops, 1,700 vehicles, and much needed military cargo on board 55

---

[2] U.S. Secretary of State, Dean Acheson "Speech on the Far East," 12 January 1950, http://teachingamericanhistory.org/library/index.asp?document=1612, (accessed 2 February 2011).

[3] Importance of Pusan: Robert H. Ferrell, *Truman and the Cold War Revisionists,* (Columbia, Missouri: University of Missouri Press, 2006), 93.

ships. This initial toehold on the southeastern tip of the peninsula would eventually lead to a flood of troops, equipment, and supplies in the following weeks and months. If the North Koreans had sunk a ship or two at the entrance to Pusan's harbor, the allied effort would have been greatly imperiled.[4]

With no warning and a dearth of naval assets, the Western powers were able to cobble together a strategy that helped save South Korea from communist aggression. The small allied naval force lacked adequate military intelligence and faced the threat of formidable air and submarine power had the Soviets chosen to back their client state with their military might. Moreover, the world was just beginning to sort out what it meant to go to war with the specter of atomic weaponry in the arsenals of the two emerging super powers. As a later American Secretary of State Henry Kissinger noted in 1957:

> [W]e added the atomic bomb to our arsenal without integrating its implications into our thinking. Because we saw it merely as another tool in a concept of warfare which knew no goal save [sic] total victory, and no mode of war except all-out war.[5]

---

[4] Pusan in the first two weeks of the war: Duk-Hyun Cho, "Don't Give Up the Ships: United States naval operations during the first year of the Korean War," Thesis (Ph.D.) -- Ohio State University, 2002, 2003; South Korea, *The History of the United Nations Forces in the Korean War*, [Seoul]: Ministry of National Defense. Republic of Korea, 1972, Vol. 2, 209-10.

[5] The struggle of integration of atomic warfare into U.S. policy: Henry Kissinger, *Nuclear Weapons and Foreign Policy*, (NY: Published for the Council on Foreign Relations by Harper, 1957), 12.

By default The U.S. Navy had become the "tip of the sword" in responding to Communist aggression scenarios around the world. The new and emerging "Containment" strategy, supplemented by the conventional military considerations annunciated in the NSC Memorandum #68 (NSC-68), became the American answer to the antagonistic Soviet expansion policies and actions since the end of the Second World War.

There are two schools of thought as to why the Soviets did not militarily come to the aid of North Korea once the United States had entered the conflict on the side of the South Koreans. The United States believed strongly that the invasion by North Korea was yet another test by the Soviet Union of American resolve. The Truman administration saw the invasion as the Soviets using a client regime to expand their influence in Asia as they had been doing in Europe since the end of World War II. Based on that perception, the President drew a line in the sand. This initial action was completely consistent with his policies (Truman doctrine and Containment strategy) dating back to 1947 that provided aid and assistance to those around the world who were being confronted by Communist aggression, whatever its form. Most importantly, his commitment was now consistent with the ideas found in NSC-68 that sought a conventional arms build-up to confront the realities of Soviet power and their expansionist aims. The traditional view as to why the Soviets did not openly support the North Koreans, especially after the spectacular initial successes of the In Min Gun, was that Stalin when confronted with American resolve and might backed down.

Since the fall of the Soviet Union twenty years ago, new Russian archival material has become available that may point to another view as to Soviet inaction at the start of the Korean War. As already noted, both traditional and newer arguments agree that the speech given by then Secretary of State Dean Acheson, discussing an American Pacific defense perimeter that excluded South Korea, greatly helped Stalin in his decision to finally give the go-ahead to Kim Il Sung's request to invade South Korea. However, beyond this point the theories diverge. Today a growing number of historians believe Stalin never considered participating in the Korean War. The reasoning for this belief follows a two-step process. In the months leading up to the Korean crisis Stalin feared Communist China was about to attack the Chinese Nationalists on the island of Formosa. If Mao Tse-tung, the leader of the People's Republic of China, succeeded in defeating Chiang Kai-Shek's Nationalists, it might lead to a possible rapprochement between China and the United States. Much of the newer research points to this fear as to the turnabout by Stalin in giving the okay to North Korea to invade South Korea. It was a strategy to preempt the Chinese Communists from invading Formosa. Secondly, it has also been argued that allowing the North Koreans to invade South Korea would eventually pull Communist China into the fray. History shows that the war in Korea eventually did draw the Communist Chinese into the war in 1951. It is claimed that, in the end, the Chinese participation in the Korean War forced Mao into a dependency on the Soviet Union for almost a decade.[6]

---

[6] New views regarding why the Soviet Union did not commit military forces to the Korean conflict: Sergei N. Goncharov, John W. Lewis, and Xue Litai, *Uncertain Partners: Stalin Mao, and the Korean War*, (Stanford, California: Stanford University Press, 1993), Chapter 5; Thornton, *Odd Man Out,* 4-5;Weathersby, "Soviet Aims in Korea and the Origins of the Korean War," 33-36.

It must be said that, at least on the surface, this line of reasoning where Stalin appears to see the future so clearly, that is, as to how events would play out seems to this writer to be uncertain at best.

Whatever the final judgment history draws as to Soviet motives behind the Korean crisis, there is little question that had Stalin used his naval power, even if only surreptitiously, or conceived a better plan for the North Koreans, one involving a strong amphibious assault on Pusan could have resulted in a quick capture of the critical port city. Had this happened a very strong argument could be made that a swift completion of the invasion would have ensued leaving the Western powers with few options for saving the Republic of South Korea. As one famous World War II U.S. Admiral, Arleigh Burke, stated, "If our control of the sea had been contested just a little bit, [South] Korea would have been lost very fast."[7] Hats off to those ships and sailors present at the outbreak of the war who helped deny victory to the communist-inspired invasion.

Operation Bluehearts

The aircraft carrier *Triumph*, fresh from the air strikes in and around Pyongyang, retired to the American naval base at Buckner Bay in Okinawa. There she was refueled by Royal Fleet Auxiliary (RFA) ship *Green Ranger* and then took on fresh stores from RFA *Fort Charlotte*. For all the effort the crew of *Triumph* had gone through, flying their aircraft around *Valley Forge* and the Seventh Fleet during that first

---

[7] Admiral Arleigh Burke remark cited in Lisle Rose, *Power at Sea: Vol. 3 A Violent Peace, 1946-2006,* (Columbia, Missouri: University of Missouri Press, 2007), 105; and in Stephen Howarth, *To Shining Sea: A History of the United States Navy, 1775-1998,* (Norman, Oklahoma: University of Oklahoma Press, 1999), 491.

combined air strike U.S. naval commanders still feared the aircraft would be mistaken for the enemy and told the British as much. While at Buckner Bay *Triumph's* crew took the time to paint additional wide black and white stripes on the wings and fuselage of the Seafires and Fireflies to address the problem. With the striping scheme, the British aircraft ceased to resemble the North Korean Soviet-built Yak-9. After about a week, the light carrier was again ready for action. *Valley Forge* had also retired to Buckner Bay and replenished. On 18 July, Task Force 77, the combined U.S. and British carrier group, was back in action covering the amphibious landing of American troops, equipment, and ammunition at Pohang.[8]

14-1 British Fighter with Special Black and White Striping

---

[8] Amphibious landing at Pohang: *Valley Forge*, Deck Log, 18 July 1950; Field, *Naval Ops Korea*, 107; Lansdown, *With the Carriers*, 17; James Paul and Martin Spirit, Britain's Small Wars: The History of British Military Conflict since 1945, http://www.britains-smallwars.com,"Korea," (accessed 17 July 2009).

The U.S. submarines continued to provide support for the Western naval forces through the gathering of intelligence on Soviet naval activity especially around Vladivostok. They also kept an eye on the Chinese Communists and Nationalists regarding the island of Formosa. Even the minesweepers got in on the action. The wooden minesweepers immediately began performing such tasks as picket duty and harbor defense for ports in Japan and Pusan. They also provided escort for those ships transporting men, equipment, ammunition, and supplies between Japan and Pusan.[9]

The 24th and then the 25th Divisions of the U.S. 8th Army began arriving in force at Pusan after the Battle of Chumunjin and the Task Force 77 airstrikes in North Korea. Forced into the front lines pell-mell in order to shore up the shrinking Pusan perimeter, the 24th Division came under immediate heavy attack as the North Koreans furiously pushed south while also continuing to wear down the ROK divisions falling back. The American 24th was one-third under strength, short of artillery, and had only a few light tanks that did not measure up to the Soviet-built T-34 tanks employed by the North Koreans. When the U.S. 25th Division landed in Pusan they found the port facilities overwhelmed and the transportation routes between Pusan and the front in all directions to be clogged and dramatically slowed with troops, equipment, and supplies. The U.S. Army wanted to move the American 1st Cavalry Division into Korea quickly but saw that Pusan, for the present, was not the answer.

---

[9] Submarine and minesweeping activity during the first month of the war: Utz, *Assault from the Sea*, 11; Field, *History of Naval Operations*, 54; Cagle and Manson, *Sea War in Korea*, 44.

On 9 July provisional planning began with an eye to landing the U.S. 1st Cavalry Division at the port city of Pohang located 70 miles north of Pusan on the Sea of Japan. The small port city sat at the head of six-mile wide Yongil Bay. The bay, surrounded by steep hills and cliffs, had some of the most accessible beaches in all of South Korea. The next day ships were selected and loading begun for the amphibious force to sail by the 14th and 15th. Vice Admiral Joy issued official orders on the 12th, based on MacArthur's instructions of the 11th, stating "U.S. Naval Forces Far East will seize, occupy, and defend by amphibious assault a beachhead in... the vicinity of Pohang."[10] The undertaking became "Operation Bluehearts." As initial elements of the 1st Cavalry Division began moving out of ports in Japan on the 14th, U.S. Naval Forces Far East wooden minesweepers of the "Bird" squadron including *Redhead*, *Mocking Bird*, *Osprey*, *Partridge*, *Chatterer*, and *Kite* arrived at Pohang and began sweeping the approaches to the port and Yongil Bay in preparation for the landing. *Juneau* and *Collett* along with some other warships operated with the landing's Gunfire Support Group. By the night of the 15th, all of the amphibious assault vessels were at sea. The landing at Pohang took place on the 18th. Three regimental-sized combat teams, an artillery group of three battalions and some smaller units totaling about 10,000 troops, 2,000 vehicles and other equipment, as well as 3,000 tons of supplies successfully came ashore. The 1st Cavalry Division proceeded from Pohang to the front lines that were less than ten miles from where they landed.[11]

---

[10] Karig, Cagle, and Manson, *Battle Report*, 91.

[11] Amphibious landing at Pohang, South Korea of the U.S. Army 1st Cavalry Division: Field, *U.S. Naval Operations*, 102-103, 107; Karig, Cagle, and Manson, *Battle Report*, 90,96; Cagle and Mason, *Sea War in Korea*, 39.

The whole operation from conception to completion took just a week and a half. The startling speed with which the U.S. Navy put together and then delivered on its mission allowed the landing to be unopposed. Operation Bluehearts foreshadowed and pointed the way to the landing at Inchon in September. It also dramatically showed, though overlooked by the press and other media, that control of the sea, in this case the littorals of the Korean peninsula, was an invaluable factor in the success on land in the coming months. Without it South Korea would have fallen. As British maritime doctrine states:

> Sea control is the condition in which one has freedom of action to use the sea for one's own purposes in specified areas and for specified periods of time and, where necessary, to deny or limit its use to the enemy. Sea control includes the airspace above the surface and the water volume and seabed below.[12]

Vice Admiral Joy stated, "I do not believe the [Pusan] perimeter could have been held without the *timely reinforcement* [emphasis added] of our forces by the 1st Cavalry Division."[13] Indeed as one author phrased it,

> In retrospect, it is clear that the unspectacular and unpublicized amphibious landing at Pohang on 18

---

[12] Great Britain, *British Maritime Doctrine: BR 1806*, (London: Stationery Office, 2004), 289.

[13] Cagle and Manson, *Sea War in Korea*, 44.

July did as much to preserve the perilous Korean toehold as any single event.[14]

Sea Power

Sea power after the Second World War has become the ability to "shape and influence the course and outcome of conflicts occurring on land."[15] With the Korean War, the focus of naval warfare shifted away from the open sea and to the littoral. As a U.S. and a Royal Navy officer writing in an American naval magazine described it:

> In the littorals, sea-control challenges are often asymmetric in nature, with military objectives...tied to the broader context of influencing events on shore. A simple definition of sea control that covers the full range of operations, therefore, is the use of the sea as a maneuver space to achieve military objectives.[16]

Today, most of the world's population lives, and commerce moves, within 50 miles of a coastline. The American and British naval forces were immediately able to project power in Korea by using their guns, and air power from carrier decks, against North Korean troops, supplies, communications, and transport, which were all located on land. They could also provide close-air support for allied

---

[14] Cagle and Manson, *Sea war in Korea*, 41.

[15] Colin S. Gray, *The Leverage of Sea Power: the Strategic Advantage of Navies in War*, (NY: Free Press, 1992), 1.

[16] Captain Victor G. Addison Jr., USN and Commander David Dominy, RN, "Got Sea Control," USNI website, http://www.usni.org/magazines/proceedings/2010-03/got-sea-control.

troops.[17] During and since the Korean War, as one author puts it: "[W]hen war initially breaks out, the Navy, its ships and sailors go into harm's way as they are, where they are, and do what needs to be done."[18]

And so it was that a small number of naval vessels and even merchant ships briefly took center stage as the curtain rose on a most serious play. The Korean War was only the first act in what would be a struggle more than four decades long known as the Cold War. It was by circumstance and chance that these particular ships came together and did what was necessary in serving the interest of their nations.

In the following weeks and months, many more naval vessels would join the original naval forces in the Korean theater as the war played out over the next three years. Each of the ships on station in those opening days of the war still had missions to fulfill as the war progressed. Some of these ships present at the beginning would pay a higher price...

---

[17] Power projection by today's naval forces: Howarth, *To Shining Sea*, 569-70; Michael J. Varhola, *Fire and Ice: The Korean War, 1950-1953*, (Mason City, Iowa: Savas, 2001), 52.

[18] CDR Salamander, "Fullbore Friday, USS *Juneau* CL-119, 1 August 2006," A Naval Blog, http://cdrsalamander.blogspot.com/2006_08_18_archive.html (accessed 13 May 2008).

Chapter 15

"[N]ecklace of gun flashes..."[1]

MacArthur's Counter-Stroke

In late July and early August 1950, many more ships began to arrive in the Korean theater. Larger gunned warships such as heavy cruisers and even American battleships joined the blockade and provided punishing bombardment capability along the Korean peninsula's coastline. Heavy cruisers like *Rochester* that had provided support for *Valley Forge* in Task Force 77 and *Toledo* to which Admiral Higgins had moved his flag from *Juneau* in late July, took over the bombardment duties. As an example, the U.S. Iowa class battleships with their 16-inch guns, whose high explosive shells weighing 1,900 lbs and their armor piercing variety 2,700 lbs, were capable of attacking targets 20 plus miles inland all along the Korean coast.

15-1 Heavy Cruiser *Toledo* and Light Cruiser *Juneau* (note the difference in size)

---

[1] U.S. Navy Combat Veterans of the Sitting Ducks of Inchon, "Sitting Ducks" Squadron Quest for the Presidential Unit Citation, Part 1, Welcome Aboard the USS *Collett* (DD-730),http://www.usscollett.com/history.htm, page 2, (Accessed 23 August 2011)

15-2 *Juneau* Moored in Foreground with *Valley Forge* nearest to Her in Sasebo, Japan (late 1950)

The original warships of the U.S. Naval Forces Far East and the British Far East Fleet continued to play a significant role in the war. The next few months found the veterans of the opening days of the conflict involved in many a perilous situation.

On just the fifth day of the crisis, General MacArthur had flown to Korea to assess the situation. Once there he took a jeep and was driven north to the Han River where the South Korean forces were retreating. He climbed a small hill and his view became that of the river with Seoul to the north. In *American Caesar*, William Manchester's superb biography of MacArthur, the author picks up the story at that point.

> Mangled corpses littered the south bank of the Han...[L]ater the General would reveal that during his twenty minutes on that little knoll he had conceived a

great amphibious landing...behind the North Koreans.[2]

Indeed the war turned in mid September with a stunning combination of strategy and display of sea power. The Inchon amphibious assault was a classic flanking maneuver where MacArthur planned to go well around and behind the enemy now dug in along the Pusan perimeter, landing U.S. Marines at the South Korean port city of Inchon 18 miles from Seoul. When MacArthur proposed the plan, it met with much resistance from the Joint Chiefs of Staff. The head of the Joints Chiefs, World War II hero General Omar Bradley, argued, "A failure at Inchon could very well so inspire the North Koreans that they would overrun the Pusan perimeter."[3] There was no love lost between the two five-star army generals. Just weeks before making the Inchon landing proposal, MacArthur had confided to Admiral James Doyle, who had drawn up the naval aspects

---

[2] General MacArthur surveying the Korean situation: William Manchester, *American Caesar: Douglas MacArthur 1880-1964*, (Boston: Little, Brown, and Company, 1978), 555.

Another view of the conception of the Inchon operation is offered by author Gordon Rottman who argues that the real Inchon landing idea came from a Pentagon staffer, Donald McB. Curtis, who less than a week before the war started developed and submitted contingency plan SL-17. This plan, to quote Rottman, "presupposed an NK invasion, a retreat south, establishment of a perimeter at Pusan, *and an outflanking amphibious landing to support a counter offensive once Pusan was reinforced* [emphasis added]." Gordan L. Rottman, and Peter Dennis, Inch'on 1950: The Last Great Amphibious Assault, (Oxford: Osprey, 2006), 42.

[3] Omar Bradley's assessment: Michael D. Pearlman, *Truman & MacArthur: Policy, Politics, and the Hunger for Honor and Renown*, (Bloomington and Indianapolis, IN: Indiana University Press, 2008), 79.

of the proposed landing, that "Bradley was a farmer."[4] However, Truman supported the idea, overruled the Joint Chiefs, who then in turn scheduled the assault for the middle of September.

Even before the assault by the Americans from the Yellow Sea, the North Koreans were beginning to experience grave problems with their offensive in the south around the Pusan perimeter. The North Koreans were not replacing men at the rate needed to defeat the South Korean and American forces that were growing with the daily arrival of men, equipment, and supplies at Pusan. Those reserves that the North Koreans did manage to send had much less training than the original troops of the In Min Gun. Shortages of just about everything began to appear in the NKPA supply lines, now extended and straining over several hundred miles. Heavy tank losses and a much-depleted air force had left the North Koreans in a precarious position, so close and yet so far away from their objective.

Naval Bombardment of Wolmi-do

The daring plan to land American troops at Inchon was set to occur on 15 September. However, before the landing, now code named "Chromite" could take place, gun emplacements located on the island of Wolmi-do, which sits directly in front of the port, needed silencing. Wolmi-do is a triangular-shaped island that is directly connected to the mainland via a 900 foot long spit. The Koreans call it "Moon Tip Island." The land mass rises up out of the water to a height of 350 feet and dominates the surrounding landscape and the approaches to Inchon. The island

---

[4] MacArthur's retort to the Bradley comment: David Halberstam, *The Coldest Winter: America and the Korean War*, (New York: Hyperion, 2007), 296.

appeared to the U.S. Navy as an unsinkable battleship with gun emplacements hidden throughout its length and breadth. The batteries on the island controlled the entire bay and all of the proposed landing zones for the operation. The strategy was to drop bombs on the island from the air at night and then bombard it during the day from the sea. Extreme tidal conditions at Inchon dictated that the Wolmi-do bombardment would require the American warships to come in with the flood tide and anchor one after another in a row, leaving the destroyers as sitting ducks for enemy gunfire. In spite of these adversities, the elimination of the guns on the island was paramount for the well-being of the United Nations' troops landing at Inchon. Air and naval bombardment of the island would begin on 13 and 14 September.

The problems and challenges associated with the naval bombardment of Wolmi-do were endless. The slight maneuvering room and narrowness of the channel leading into the harbor plus the possibility of mines precluded the use of larger warships. The decision to use the smaller and more agile destroyers for the gunfire mission became obvious. The original four destroyers *Mansfield*, *Collett*, *De Haven*, and *Lyman K. Swenson* along with two newer Gearing class destroyers *Gurke* and *Henderson* would provide the firepower for the bombardment. The differences between the Gearing and Sumner classes were slight. The Gearings were newer and 14 feet longer amidships to make room for more fuel storage. Consequently, the Gearings were known as long-hulled and the Sumners as short-hulled. There were compelling reasons for the selection of the Sumners: first, they had been in action since the beginning of the conflict and thus had the experience of wartime operations recently. During the blockade beginning in July, they had sharpened their gunnery skills. Lastly, they were comparatively older destroyers to those now arriving in the theater thus making them more expendable should the North Korean defenses on Wolmi-do prove to be stronger than hoped.

The aerial night attack proceeded as scheduled but the unguided aerial bombs available in 1950 proved to be less effective than hoped. The ships did not enter the channel at night because of the aforementioned problems of room to maneuver and mines and then had to add the issue of recognizing gun emplacements on the island in the darkness before being exposed themselves.

15-3 USS *Lyman K. Swenson* off Wolmi-do during Pre-invasion Bombardment 13 September 1950 (40-mm guns in foreground)

The next morning, 13 September, the destroyers entered the channel on the flooding tide. They proceeded in single file with *Mansfield* in the van, followed 700 yards astern by *De Haven*, *Swenson*, *Collett*, *Gurke*, and *Henderson*. The weather presented with low cumulus clouds and calm to moderate seas. Not very far into the channel, *Mansfield* reported a string of floating mines to port. Minesweepers were two days away, and the bombardment could not wait, so they pressed on. *Henderson,* the last of the destroyers to enter the channel, received instructions to deal with as many of the exposed mines as possible, while the remaining five destroyers continued on course through the passage known as Flying Fish channel.

Because of extremely swift moving current through the channel, once the destroyers reached the designated area off the island, they dropped anchor to hold their tenuous positions. *De Haven* moved into designated position "fire support station #2"[5] paying out "30 fathoms of the starboard anchor chain."[6] The destroyer hooked bottom in nine fathoms of water. The fire support stations were as close to Wolmi-do as they dared and then the shelling of the island began with *De Haven* opening fire first, followed by *Collett*. Being tethered, so to speak, to their stations did not allow for any movement or maneuvering, as the destroyers were accustomed to doing when trading fire with an enemy. Some of the ships were within 700 yards of the shoreline. The destroyers in that setting were sitting ducks. As guns on Wolmi-do returned fire, the destroyers pinpointed their location and redirected their own fire. Shells were flying back and forth with expended powder charges creating much smoke.

A 20-year-old radar man on board *De* Haven, Bob Sauer, described the exchange of gunfire this way:

> Those 58 minutes or so that we were in there that day seemed like a very long time to me, and I imagine to the rest of the men aboard. It made me think that

---

[5] USS *De Haven*, Deck Log, 13 September 1950.

[6] USS *De Haven*, Deck Log, 13 September 1950.

INITIAL BURDEN

old familiar thought that millions of young Americans had experienced before us — something like: what the hell am I doing here?[7]

Some miles out to sea on board the heavy cruiser *Toledo*, Associated Press correspondent, Relman Morin, who was watching the action using binoculars, later described the enemy fire as a "necklace of gun flashes... soon they came so fast the entire slope [of the island] was sparkling with pinpoints of fire."[8] A lieutenant John W. Lee, also on *Toledo* observing the gunfire spoke out regarding the destroyers, "My God, they're sacrificing these guys."[9] As the "tin cans" and the shore batteries on Wolmi-do continued to swap shellfire, the North Korean gun emplacements on the island focused their attention on *Swenson*, *Collett*, and *Gurke*. A Gunner's Mate 1st Class, Joe Carrillo, on board *Collett*, described the action in this fashion:

> We were now at "Bore Sight" range, or for better words, "Sitting Ducks".... As I watched, I could see a solid row of red and yellow flashes along the face of Wolmi-Do. It appeared as if the whole island was on fire.... The artillery had found our range and a lucky shot had struck our oil storage compartments, another one had entered CIC wounding several men and knocking out our main battery computer, which forced the main battery into Local Control. My gun

---

[7] Bob Sauer, "Bob Sauer Remembers," USS *De Haven* Sailors Association, http://ussdehaven.org (accessed 23 August 2011).

[8] U.S. Navy Combat Veterans of the Sitting Ducks of Inchon, "Sitting Ducks" Squadron Quest for the Presidential Unit Citation, Part 1, page 2.

[9] Ibid.

crew was made up of untested men in combat, they were now facing death as a reality and it showed. Only a fool would deny his fear of death. It seemed like the battle would never end, the air was thick with enemy shells screeching over our heads.... The battle was now ferocious with rifle and machine gun fire hitting and passing overhead.... I noticed that my gun Mt. [mount] was firing above zero elevation and soon realized that *Collett* was listing to portside, due to enemy shells striking our fuel compartments....[10]

In fact, nine shells had struck *Collett*. One shell struck forward on the port side penetrating the thin armor and exploding in the crew's quarters. Fortunately, all the sailors were at their battle stations. Struck at the water line, another shell created a two-foot hole flooding the steward's living compartment with oil and water. One author described the next shell to strike *Collett* in this manner:

> Twenty minutes after the first wound, *Collett* took hit number three, this one in the wardroom. It was a dud shell, which walked through the door, knocked down a shelf of books, dented the opposite steel bulkhead, and fell to rest on the wardroom sofa.[11]

The most damaging blow came next. A 75-mm armor piercing shell broke in half upon impact with half of the shell ripping into the fire room rupturing an air line. The

---

[10] Joe Carrillo, "Desron Nine and the Odyssey of the "Sitting Ducks," Welcome Aboard the USS *Collett* (DD-730), http://www.usscollett.com/history.htm (Accessed 21 March 2012).

[11] Malcolm W. Cagle, "The Taking of Wolmi-do," Sea Classics, Vol. 33, No. 10, October 2000.

other half of the shell sliced into the plot room destroying the computer that fired the 5-inch guns and wounded five sailors. At that point, control of the guns shifted to each individual gun mount. Five more hits amounted to no more than splinter damage. Joe Carrillo picks up the story again:

> After almost one hour of continuous fire, *Collett* signaled for help from sister ships, Commodore Allen, now ordered all Destroyers to withdraw from the battle, *Collett* was denied help, when all of the Destroyers were ordered to withdraw independently. Captain Robert H. Close was concerned about damage control and the possibility of sinking in the harbor. He ordered full speed astern and commenced hoisting the anchor at the same time. Soon I saw our sister ships speed by on our stern, waving and cheering loudly; they could see that we were in trouble. Still under fire, *Collett* maneuvered to the outer harbor and seaward.[12]

A bluejacket, Ed Shumer, described what the crew did next:

> Some of us focused on the engine rooms, while others had their hands full in the Stewards quarters below the mess decks. Oil was pouring out of a fuel tank and saltwater was pouring in where a shell had penetrated below the waterline. It took about 12 hours to get the tank hole plugged to keep the oil from leaking out and to get a temporary plug in place to keep the salt water at bay.[13]

---

[12] Carrillo, "Desron Nine and the Odyssey of the 'Sitting Ducks,'" n.p.

[13] Ed Shumer, "1949-1952: My Time On board the USS *Collett*," March 2010, Welcome Aboard the USS *Collett* (DD-730), http://www.usscollett.com/history.htm, (Accessed 23 August 2011).

Collett's action report for that day would read in part, "In view of the great number of projectiles which landed in our immediate vicinity, God must be credited with keeping a watchful and protective eye on us."[14]

During the bombardment, *Gurke* was struck by enemy fire three times leaving two sailors wounded. The ship overall though had suffered only minor splinter damage. *De Haven* took a .50 caliber round severing both an emergency power cable and a fire hose. *Swenson*, not directly hit, still suffered casualties as a shell exploding close to the ship caused fragments to spray the deck wounding one crewman and killing another.

The following day five of the original six destroyers returned to the island to eliminate the remaining gun emplacements. *Collett* did not participate because of the damage to her fire control system. Before they re-entered Flying Fish channel the destroyers paused as they moved by *Toledo*, which had taken on board the wounded and dead from the previous day's action. All the ships displayed their colors at half-mast[15] and observed a minute of silent prayer[16] for Lieutenant Junior Grade W. H. Swenson killed in action less than 24 hours before. *Toledo* provided full military honors beginning with a Boatswain's mate piping all hands to bury the dead, followed by "a simple service, a Marine rifle salute, and the playing of Taps" after which the young officer's remains were committed to the deep.[17] On this

---

[14] Cagle, "The Taking of Wolmi-do," Vol. 33, No. 10, October 2000.

[15] USS *De Haven*, Deck Log, 14 September 1950.

[16] Ibid.

[17] Charles A. Utz, *Assault from the Sea: the Amphibious Landing at Inchon*, (Washington D.C.: Naval Historical Center, Department of the Navy, 1994), 26.

second day of bombardment, the destroyer fire was deadly, silencing the remaining guns on the island in just a little over an hour with no new damage to the ships. In two days, the "sitting duck squadron" expended over 3,000 shells. With the guns of Wolmi-do silenced, the amphibious landing at Inchon took place the next day, 15 September.[18]

MacArthur was not known for his genial relations with the Navy. He had complained during the Second World War that too many admirals were more interested in protecting their ships than fighting the enemy with them. But after the assault at Inchon the general told Rear Admiral James H. Doyle, who was in charge of the amphibious landing, that "The Navy and Marines have never shown more brightly than this morning."[19]

U.S. Navy Presidential Unit Citation Ribbon (Blue, Gold, and Red)

In 2003 the U.S. Navy Combat Veterans of the "Sitting Ducks" Squadron of Inchon, Petitioned the Government for the Presidential Unit Citation

---

[18] The bombardment of Wolmi island: Karig, Manson, and Cagle, *Battle Report*, 192-93, 202, 206-209; Cagle and Manson, *Sea War in Korea*, 91-92; Field, *History of Naval Operations*, 191-93; Utz, *Assault from the Sea*, 26.

[19] Douglas MacArthur, *Reminiscences*, (New York: McGraw-Hill, 1964), 353.

INITIAL BURDEN

15-4 Inchon Landing 15 September 1950 (*De Haven* in foreground)

The NKPA — so close to pushing the allies out of South Korea at Pusan — now completely outflanked, found their supply lines in serious jeopardy. The In Min Gun began falling back from the Pusan perimeter leaving much of their armor and artillery behind. Seoul fell on the 27th to MacArthur's forces 12 days after the landing at Inchon. By the end of September, the now routed North Korean forces had returned to positions north of the 38th parallel. United Nations forces took up positions along the parallel and waited for orders. After three months of fighting, everything was back to square one.

15-5 *Collett, Lyman K. Swenson, Mansfield,* and *De Haven*

Truman's Fateful Decision

At the beginning of the war, President Truman's objective had been to reestablish the status quo between North and South Korea. In his words, he wanted "to restore peace there [Korea] and *restore the border* [emphasis added]."[20] With the Navy now in complete control of the seas surrounding the Korean peninsula and the UN forces firmly established just below the 38th parallel, Truman could have walked away from the conflict and chalked it up as a tactical victory snatched from the jaws of defeat. He could have made a very strong case that it was a strategic vindication of the Truman Doctrine and the NSC-68 memorandum enhanced Containment policy for U.S. foreign affairs. He could have easily told the world it was a triumph of

---

[20] Manchester, *American Caesar*, 583.

democracy over communist aggression. His leadership in such a high stakes affair would surely have improved his re-election chances the following year. Nevertheless, Truman did not declare victory and end the fighting.

Instead, it was at this time the United States and her allies saw the opportunity to reunite the two Koreas on their terms and not Moscow's. When Inchon turned into a much more than hoped for success the impulse to cross into North Korea, destroy the NKPA, and establish a democratic and united Korea became palpable. Truman jumped at the opportunity. On 27 September, using a National Security Council memorandum (NSC-81/1) developed a few weeks earlier as a basis, Truman ordered MacArthur to cross the 38th parallel in an attempt to defeat the North Korean forces.[21] Although the Korean conflict was ostensibly a United Nations effort, that body did not approve the President's order until 7 October. By then the United Nations' forces had been in North Korea for over a week. The strategy chosen by Truman was politically and militarily fraught with risk because attacking North Korea raised the specter and possibility of Communist China, the Soviet Union, or both entering the conflict.

There are differing thoughts as to why Truman chose the course of action that he did. In his memoirs, former Secretary of State Dean Acheson contends that he recommended to the president, and Truman made the decision, to go into North Korea based solely on the merits of military tactics and possible outcomes — destroying the

---

[21] Truman orders ground forces into North Korea: Paolo E. Coletta, *The American Naval Heritage*, Third Edition, (Lanham, Maryland: University Press of America), 476; Donovan, *Tumultuous Years*, 273. A copy of NSC 81/1 can be found on-line at The Cold War Files, http://legacy.wilson center.org/coldwarfiles/files/Documents/Truman-library.NSC.81-1.pdf.

NKPA and possibly restoring unity.[22] Many looked to United Nations Security Council Resolution 82 issued at the beginning of the North Korean invasion that spoke to the UN's already stated objective of "the complete independence and unity of Korea."[23] Another view raised the issue that political pressure at home (mid-term elections) could have possibly influenced Truman into looking for not just a good outcome but also a potentially great outcome to the war.[24] The United States' allies were behind the action. British Foreign Secretary, Ernest Bevan, stated, "[T]here should be no perpetuation of that division [between the Korean peoples]."[25] One author has gone as far to say that it was "a decision that made itself" and "had a momentum of its own."[26] It is always possible that to some degree Truman, having achieved his original objective, and bolstered by the initial success of stopping the North Koreans from reaching Pusan simply succumbed to the psychological phenomenon known as "victory disease." Another term used by the military for this is "mission creep" — as too many former world leaders, generals, and admirals

---

[22] Argument for authorizing troops to cross into North Korea as purely a military tactical decision: Dean Acheson, *Present at the Creation: My Years in the State Department*, (NY: W. W. Norton, 1969), 453.

[23] UN Security Council, *Resolution 82 of 25 June 1950*, available at: http://www.unhcr.org/refworld/docid /3b00f15960.html [accessed 15 October 2011]

[24] Argument for authorizing troops to cross into North Korea as possibly being influenced by domestic politics: Richard F. Haynes, *The Awesome Power: Harry S. Truman as Commander in Chief*, Baton Rouge, Louisiana, Louisiana State University Press, 1973), 196-97.

[25] John W. Spanier, *The Truman-MacArthur Controversy and the Korean War*, Cambridge, Massachusetts: Belknap Press, 1959), 102.

[26] Halberstam, *The Coldest Winter*, 323.

throughout history were painfully aware. In the end, it was his responsibility and his decision alone in authorizing the crossing of the 38th parallel. Truman's decision to not declare victory and instead carry the fight into North Korea in the end proved to be disastrous for the United States. The approved operation was supposed to take just weeks with the soldiers and sailors home by Christmas. In fact, the war would last another two and one-half years.

Chapter 16

"[T]he...water had ceased falling"[1]

Mine Warfare

MacArthur received the go ahead to cross the parallel to destroy the North Korean Army on 27 September. The General's plan had been put together prior to the orders so that, if needed, it could be implemented quickly. As part of this operation, MacArthur had planned yet another amphibious flanking maneuver, this time on the east coast of the Korean peninsula. He had decided to land troops at the North Korean port of Wonsan. From there they would push northward toward the Yalu River that marked the border between North Korea and China, and eventually link up with the UN forces advancing north of Seoul. The intent of the operation was, as per the new mission, to destroy the NKPA. MacArthur ordered the forces for the landing at Wonsan to be quickly assembled. These forces were then embarked on amphibious landing vessels. A great minesweeping effort to clear and make safe the approaches to Wonsan was to precede the operation.

By the end of the Second World War, the United States possessed over 500 ships dedicated to mine warfare. By the start of the Korean War, the U.S. Navy's mine warfare ships stood at around 50. The small group of sweepers in the Far East did not possess the latest communications and sonar

---

[1] C. E. McMullen, "Report of the Loss of USS *Pirate*," Naval History & Heritage Command website, http://www.history.navy.mil/faqs/faq103-3.htm (accessed 19 February 2009).

equipment the Navy had to offer. Moreover, of the four larger Admirable class sweepers stationed in Japan at the outbreak of hostilities only one, *Pledge*, had been available for duty. It had taken almost another two months to obtain parts and even crewmen to fill out and make ready *Pirate* and *Incredible*. The two sweepers were finally recommissioned in the middle of August. Even then, *Mainstay*, the fourth of the larger sweepers, was unable to join her sisters for duty still lacking the correct parts to make her serviceable.[2]

Historically, expertise in mine warfare is a known strength of the Soviet Navy. During the Russo-Japanese War of 1904-5, Russian mines sank two Japanese battleships. At the end of the Second World War, the Soviets captured all o the mines that Germany had not had time to deploy. These mines, added to the Soviets' already large inventory, created an extensive stockpile of defensive weapons.

As part of their post-WWII build up of military forces, the Soviets emphasized advanced mine warfare education and training. Before the Korean War began, undetected by Western intelligence, the Soviets had moved thousands of mines into North Korea by rail from Vladivostok. Soviet mine warfare officers as advisors helped the North Koreans lay mines at Chinnampo on the Yellow Sea and at Wonsan. They taught the North Koreans how to assemble the magnetic mines. The same advisors planned the design of the minefields and supervised the planting operation. Motorized sampans that operated as minelayers towed barges. Local labor loaded and then rolled the deadly

---

[2] The state of U.S. Naval mine warfare early in 1950: Edwards, *Small United States and United Nations Warships in the Korean War*, 151,159.

weapons off the sterns of the barges in a predetermined order. Contact, magnetic, and controlled mines made up the two to three-thousand explosives planted in a 400 square mile minefield that encompassed the harbor and the seaward approaches to Wonsan.[3]

During the run-up to the amphibious landing at Wonsan, the destroyers *Mansfield* and *Swenson* were part of a gunfire support group working to the south of Wonsan in the Chumunjin area. Around noon, on 30 September they received orders to detach from the group and proceed north to latitude 38 degrees 45 minutes to attempt the rescue of the crew of a downed American B-26 bomber. After making their way up the coast into North Korean waters not too far south of Wonsan the two American destroyers began their search. As *Swenson* covered *Mansfield's* approach, machine gun and small arms fire chattered noisily from the direction of the beach. *Swenson* had stopped at the fifty-fathom curve. *Mansfield* inched closer to the beach. Two aircraft had now arrived and were reporting that *Mansfield* was within 2,200 yards of the plane wreckage, clearly visible now in about twelve fathoms of water. Suddenly a deep explosion under the bow shook the entire ship. The detonation and concussion of the blast sent a geyser of water hurtling high into the sky. After a moment of shock, *Mansfield* began to draw back from the spot of the explosion. The bow began sinking. The damage control parties made their way to the compartments

---

[3] Soviet mine warfare: Tamara Moser Melia, *Damn the Torpedoes: A Short History of U.S. Countermeasures Naval Mine, 1777-1991*, (Washington D.C.: Naval Historical Center, Department of the Navy, 1991), 72; Uhlig, "The Threat of the Soviet Navy," 444-454; Field, *History of U.S. Naval Operations*, 237.

forward in the ship where they found 27 wounded sailors and quickly moved them to safety. Next, water began flooding spaces below the first platform deck. This precipitated a shoring operation on all of the below decks. *Mansfield's* awning stanchions and magazine stowage supports supplemented the wood stored on board in this effort. The crew even employed welding torches to finish the protective work. The captain then ordered pumping the forward ballast tanks empty and the aft tanks full in order to keep *Mansfield's* bow as high in the water as possible. Finally, the destroyer's bow trim improved by uncoupling and letting go the port anchor. After these repairs *Mansfield,* although sitting about as low in the water as possible, was able to make eight to ten knots and retire to the south heading toward Japan. Once there, the destroyer received a temporary patching job. Eventually, the wounded warship made her way stateside for major repairs. Miraculously all of the twenty-seven injured sailors survived.

Shortly after the *Mansfield* mining incident, the Americans discovered another mine that had obviously loosened its mooring and ascended to the surface in the approaches to the port of Wonsan. Ominously, the mine was clean with what looked like fresh paint on it — a sign that it had been in the water a very short time.[4] The two events alerted Admiral Joy that the seaward path to Wonsan would not be the same as that to Pohang or even Inchon. Getting the

---

[4] The mining of USS *Mansfield*: Karl Kristiansen, "USS *Mansfield* DD-728 Mine Incident," Karl's Korner, USS *Mansfield* DD-728, Ship's History and Photos, http://web.meganet.net/kman/nfmine.htm (accessed 22 March 2012); Cagle and Manson, *Sea War in Korea*, 132-133.

amphibious forces to the beaches at Wonsan would present the U.S. Navy with a much greater challenge.

Wonsan Minesweeping Operation

The Wonsan amphibious landing with its 250-ship contingent was code-named "Operation Tailboard." The mine sweeping task group within this larger operation consisted of just two dozen vessels (for perspective, the landing at Normandy in France during 1944 had used some 300 mine sweeping ships and during the whole of the Second World War the United States had never cleared even a small harbor without at least 30 anti-mine vessels). Wonsan was no small harbor. The landing had originally been set for 20 October, but the Army, adding to the growing pressure, requested the date moved up by five days to the 15th. Finally, intelligence regarding the enemy, the harbor, and its surroundings was sorely lacking. *Collett*, which had undergone repairs in Japan since sustaining damage during the bombardment of Wolmi-do back in September, was designated as the flagship of this small band of sweepers. *Collett's* selection as flag was due to her extensive and varied assignments during the opening days of the war and because her captain, O. B. Lundgren, was a mine warfare expert. The group departed Sasebo on 6 October and arrived just outside Wonsan in the cold and gray early morning hours of 10 October.[5]

Collett took her position and immediately began to direct the operation. There were two ways to the landing beaches. One route into the harbor and the beaches called the Russian navigation channel used a northerly approach. The

---

[5] Preparation for minesweeping effort at Wonsan: Cagle and Manson, *Sea War in Korea*, 133; Field, *History of Naval Operations*, 220-21; Karig, Manson, and Cagle, *Battle Report*, 311, 315.

INITIAL BURDEN

other option was to attempt to head straight from the 100-fathom curve at the southern edge of the harbor directly to the beaches where the landing was to take place. The sweepers received direction to head directly towards the beach using the southern approach. It was a much shorter route than the Russian navigation channel and, if they could make it, they would be in a position to complete their sweeping chores in time to facilitate the Army's new landing deadline.

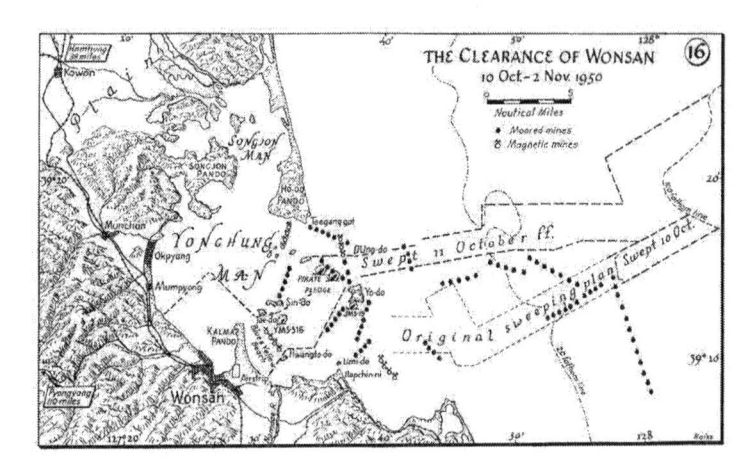

16-1 Direct Channel (lower) and Russian Channel (upper) Leading to Wonsan, North Korea

The plan was to have the three larger steel-hulled minesweepers lead the way. *Pledge* took the point with *Incredible* astern of her. Unfortunately, the third sweeper *Pirate* was experiencing trouble with her port engine and radioed she would have to remain behind until she could sort out and repair the problem. Behind the two "big steel jobs," as the Admirable class sweepers were known, came four of the smaller wooden-hulled sweepers *Osprey*, *Mocking Bird*, *Chatterer*, and *Partridge*. *Chatterer* was to mark the outer limits of the swept area with orange buoys while *Partridge's* job was to use gunfire to destroy any mines brought to the surface by the other minesweepers. Also — and this was a first — a helicopter from the American cruiser *Worcester* was positioned above and in front of the sweepers to attempt to spot mines from the air. During the Second World War planes used as spotters compiled a record of mixed results at best.

The small band of vessels began working their way toward shore. It was particularly ticklish work but by late mid-afternoon, the group had made excellent progress. The sweepers had cleared a path towards the beach of about ten to twelve miles. They had gone from the one-hundred fathom curve to about thirty fathoms from the shore. They had found and destroyed twenty-one contact mines with no mishaps. About midday, with *Pirate's* engine repaired, *Collett* directed her and a few of the wooden sweepers on an exploratory sweep of the Russian navigation channel in case any insurmountable problems arose with the current southern route. Just as late afternoon arrived and *Collett* was poised to recall the sweepers for the day, the lone helicopter moved down closer to the water and then after a few minutes regained some altitude. The helicopter notified the sweeping vessels and *Collett* that five lines of mines were clearly visible just ahead of *Pledge*. The lines, each with hundreds of mines sown to them, were between the thirty-fathom curve and the beach. This was the worst sort of discovery. *Collett* radioed, to the sweepers clearing the direct or southern channel, to withdraw and wait until the following morning for orders. The group that was attempting to clear the Russian navigation channel received instructions to continue their efforts into the evening hours. By midnight, the second group had made good progress. Based on this success and the discovery of the heavily planted minefield to the south, the sweepers abandoned operations on the direct approach. With more time, the original route could have been cleared, but there was a sense of great urgency with the landing date scheduled for just a few days hence. All of the minesweeping assets would now focus their efforts on the Russian navigation channel. The sweepers worked hard that second day and as evening approached they had moved to within about four miles of the shore. They retired for the night again.

On the third day of the operation, 12 October, the U.S. Navy attempted to augment the sweeping effort through aerial countermining. Over three dozen aircraft from American carriers *Philippine Sea* and *Leyte* participated in the effort. Skyraiders with three 1,000 lb general purpose bombs each and Corsairs with one 1,000 lb bomb each dropped their payloads over the remaining four miles of the Russian channel. The bombs, fused to explode a couple dozen feet below the surface of the water, splashed into the channel and erupted with great explosions. At the end of the rather spectacular-looking endeavor, the bombs' effectiveness in destroying mines was, of course, difficult to assess.

It was time again for the sweepers to move in and see what they could do. Because of the aerial countermining effort that morning, the sweepers did not arrive at the spot of their most forward progress in the channel until about 1100 hours. *Pirate* took the lead with *Pledge* and *Incredible* astern. Behind them, two of the smaller wooden-hulled sweepers, *Redhead* and *Kite,* operated as the "danning" vessels, that is, assuming the duties of laying a perimeter of dan buoys around the minesweeping area.[6] The two vessels also performed the function of destroying mines brought to the surface. It was just after noon when *Pirate's* sweeping gear cut six mines and all of them came bobbing to the

---

[6] The word "dan," used in fishing and minesweeping, dates from the late 17th century. However, its specific origin is unknown. See *Shorter Oxford English Dictionary*, 5th Edition.

INITIAL BURDEN

surface. Astern, *Incredible* cut four more mines loose. *Pledge* also began finding and cutting mines. Because of the outdated communications gear on board the sweepers, a message from the circling helicopter spotting a cluster of mines dead ahead, took extra valuable seconds to reach them. *Pirate* was now uncomfortably deep in an area of both bobbing and submerged mines. *Pirate's* starboard bow lookout reported a shallow mine close to that side of the ship. Moments later, there was a terrible explosion. *Pirate's* stern rose up out of the water, tossing some men overboard, and then crashed back down, the ship's back broken by the force of the blast. She then pitched over on her port side exposing about forty feet of her keel forward. The explosion rendered *Pirate's* Commanding Officer C. E. McMullen unconscious for a period of approximately 30 seconds. He regained his senses as he says after "the column of water had ceased falling."[7] McMullen then described what happened next.

> At that time the vessel had a port list of about 20 degrees and was righting herself rapidly. [I] asked for an estimate of the damage; none was received because communications were out, and the phone talkers temporarily dazed. The vessel commenced listing to starboard at a steady rate with no indication of slowing and the stern settling at the same time. The vessel was ordered abandoned when the list reached approximately 15 [degrees], the order being passed by mouth and the whistle cord pulled without results...[8]

---

[7] C. E. McMullen, "Report of the Loss of USS *Pirate*," n.p.

[8] Ibid.

The crewmen injured and dazed went over the side and into the water. She sank in just four minutes.

16-2 *Pirate* (far right) in Her Final Moments before Sinking

The explosion inspired North Korean shore batteries to open fire. *Pledge's* captain instinctively turned to starboard to place the vessel between the shore batteries and the men in the water. She began to return the fire with her 3-inch gun as well as her smaller guns. However, *Pledge*, like *Pirate,* was doomed. She had just lowered her whaleboat in an attempt to rescue crewmembers of *Pirate* when the fire from the shore began to bracket her. *Pledge* began to maneuver seaward and away from the shore fire but was in the midst of a dozen or so mines. She promptly struck one near her forward engine room and suffered *Pirate's* fate. *Incredible* started to come to the rescue of her two sister ships, when at the height of this disaster, she experienced complete engine failure and lay dead in the water. It may have saved her. Later that day, *Incredible*, powerless but in one piece, was towed back out of the channel.

By early evening rescue of the crewmen of both *Pirate* and *Pledge* was complete with a final toll of one sailor dead and another 12 men missing in action and presumed dead. Eighty crewmen sustained injuries. Remarkably only one of the injured survivors subsequently died of his wounds. Days later, a South Korean sweeper would also strike a mine and sink during operations at Wonsan. It would take another 12 days to clear a channel wide enough to allow for the landing of the Americans to take place — ten days longer than had been planned.

16-3 South Korean Minesweeper Striking Mine in Harbor at Wonsan Six Days after Destruction of *Pirate* and *Pledge*

In summarizing the mining of the port of Wonsan and the loss of *Pirate* and *Pledge* Rear Admiral Allen E. Smith stated, "We have lost control of the seas to a nation without a navy, using pre-World War I weapons, laid by vessels that were utilized at the time of the birth of Christ." The out of date communications gear and sonar equipment as well as a dearth of mine warfare ships contributed greatly to the loss of the two ships. A grim statistic was that minesweeping personnel made up less than 2% of the forces in Korea, yet they accounted for over 20% of the war's naval casualties. It is also fair to say that the reputation the Russians had in the use of mine warfare remained unchallenged.[9]

Truman, MacArthur, and the Navy

On 25 October, the American 10th Mountain Division came ashore at Wonsan and began their advance north. The other prong of the pincer movement, the United Nation's troops who had come ashore at Inchon, recaptured Seoul, then captured the North Korean capital of Pyongyang, also had pushed back NKPA defenders to the north. The two forces finally cornered the remaining NKPA units up close to the Yalu River, the border with China.

It was at this point it all went wrong. In November with the NKPA close to capitulation, the Chinese communists thought MacArthur's advance much too close to their country for their liking and made the decision to attack the UN forces with, eventually, an estimated one million combat soldiers. The UN forces fell back against the mass of Communist Chinese troops. The Chinese pushed as far south as to recapture Seoul. MacArthur rallied his forces at

---

[9] The losses of *Pirate* and *Pledge* at Wonsan: Cagle and Manson, *Sea War in Korea*, Chap. 4; Field, *History of Naval Operations*, 219-37; Karig, Manson, and Cagle, *Battle Report*, 311-15; Edwards, *Small U.S. and UN Warships*, 151-52, 154, 159, 162; Melia, *Damn the Torpedoes*, 73; A. Carleton, "USS *Pledge*, Bulletin Board at Korean War Project," posted 22 May 2000, https://www.koreanwar.org/html/units/navy/usspledge.htm (accessed 19 February 2009); McMullen, "USS *Pirate*: Report of Loss of USS *Pirate* (AM-275)," http://history.navy.mil/faqs/faq103-3.html, (accessed 19 February 2009; H. T. Lenton, *American Gunboats and Minesweepers*, (NY: Arco, 1974), 46; Rear Admiral Allen E. Smith quote: cited in James L. George, *History of Warships: From Ancient Times to the Twenty-First Century*, Annapolis, MD: U.S. Naval Institute, 1998, 234.

this point and once again retook the decimated South Korean capital. The front lines of this back and forth campaign finally, though tenuously, solidified around the original starting point — the 38th parallel.

The forces of democracy, instead of destroying the NKPA and re-uniting Korea, were now engaged in a major conflict with Communist China. This had not been Truman's or the United Nation's plan. MacArthur argued for the ability to bomb bases across the Yalu River in China that were supplying the Red Chinese Army in North Korea. The president refused. Truman, his administration and fellow United Nation's participants desperately began looking for ways to end the affair. MacArthur saw his casualties rise to numbers well exceeding 1,000 per week. Hemorrhaging troops, he argued in the press that the war should be waged to be won not fought in order not to lose. Truman now faced the reality of a so-called limited war. He had never asked Congress for permission to declare war against the North Koreans and MacArthur was now publically assailing the president for not doing what was exigent and necessary in order to gain victory. Truman, incensed with MacArthur, fired the five-star general in April 1951.[10] For two more years, there was a bloody and costly standoff and then, finally, a cease-fire in 1953. The Republic of South Korea had been preserved — but at a frightful cost.

---

[10] This action and the stalemate in Korea contributed greatly to Truman's popularity plummeting. Soon after the Korean setback, he lost the New Hampshire Democratic primary to Estes Kefauver thus effectively ending his re-election bid. In the 1952 election, the Republican Dwight D. Eisenhower defeated Truman backed Democrat, Adlai Stevenson, for the presidency. Eisenhower's winning campaign consisted of ignoring Stevenson and focusing on, what Eisenhower termed, Truman's failed efforts in Korea and against Communism in general.

The Navy, for its part, had performed extremely well during the conflict. They had established control of the waters surrounding the Korean peninsula that had allowed the UN forces to move men and material at will between Japan and South Korea. The original ships of U.S. Naval Forces Far East, the U.S. Seventh Fleet, and the British Far East Fleet had acted as the "tip of the sword" in those opening days and weeks of the conflict. With skill and bravery, they carried out the initial necessary actions in the defense of South Korea.

Looking back and assessing Truman's relationship with the Navy as president: he had never been considered a friend. For example, one newspaper media report explained that privately Truman believed that "the navy is not profiting by the lessons of airpower but is bulling ahead with...aircraft carriers that are obsolescent before they hit the blueprints."[11] In 1948 he proposed disbanding the Marine Corp and the following year approved the Secretary of Defense Louis A. Johnson's cancellation of the Navy's new "super" carrier USS *United States* (the keel had already been laid). This prompted a number of high-ranking admirals to resign in protest in what became known as the "Revolt of the Admirals."[12] Despite Truman's attempt to diminish the role of the Navy, in 1996 Secretary of the Navy, John Howard Dalton, appointed by President Clinton, with just perhaps a bit of political and historical asymmetry, honored the former president by changing the name of a newly authorized nuclear-powered Nimitz class aircraft carrier, USS *United States*, to that of the USS *Harry S. Truman*.

---

[11] *Miami Daily News*, 28 March 1946, A18.

[12] See the following: Barlow, *Revolt of the Admirals;* and Coletta, *The U.S. Navy and Defense Unification, 169-203.*

Fate had brought elements of the American and British fleets together at the beginning of the Korean War. Many of the warships present at the start of the conflict went on to serve multiple tours of duty between 1950 and the armistice in 1953. The Korean War cost the lives of 657 American sailors with another 1,576 wounded. The U.S. Navy lost five ships during the conflict while another 87 ships received damage. After the war each of the remaining original ships would go their separate ways and finish their careers — some quite interestingly.

Epilogue 1

Beyond the Nexus

The Korean War ended in 1953. However, it was not the end for the ships present at the beginning of the war. Each of the surviving ships went on to serve their nations admirably during the mid to late 20th century. Some even served other countries.

Merchant Ships

The four merchant ships that figured prominently in the evacuation of American dependents during the first days of the Korean conflict went on to varied careers. *Jesse Lykes*, one of the evacuation ships at Pusan, had gone on transporting goods to the ports of the world during the 1950s. In 1959, both *Jesse Lykes* and another merchant ship, *President Hoover*, found themselves in a typhoon in the central Pacific as they were crossing the International Dateline. During the storm, she recorded wind speeds at over 90 knots and both ships were thankful to have escaped. Based out of Houston, *Jesse Lykes* plied her trade until 1971 before being scrapped.[1]

---

[1] Post-war information for *Jesse Lykes*: "The 1959 Central Pacific Tropical Cyclone Season," U.S. National Weather Service, Central Pacific Hurricane Center, http://www.prh.noaa.gov/cphc/summaries/1959.php#Patsy (accessed 14 January 2011). Three days earlier Typhoon "Patsy" had reached wind speeds of over 150 knots; New York Times, 16 January 1955; Ship historical data: The Ships List website, "Lykes Brothers Steam Ship Company / Lykes Lines," The Ships List: Passengers, Ships, Shipwrecks, www.theshipslist.com/ships/lines/lykes.htm (accessed 14 January 2011).

Pioneer Dale, the other merchant ship used to evacuate American dependants from Pusan, also continued to move cargo around the world at least into the mid 1960s.[2]

Reinholt, the Swedish built merchant ship that had evacuated U.S. nationals from Inchon was sold to Bulgarian interests in 1965. She continued for some time after that to transport cargo on the Black Sea.[3] *Norelg*, the American-built merchant deemed too unsanitary for evacuation purposes at Inchon, in 1955 was reportedly sailing as the *Chung Hsing I*. Shortly after that, she disappeared from shipping registers.[4]

HMS *Black Swan*

As for the naval vessels, for a few, time simply caught up with them. *Black Swan*, the speed challenged British frigate, remained in the Korean theater for another year. During that time, she was credited with firing at enemy positions near the small port of Sonjin located on the eastern coast of North Korea. *Black Swan* left the British Far East Fleet returning to Plymouth on 13 September 1951. Moved to Troon, Ayrshire on the west coast of Scotland in September

---

[2] *Pioneer Dale* post-war data: "SS *Pioneer Dale*," Maine Memory Network, Maine's Statewide Digital Museum, http://www.mainememory.net/bin/SwishSearch?Keywords=SS%20Pioneer%20Dale, (accessed 14 January 2011).

[3] Fate of *Reinholt*: Siri Holm Lawson, "M/S Reinholt" http://warsailors.com/singleships/reinholt.html (accessed 14 January 2011).

[4] Fate of *Norelg*: Siri Holm Lawson, "M/S Norelg" http://warsailors.com/singleships/norelg.html (accessed 14 January 2011).

of 1956, the 17-year-old frigate was un-ceremoniously scrapped. It was a straightforward matter of her being too slow and worn out.

USS *Incredible*

Incredible, the American Admirable class minesweeper that had rescued twenty-seven sailors from the sinking of *Pirate* in Wonsan harbor in October of 1950 was also struck from the Navy List in 1959. Sold, she was then scrapped at Terminal Island, California in 1960.

USS *Juneau*

Other ships became victims of the relentless march of technology. During the 1950s, guided missiles dramatically replaced the need for big gun ships. As new classes of guided missile cruisers were built, older gunnery-based cruisers had to go. Light cruiser *Juneau*, one of a few ships that had earned the colloquial title "Galloping Ghost of the Korean Coast" for her exploits during the opening month of the war, operated for a few more years in the early to mid 1950s with the U.S. Sixth Fleet in the Mediterranean. She also served for a shorter period in the Caribbean and on the East Coast of the United States. Though relatively young, as far as naval vessels go, *Juneau* was de-commissioned during

Epi-1 USS *Juneau* w/Crew in Summer Whites on Deck 1951

the summer of 1956, struck from the Navy List in 1959, and scrapped by New York's Union Metals & Alloys in 1962.[5]

HMS *Belfast*

The British cruiser *Belfast* hung on until recalled in 1962 while on another tour in the Far East. On her return to Great Britain, she visited Victoria, British Columbia, and Seattle as representative of one of the last vestiges of a byegone era. *Belfast,* the flag ship of the British Far East Fleet at the beginning of the Korean War, had provided support for *Triumph* and *Valley Forge* during Task Force 77's first naval air attack on North Korea. She also had pounded Korea's east coast with her 6-inch guns during that first month of the war. Between 1956 and 1959, *Belfast* underwent modernization with the addition of guided-missile launchers. Sadly, due to the fiscal woes of the government, she would only remain in commission until 1963. Then the proud ship was rather ignominiously reduced to what was generously called an "accommodation vessel" — a fancy

---

[5] USS *Juneau* during the mid to late 1950s: "CL-119 *Juneau*," The Dictionary of American Naval Fighting Ships Online, http://www.hazegray .org/danfs/ cruisers/cl119.htm (accessed 27 February 2011). "Galloping Ghost" reference: "4th of July, Huntington Beach & the USS *Juneau*," Orange County History Roundup, http://ochistorical .blogspot.com/2009 /07/4th-of-july-huntington-beach-uss-juneau.html (accessed 5 January 2011); HMS *Jamaica* also shared this nickname; Michael Stephens, "The Galloping Ghost of the of the Korean Coast," Britain's Small Wars, http://www. britains-smallwars.com/korea/Jamaica .html (accessed 5 January 2011).

The term "Struck from the Navy List" simply means the ship was removed from the official U.S. Navy inventory. The origin of the List goes back to the 1880s. Today it is officially known as the United States Naval Vessel Register or NVR.

way of saying a barracks for reserve naval personnel while on duty at Portsmouth.

HMS *Jamaica*

The British cruiser *Jamaica,* however, had one last mission to perform before her demise. In July of 1956, Egyptian President Gamal Abdul Nasser had taken over exclusive control of the Suez Canal by nationalizing that most important waterway. In response, the British and French, with the help of Israel, mounted a military expedition to occupy the Canal Zone and remove the threat to maritime traffic the Egyptian action had created. As part of "Musketeer," the operation to seize the Suez Canal zone, *Jamaica,* another cruiser, and six destroyers were selected to provide the naval gunfire support for the landing of British commandos at Port Said.

It was sunrise 6 November 1956. *Jamaica* steamed toward the beach at Port Said with three Daring class destroyers in line ahead formation astern. The local weather had deteriorated since the previous day and the Mediterranean Sea now had a moderate chop to it as the ships proceeded on their mission. As daylight broke, the port itself was somewhat hidden by smoke caused by associated tactical air operations. All in all the conditions were still acceptable for the amphibious landing. As part of the operation, the British warships were to bombard the beach areas to clear the way for the commandos to come ashore. When the venerable Colony class cruiser reached a position just inside two miles from the landing beach she began slowly turning to port establishing her in a parallel position to the shoreline. The Daring class destroyers, directly behind *Jamaica,* did not follow her as she turned to port. Instead, the destroyers, *Duchess*, *Diamond*, and *Decoy* pressed even further toward shore before they too finally swung about parallel to the shoreline within a mile of the beach. Once they had completed their turn, the destroyers opened fire with their 4.5-inch guns directed at the beaches chosen for the landing. *Jamaica*, sitting a mile behind the destroyers did not join in.

Many of those on board *Jamaica* that day began to ask when the cruiser was going to open fire with her larger 6-inch guns. The answer was disappointing. It turned out the orders had been changed a few days before the landing. With the idea of minimizing as much as possible civilian casualties, the political leaders, including British Prime Minister Anthony Eden, had decided that only the smaller guns on board the destroyers would be used. Consequently, the destroyers bombarded the beaches while the two British cruisers' guns remained silent. The decision was purely political. However, it was never explainable to the British soldiers who had to risk their lives going ashore that morning supported by less firepower than was available.[6] Soon the whole Suez affair turned into a debacle with the United States forcing the British and French to abandon their efforts in the region.

On 5 September 1958, less than two years after the Suez fiasco, *Jamaica* was "paid off."[7] *Jamaica*, which during the

---

[6] *Jamaica* and Operation Musketeer during the Suez Crisis: Derek Varble, *Essential Histories: The Suez Crisis 1956*, (Oxford: Osprey Publishing, 2003), 64-65; Grove, *Vanguard to Trident*, 190-91; James Robinson, "Assault on the Canal: H.M.S. Jamaica," Britain's Small Wars, http://www.britains-smallwars.com/suez/Jamaica.html (accessed 25 November 2010).

[7] The term "paid off" is used by some navies, most particularly the British Royal Navy. It refers to an old practice of paying off the crew before they left the ship, in this case for the last time. The United States Navy uses the term "decommission." Both terms indicate a ship is no longer in active service.

Second World War had participated in the Battle of the Barents Sea, the Battle of North Cape, and the Battle of Chumunjin in Korea, was rendered inactive and turned over to the Royal dockyard control. There she languished tied up to a pier until 1960 when she was sold for demolition. The breaking up of *Jamaica* for recycle and scrap was performed in Dalmuir, Scotland and was completed on 15 August 1963.

HMS *Triumph* and USS *Valley Forge*

After Korea the British and American aircraft carriers of Task Force 77, *Triumph* and *Valley Forge*, each performed service for their respective countries for another two decades.

Triumph operated as a light fleet carrier until 1956. She was then was reduced to reserve-status pending conversion for use as a heavy repair ship. Due to the on-going post WWII strain on Great Britain's financial resources, the conversion was not completed until 1965. *Triumph* performed her new duties with the fleet until 1972 when she was withdrawn from service, placed in reserve, and eventually broken up in 1980.[8]

The American aircraft carrier *Valley Forge* operated in the Atlantic and the Mediterranean during the 1950s. During the 1960s, she spent a great deal of time off the coast of Vietnam participating in multiple operations in that confusing conflict. She was decommissioned in 1970. In 1971, *Valley Forge* was used in the shooting of a Hollywood science fiction movie entitled "Silent Running." Her former

---

[8] Post Korean War uses of *Triumph*: Geoffrey B Mason, "HMS *Triumph* - Colossus-class Light Fleet Aircraft Carrier" Naval-History.net, http://www.naval-history.net/xGM-Chrono-04CV-Triumph%20(ii).htm, (accessed 11 January 2011).

hangar deck and flight command areas were used to represent a cargo hold, control room, and living quarters for a fictional space ship crew. Following the shooting of the movie "Happy Valley" was sold for scrap and broken up.

U.S. Sumner Class Destroyers

The Sumner class destroyers had kept active during the 1950s, and around 1960 each of the four ships *De Haven*, *Mansfield*, *Collett*, and *Swenson* underwent major refits. The refits focused on antisubmarine warfare. With their large size, they were especially suited to adding a helicopter flight and hangar decks to their superstructures. The Sumners all saw duty in Vietnam. The refits served them well for another decade but by the early 1970s, it was the end of the line. All four of the destroyers were decommissioned. Argentina purchased *Mansfield* and *Collett* in the summer of 1974. The same year *Swenson* was sold to Taiwan. She was used by the Navy of Taiwan as spare parts for other destroyers that nation had purchased from the United States. *De Haven* was transferred to the Republic of Korea in 1973. There she was re-commissioned and renamed *Inchon*. It was at Inchon that she had participated with the "sitting ducks" squadron during the silencing of the guns at Wolmi-do. She served in the South Korean Navy for the next twenty years finally being decommissioned and scrapped in 1993.

U.S. Submarines

The American submarine *Remora*, present at Yokosuka the day of the North Korean invasion, and *Catfish*, which provided support in the Yellow Sea for *Valley Forge's* and *Triumph's* air strikes against Pyongyang that first week of the war, both served into the 1970s. Each of the submarines had also patrolled between Japan and the Soviet Union during that critical first month of the war. *Remora* was eventually decommissioned in 1973. That same year she was sold to the Greek Navy and re-commissioned as the S-115 *Katsonis*. She was scrapped in Aliaga, Turkey in 1993. *Catfish*, decommissioned in 1971, was sold to Argentina.[9]

ROK *Bak du San*

Lastly, *Bak du San*, the South Korean, former American sub chaser, that had sunk the North Korean armed transport trying to land 600 troops in the Pusan area on the first evening of the war, was decommissioned in 1960 and later scrapped. That confrontation may have been the most significant single naval action of the war. Her mast saved and preserved, is today on display in Chinhae, at the Republic of Korea Naval Academy in remembrance of *Bak du San's* vital service to her country.[10]

---

[9] Vladivostok surveillance and post-war information for *Remora* and *Catfish*: Thornton, *Odd Man Out*, 178; Utz, *Assault from the Sea*, 11; "NavSource Online: Submarine Photo Archive," NavSource Naval History, http://www .navsource.org/archives/08/08487.htm (accessed 14 January 2011).

[10] The fate of *Bak du San* and recognition of the significance of her actions on that first night of the war: "NavSource Online:Submarine Chaser Photo Archive," NavSource Naval History, http://www.nav source.org /archives /12/010823.htm (accessed 24 January 2011); Field, U.S. Naval Operations, 51.

Epilogue 2

New Names, New War

Falklands War

Purchased by Argentina in 1974, the Sumner class destroyers *Mansfield* and *Collett* were towed from San Diego to Puerto Belgrano on Argentina's Atlantic coast. There, *Mansfield* was broken up and used for spare parts. However, *Collett* was found to be in better shape than expected and the decision was made to rehabilitate her. With three years dry dock effort and some parts from her sister ship *Mansfield*, *Collett* was finally re-commissioned in the Argentine Navy as D-29 ARA *Piedra Buena* on 17 May 1977.

The American submarine *Catfish* was also rehabilitated by the Argentine Navy. After some modernization, she was re-commissioned and renamed S-21 ARA *Santa Fe*.

In 1982, both *Santa Fe* and *Piedra Buena* found themselves facing a former ally Great Britain in what the British would call the Falklands War.[1] In December 1981, acting President Leopoldo Galtieri, head of the Argentine military junta, authorized the invasion and occupation of the Falkland Islands off the Atlantic coast of that most southern South American country. The British had controlled the islands since the 1840s. Since that time, Argentina had always claimed the islands and the dispute had remained a source of tension between the two nations. The Junta's strategy of

---

[1] The Argentines call the islands the Malvinas.

forcing a resolution to the long-standing issue over the islands was to create a cause célèbre to deflect attention from the severe economic and human rights issues plaguing the military government.

ARA *Santa Fe* — Port Stanley

At first light on 2 April 1982, *Santa Fe* slowly surfaced inside Yorke Bay north of the airport located just outside of the capital city of Port Stanley on East Falkland Island. Ten commandos launched a raft and came ashore. Their job was to make sure the beach was clear. Receiving a signal from the men on shore, another vessel moved into the small bay and unloaded 19 amphibious tracked vehicles and soldiers that in turn began the assault on Port Stanley.

The Argentine military forces were forcefully taking possession of the Falkland Islands two-hundred miles off Argentina's southeastern coast. Originally, *Santa Fe's* orders had been to land the commandos at Cape Pembroke lighthouse on the eastern tip of the peninsula. However, the Argentines had discovered that the defenders at Port Stanley had reinforced the lighthouse and so changed the landing to the beach at Yorke Bay, three and one half miles west of the lighthouse. *Santa Fe* had departed Mar del Plata on the Argentine coast a week earlier. Multiple landings had taken place in and around Port Stanley at about 0600 that morning and by 0930 the volunteer home defense force of Falklanders at Stanley, all dependents of the United

Kingdom, had surrendered. Argentina now controlled the Falkland Islands[2]

Led by the Tory Prime Minister Margaret Thatcher, the British, (much to the surprise of the Argentine government) did not acquiesce to what was presented as a *fait accompli* as the Galtieri led junta had hoped. Instead, the government of Great Britain moved immediately to restore the British dependency. As part of the invasion, Argentine forces, some 1,000 miles further to the southeast of the Falklands, had also come ashore and occupied South Georgia another British island dependency. Within a week of the taking of Port Stanley by the Argentines, the British were in the process of assembling an armada of sorts to retake the islands. In short order the British fleet of ships and troops headed for the South Atlantic.

ARA *Santa Fe* — South Georgia

After the successful occupation of the Falkland Islands, *Santa Fe* returned to her base at Mar del Plata. There she took on provisions for a sixty-day patrol. However, events were moving fast. The British proclaimed a two-hundred mile exclusion zone around the Falklands meaning any Argentine ships found in that zone would be sunk. In order to reinforce troops on South Georgia, *Santa Fe* took on the task of resupplying and moving a detachment of soldiers to that island to augment the original forces put ashore. As a

---

[2] ARA *Santa Fe* at the beginning of the Falklands' War: Steven R. Harper, "Submarine Operations During the Falklands War," An Unclassified Paper, U.S. Naval War College, Newport, Rhode Island, Department of Operations, 17 June 1994, 9-10; Martin Middlebrook, *Operation Corporate: The Story of the Falklands War, 1982*, (London: Viking, 1987), 48-49.

submarine, it was hoped that she could avoid detection while traversing through the exclusion zone. She departed on the night of 8 April. During her 1,200-mile passage to South Georgia, *Santa Fe* detected active sonar hunting for her but she was not discovered.

South Georgia and its assorted bays and harbors had been the site of a number of whaling stations dating back to the 19th century. Now abandoned, the island boasted a variety of landscapes and wild life. In late summer the island was particularly breath-taking with its snow covered mountain peaks and magnificently green mountain slopes and hillsides. Since the passing of the whaling industry, the island had been used as sites for a few British scientific stations and not much else.

Santa Fe arrived at 2200 hours the evening of 24 April, coming to the surface in Cumberland East Bay just outside the harbor of Grytviken, the capital of South Georgia. Met by a small number of launches early the next morning, the 20 military personnel and supplies were off-loaded. It was almost 0900 the next morning before the submarine was ready to put to sea again. As *Santa Fe* began moving northwest out of the bay into to deeper water in order to submerge, she was spotted by a Wessex helicopter launched from a British surface ship over a hundred miles out to sea. The Wessex immediately attacked, sweeping down to within 1,000 feet of the submarine before releasing two Mark XI depth charges. The first exploded near the stern of *Santa Fe* while the second clanked off the deck and exploded alongside her. Damaged, *Santa Fe* turned around and headed back for the harbor, oil trailing from her stern. Two more helicopters arrived and fired a homing torpedo and AS12 rocket missiles at her. *Santa Fe* ended up next to the jetty at King Edward Point at the entrance to Grytviken harbor. There the crew abandoned the submarine and made for the relative safety of the town using a road that skirted the edge of the harbor. A British detachment landed later that day and quickly secured the island.[3]

Later, the British towed *Santa Fe* into the harbor and left her at one of the docks. There was conjecture among some in the Royal Navy that she might be worth restoring. However, upon further inspection that idea was discarded. After the war, a salvage tug tried to tow her back to the Falklands but the lines between *Santa Fe* and the tug parted and the vessel sunk at the entrance to Grytviken harbor. A red buoy marked the spot of her sinking for a few years until she was finally raised, taken to deeper water and scuttled in 1985.[4]

ARA *Piedra Buena*

Augmented with many of her old sister ship *Mansfield's* parts the former *Collett,* now *Piedra Buena,* had participated the month before in the amphibious assault on Port Stanley. She had then joined heavy cruiser *General Belgrano* and destroyer *Hipolito Bouchard* in Ushuaia. As noted, *Piedra Buena* had undergone a major refit between 1974 and 1977. During that time a modern French-developed Exocet medium range ship-to-ship guided missile

---

[3] Action off Grytviken 25 April 1982 involving *Santa Fe*: Robert L. Scheina, *Latin American Wars Volume II: The Age of the Professional Soldier 1900-2001*, (Dulles, Virginia: Potomac Books, 2003), 310; Gordon Smith, *Battle Atlas of the Falklands War 1982*, (Penarth, UK: Naval-History.Net, 2006), 51; Middlebrook, *Operation Corporate*, 109-111; Harper, "Submarine Operations during the Falklands War," 10.

[4] The scuttling of *Santa Fe*: Robert Fox, *Antarctica and the South Atlantic: Discovery, Development, and Dispute*, (London: British Broadcasting Corp., 1985), 29.

system, with four launchers, was installed. Upgraded, with a newer search and fire control radar and variable depth sonar to improve her anti-submarine performance, *Piedra Buena* was a serious naval platform.[5]

It had been a month since the start of the hostilities in the South Atlantic. The British had announced that beginning 12 April they were establishing a Maritime Exclusion Zone 200 miles around the Falkland Islands.[6] Any warships entering the zone would be attacked. Later that month, news of the expected arrival of the British task force within a few days, resulted in the putting to sea of the bulk of the Argentine Navy on 27 April. The old ex-American 13,000-ton cruiser *General Belgrano*, and the destroyers *Piedra Buena* and *Hipolito Bouchard*, were tasked with stopping British warships coming round Cape Horn from the Pacific and any possible Chilean military interference. *Piedra Buena* and *Hipolito Bouchard* (another ex-American destroyer) were assigned with providing protection for *General Belgrano*. The surface group had positioned itself two-hundred and fifty miles southwest of the Falklands close to the underwater Burwood Bank. Both of the destroyers had been using their sonar equipment in passive mode at different distances from *General Belgrano* in an attempt to establish the range that a British submarine might detect the large cruiser. The surface group's dilemma was if it moved over the bank, it would be dangerously close to the 200-mile exclusion zone in which the British had vowed to sink any enemy vessels. On the other hand, the bank, a shallow area where the lack of depth on top of the

---

[5] Information regarding *Piedra Buena's* modernization: Mike Rossiter, *Sink the Belgrano*, (London: Transworld, 2007) 192.

[6] Martin Middlebrook, *Argentine Fight for the Falklands*, (Barnsley, South Yorkshire: Pen & Sword, 2009), 67.

submerged ridge of sand was critical to the group's survival, because it would force any British submarine to operate in shallower water thus being more easily detected by the Argentine destroyers.

Early in the Falkland's crisis, the British had ordered three of their nuclear powered submarines to the South Atlantic. One of the three submarines, HMS *Conqueror*, operating independently, detected the *General Belgrano* surface group on 1 May. *Conqueror* immediately asked for permission to attack, fearing the group might move northward over the Burwood Bank. The British War Cabinet approved the action the next morning. *Conqueror* moved into position for an attack on the large Argentine cruiser.[7]

In the late afternoon of 2 May, the weather worsened. Snow was falling. Visibility was decreasing in the gloom. The Argentine group was zigzagging at about 13 knots. The destroyers were out of visual contact with *General Belgrano*. They were unable to detect the presence of *Conqueror* who had been stalking the cruiser since the morning and was now less than 2,000 yards away. At 1557 *Conqueror* fired a spread of three, 1943 vintage, Mark 8 torpedoes. The Second World War weapon traveled at a speed of 45 knots. The torpedoes used in the attack were

---

[7] There has been some discussion over the years that there was some consideration given to not attacking *General Belgrano* but rather the two escorting destroyers, *Hipolito Bouchard* and *Piedra Buena*. This is because they were in many ways possibly more dangerous to the British task force: the two destroyers with their Exocet missile systems and 35-mile range as opposed to *General Belgrano's* 6-inch guns with their 13-mile range. Nevertheless, in the end the cruiser was targeted. See: Arthur Gavshon, and Desmond Rice, The Sinking of the *Belgrano*, (London: Martin Secker & Warburg, 1984, 101.

not sophisticated. Nevertheless, by late twentieth century standards, the older torpedoes carried more explosives than the latest versions that were specifically built to sink newer ships with much thinner skins. The old American heavy cruiser had a six-inch belt of armor at the waterline. The first and second torpedoes struck *General Belgrano* fore and aft. That was all it took: the old cruiser went ingloriously to the bottom in just 45 minutes.

With the early onset of darkness in the far southern latitudes and snow falling, neither of the destroyers had witnessed *General Belgrano* under attack. However, the third torpedo fired by *Conqueror* in the original spread, missed the heavy cruiser, and instead hit one of the destroyers *Hipolito Bouchard*. Luckily, for her, the charge did not explode. Surviving the torpedo hit, *Hipolito Bouchard* radioed that she too had come under attack and began to withdraw from the area. *Piedra Buena* began depth charging in the direction of the attack. *Conqueror* took evasive action. After an hour, she rose to periscope depth about 20 miles from the stricken Argentine cruiser. However, as soon as she did *Piedra Buena* attacked her again with more depth charges. After another hour of stealth on the part of *Conqueror,* the British submarine finally escaped *Piedra Buena's* persistent attack. The destroyer returned to the site of the sinking and attempted to find survivors. *General Belgrano* had a crew of over a thousand sailors on board; 323 of them paid with their lives.[8]

---

[8] Information on the Sinking of *General Belgrano:*, Middlebrook, *Argentine Fight for the Falklands*, 104-116; Rossiter, *Sink the Belgrano*, 102, 192, 230, 232, 242; Gavshon and Rice, *The Sinking of the Belgrano*, 104-105; Max Hastings, and Simon Jenkins, *The Battle for the Falklands*, (NY: W.W. Norton, 1984), 143-150; Middlebrook, Operation Corporate, 142-152; Smith, *Battle Atlas Falklands War*, 56-57.

It was a turning point in the war. The Argentine fleet returned to its base. It never again attempted to engage the British naval task force.

Ignoble Pyre at Sea

Six years later in November 1988 during a warm and sunny spring day in the Southern Hemisphere, out at sea, the Argentine frigate *Espora* waited for the signal. When it came, a fiery MM38 Exocet surface-to-surface missile leapt from the ship's rocket launching system located on her forward deck. The missile streaked across the open water at a speed of over 300 miles per hour, and in due course, buried itself into *Piedra Buena*. The former U.S. destroyer *Collett* had survived a Japanese air attack and nerve wracking tour of Tokyo Bay during the Second World War. She had fought along the east coast of Korea in the first months of that conflict. The Sumner class warship had participated in the shelling of Wolmi-do with the "sitting ducks" squadron at Inchon receiving nine hits. She had acted as the mine sweeping command ship at Wonsan. She had bombarded the coast of Vietnam during that war and in the Falklands conflict as *Piedra Buena* had attempted to prosecute the British nuclear submarine *Conqueror* after the latter had sunk the Argentine heavy cruiser *General Belgrano*. Now, *Piedra Buena* holed, ablaze, and shipping water finally succumbed to a half century of naval service and slipped beneath the waves. Decommissioned in 1985, *Piedra Buena* had languished tied to a dock for three years before being towed out to sea earlier that day to be used for target practice in an Argentine naval exercise.[9]

---

[9] The sinking of *Piedra Buena* (ex-*Collett*): USS *Collett* Website, http://www.usscollett.com/history/many_sources/Collett_as_piedra_buena.htm, (accessed 24 January 2011).

Postscript

Two Views

Pyongyang

Today in the North Korean capital of Pyongyang, a building houses the "Museum of Victory of the Fatherland Liberation War." In the middle of a large room within this museum is a G5 motor torpedo boat with the number 21.

Post-1 G5 in Pyongyang

Every day a member of the North Korean military explains to tourists how this vessel had sunk the American cruiser *Baltimore* during the first days of the Korean War at the naval engagement off Chumunjin.

In fact, the *Baltimore* participated in the Second World War and not the Korean War. Further, she never left the United States during the time of the Korean conflict. This elaborate hoax is purely for propaganda purposes in order for the

North Koreans to tell their side of the story of the surface action off Chumunjin in South Korea on 2 July 1950.

Of course, the rest of the world knows that the American light cruiser *Juneau*, the British cruiser *Jamaica* and frigate *Black Swan* destroyed three of four North Korean torpedo boats and two motor gun boats that early Sunday morning in 1950.[1]

London

A far better example of a naval museum is located on the Thames River in the Pool of London very near to the Tower Bridge, where HMS *Belfast* now resides. *Belfast* is the last of the remaining group of ships that participated in the opening days of the Korean War some 60 plus years ago. She was designated as a preservation project after being saved from the breakers in 1971. Then in 1978, the Imperial War Museum took over ownership and moved her to London. Today, painted in her "dazzle" World War II camouflage,[2] she is proudly open to the public. She is an

---

[1] North Korean version of 2 July 1950: Lindsay Fincher, "North Korea: US Imperialists visit the Victorious Fatherland Liberation War Museum," At Home in the Wasteland, entry posted May 25, 2010, http://www.lindsayfincher.com/2010/05/north-korea-us-imperialists-visit-the-victorious-fatherland-liberation-war-museum-korean-war-museum-and-learn-how-the-korean-war-really-started.html; (accessed March 28, 2012). Image of G-5 motor torpedo boat also found at this site.

[2] Dazzle camouflage was developed during World War I and was subsequently used, though less so, during World War II. The idea was not to conceal a ship but rather to make it harder for an opposing vessel to estimate the ship's type, size, speed, and heading. Its effectiveness during wartime has been debatable but there is no doubt it makes Belfast eye catching in the Pool of London.

INITIAL BURDEN

imposing sight and most importantly a tangible and visual reminder of the value and significance of sea power.[3]

Post-2 HMS *Belfast* in the Pool of London on the Thames River

---

[3] HMS *Belfast* as a museum ship: British Imperial War Museum website - image also found here: http://hmsbelfast.iwm.org.uk, (accessed 24 February 2011).

BIBLIOGRAPHY

Documents

Acheson, Dean. "Speech on the Far East." 12 January 1950. http://teachingamericanhistory.org/library/index.asp?document=1612 (accessed 2 February 2011).

HMS *Jamaica*. Report of Proceedings 4 July to 9 July 1950 (Letter No. 191, 10 July 1950).

------. Reply #1, to Report of Proceedings 4 July to 9 July 1950 (signed by Director of Operations Division on 6 September 1950).

------. Reply #2, to Report of Proceedings 4 July to 9 July 1950 (signed by Chief of Naval Information on 15 November 1950).

------. Reply #3, to Report of Proceedings 4 July to 9 July 1950 (signed by U. S. S. on 22 November 1950).

HMS *Black Swan*. Report of Proceedings 28 June to 7 July 1950. Reference No. 39/6501. The Flag Officer Second in Command, Far East Station.

Great Britain. *British Maritime Doctrine: BR 1806*. London: Stationery Office, 2004, Open Library, openlibrary.org/books/.../British_Maritime_Doctrine_Br_1806 (accessed 15 December 2011).

Jessup, Phillip C. "Memo of Conversation, 25 June 1950." From the papers of Dean Acheson. President Harry S. Truman Library, http://www.trumanlibrary.org/korea (accessed 12 February 2009).

------. "Memorandum of Conversation, 26 June 1950." From the papers of Dean Acheson. President Harry S. Truman Library, http://www.trumanlibrary.org/korea (accessed 12 February 2009).

UN Security Council. Resolution No. 82 of 25 June 1950. Office of the United Nations High Commissioner for Refugees, http://www.unhcr.org/refworld/docid/3b00f15960.html (accessed 14 October 2011).

BIBLIOGRAPHY

U.S. Joint Chiefs of Staff. "Directive, 29 June 1950." From the papers of George M. Elsey. President Harry S. Truman Library, http://www. trumanlibrary.org/korea (accessed 12 February 2009).

------. "Army Department Message, Joint Chiefs of Staff to Douglas MacArthur, July 1, 1950." From the papers of George M. Elsey. President Harry S. Truman Library http://www.trumanlibrary.org/ whistlestop/study_collections/koreanwar/documents/index.php?documentdate=1950-07-01&documentid=ki-5-6&pagenumber=1 (accessed 1 February 2012).

U.S. Military Officials. "Teletype Conference, 25 June 1950, from the papers of Harry S. Truman: Naval Aide Files." President Harry S. Truman Library, http://www.trumanlibrary.org/ korea (accessed 12 February 2009).

------. . "Teletype Conference, 26 June 1950, from the papers of Harry S. Truman: Naval Aide Files." President Harry S. Truman Library, http://www.trumanlibrary.org/korea (accessed 12 February 2009).

U.S. Navy Combat Veterans of the "Sitting Ducks of Inchon," "The Sitting Ducks of Inchon," Letter written 15 October 2008. Welcome Aboard the USS *Collett* (DD-730), http://www.usscollett.com/ history.htm (accessed 23 August 2011).

USS *Juneau*. Deck Log: 24 June to 26 July 1950.

------. War Diary: 26 June to 6 July 1950.

------. Action Report: Personnel Participating in Landings of Foreign Territory, 14 July 1950.

------. Action Report: North Korea, Report of Operations 24 June to 6 July 1950, dated 3 August 1950.

------. First Endorsement with comments Re: Action Report: North Korea, Report of Operations 26 June to 6 July 1950 to Commander in Chief, US Pacific Fleet (signed by Commander Cruiser Division FIVE, Admiral J. M. Higgins on 2 October 1950).

------. Second Endorsement with comments Re: Action Report: North Korea, Report of Operations 26 June to 6 July 1950 to Commander in Chief, US Pacific Fleet (signed by

BIBLIOGRAPHY

Commander Naval Forces Far East, Admiral C. Turner Joy on 9 November 1950).

------. Third Endorsement with comments Re: Action Report: North Korea, Report of Operations 26 June to 6 July 1950 to Commander in Chief, US Pacific Fleet (signed by Commander Cruiser-Destroyer Force, Pacific Fleet, Admiral L. T. DuBose on 30 December 1950).

------. Fourth Endorsement with comments Re: Action Report: North Korea, Report of Operations 26 June to 6 July 1950 to Chief of Naval Operations (signed by Commander in Chief, US Pacific Fleet, Admiral John Gingrich, Chief of Staff on 16 January 1951).

USS *Collett*. Deck Log: 24 June to 26 July 1950.

------. War Diary: 24 June to 15 July 1950.

USS *De Haven*. Deck Log: 24 June to 26 July 1950.

------. Deck Log: 13-14 September 1950.

------. War Diary: 24 June to 1 August.

USS *Lyman K. Swenson*. Deck Log: 24 June to 26 July 1950.

------. War Diary: 24 June to 15 July 1950.

USS *Mansfield*. Deck Log: 24 June to 26 July 1950.

------. War Diary: 24 June to 11 July.

USS *Valley Forge*. Deck Log: 24 June to 26 July 1950.

Books

Acheson, Dean. *Present at the Creation: my Years in the State Department*. New York: W. W. Norton, 1969.

Alexander, James Edwin. *Inchon to Wonsan: From the Deck of a Destroyer in the Korean War*. Annapolis, Maryland: U.S. Naval Institute Press, 1996.

Allard, Dean C. "An Era of Transition 1945-1953." Chapter 15 in *Peace and War: Interpretations of American Naval History, 1775-1978*. Edited by Kenneth J. Hagan. Westport, Connecticut: Greenwood Press, 1978.

Appleman, Roy Edgar. *South to the Naktong, North to the Yalu: June-November 1950*. Washington: Office of the Chief of Military History, Dept. of the Army, 1961.

BIBLIOGRAPHY

Baer, George W. *One Hundred Years of Sea Power: The U.S. Navy, 1890-1990*. Stanford, California: Stanford University Press, 1994.

Barlow, Jeffrey G. *Revolt of the Admirals: the Fight for Naval Aviation, 1940-1950*. Washington D.C.: Brassey's, 1998.

Barnett, Correlli. *Engage the Enemy More Closely: The Royal Navy in the Second World War*. New York: Norton, 1991.

Barnett, Roger W. *Navy Strategic Culture: Why the Navy Thinks Differently*. Annapolis, Maryland: U.S. Naval Institute Press, 2009.

Bermudez, Joseph S. *North Korean Special Forces*. Annapolis, Maryland: U.S. Naval Institute Press, 1998.

Bishop, Chris. *The Complete Encyclopedia of Weapons of World War II*. London: Brown Books, 1998.

Blackman, R.V.B., editor. Jane's Fighting Ships, 1950-51. London: Sampson low, 1951.

Boose, Donald W. *Over the Beach US Army Amphibious Operations in the Korean War*. Fort Leavenworth, Kansas: Combat Studies Institute Press, US Army Combined Arms Center, 2008, http://purl.access.gpo.gov/GPO/LPS113721 (accessed 15 December 2011).

Boot, Max. *War Made New: Technology, Warfare, and the Course of History, 1500 to Today*. New York: Gotham Books, 2006.

Buell, Thomas B. *Naval Leadership in Korea: The First Six Months*. Washington D.C.: Naval Historical Center, Department of the Navy, 2002.

Busch, Fritz-Otto. *The Drama of the Scharnhorst*. Ware, Hertfordshire: Wordsworth Editions, 2000.

Cable, James. *Gunboat Diplomacy; Political Applications of Limited Naval Force*. New York: Published for the Institute for Strategic Studies [by] Praeger, 1971.

Cagle, Malcolm W., and Frank Albert Manson. *The Sea War in Korea*. Annapolis: U.S. Naval Institute Press, 1957.

Calhoun, C. Raymond. *Typhoon, the Other Enemy: The Third Fleet and the Pacific Storm of December 1944*. Annapolis, Maryland: U.S. Naval Institute Press, 1981.

BIBLIOGRAPHY

Campbell, John. *Naval Weapons of World War Two*. Annapolis, Maryland: U.S. Naval Institute Press, 1985, reprinted 2002.

Catchpole, Brian. *The Korean War, 1950-1953*. London: Magpie Books, 2010.

Chesneau, Roger. *Conway's All the World's Fighting Ships, 1922-1946*. London: Conway Maritime Press, 1980.

Cho, Duk-Hyun. "Don't Give Up the Ships: United States Naval Operations During the First Year of the Korean War." PhD diss., Ohio State University, 2002.

Cocker, Maurice. *West Coast Support Group, Task Group 96.8: Korea 1950-1953*. Latheronwheel, Scotland: Whittles, 2003.

Cole, Charles F. *Korea Remembered: Enough of a War, The USS Ozbourne's First-Tour 1950-1951*. La Cruces, New Mexico: Yucca Tree Press, 1995.

Coletta, Paolo E. *The American Naval Heritage*, Third Edition. Lanham, Maryland: University Press of America. 1987.

------. *The United States Navy and Defense Unification 1947-1953*. Newark, New Jersey: University of Delaware Press, 1981.

Compton-Hall, Richard. *Submarine Versus Submarine: the Tactics and Technology of Underwater Confrontation*. London: Grub Street, 1988.

Craven, Wesley Frank and James Lea Cate. *The Army Air Forces in World War II: The Pacific: Matterhorn to Nagasaki June 1944 to August 1945*, Volume 5. Chicago, Illinois: University of Chicago, 1953.

Cutler, Thomas J. *The Bluejackets' Manual*. Annapolis, Maryland: U.S. Naval Institute Press, 2002.

Donovan, Robert J. *Tumultuous Years: The Presidency of Harry S. Truman, 1949-1953*. New York: Norton, 1982.

Dunnigan, James F. and Albert A. Nofi. *Victory at Sea: World War II in the Pacific*. New York: William Morrow, 1995.

Edwards, Paul M. *Small United States and United Nations Warships in the Korean War*. Jefferson, N.C.: McFarland, 2008.

Ferrell, Robert H. *Harry S. Truman and the Cold War Revisionists*. Columbia: University of Missouri Press, 2006.

BIBLIOGRAPHY

Field, James A., and Ernest McNeill Eller. *History of United States Naval Operations: Korea*. Washington, D.C.: [U.S. G.P.O.], 1962.

Fox, Robert. *Antarctica and the South Atlantic: Discovery, Development, and Dispute*. London: British Broadcasting Corp., 1985.

Friedman, Norman. *U.S. Cruisers: An Illustrated Design History*. Annapolis, Maryland: U.S. Naval Institute Press, 1984.

Futrell, Robert Frank. *The United States Air Force in Korea 1950-1953*. Revised Edition. Washington D.C.: Office of Air Force History, United States Air Force, 1983.

Gaddis, John Lewis. *Strategies of Containment: A Critical Appraisal of Postwar American National Security Policy*. New York: Oxford University Press, 1982.

Gardiner, Robert. *Conway's All the World's Fighting Ships 1947 - 1982: Part 2, The Warsaw Pact and Non-Aligned Nations*. Annapolis, Maryland: U.S. Naval Institute Press, 1983.

Robert Gardiner and Roger Chesneau. *Conway's All the World's Fighting Ships 1922-1946*. Annapolis, Maryland: U.S. Naval Institute Press, 2001.

Gavshon, Arthur L. and Desmond Rice. *The Sinking of the Belgrano*. London: Martin Secker & Warburg, 1984.

George, James L. *History of Warships: From Ancient Times to the Twenty-First Century*. Annapolis, Maryland: U.S. Naval Institute Press, 1998.

Goncharov, S. N., John Wilson Lewis, and Litai Xue. *Uncertain Partners: Stalin, Mao, and the Korean War*. Stanford, California: Stanford University Press, 1993.

Gordin, Michael D. *Red Cloud at Dawn: Truman, Stalin, and the End of the Atomic Monopoly*. New York: Farrar, Straus, and Giroux, 2009.

Gray, Colin S. *The Leverage of Sea Power: The Strategic Advantage of Navies in War*. New York: The Free Press, 1992.

Gray, Randal. *Conway's All the World's Fighting Ships 1947-1982: Part 2, The Warsaw Pact and Non-Aligned Nations*. London: Conway, 1983.

Grove, Eric. *The Future of Sea Power*. Annapolis, Maryland: U.S. Naval Institute Press, 1990.

BIBLIOGRAPHY

------. *Vanguard to Trident: British Naval Policy Since World War II*. Annapolis, Maryland: U.S. Naval Institute Press, 1987.

------. *This People's Navy: The Making of American Sea Power*. New York: Free Press, 1992.

Halberstam, David. *The Coldest Winter: America and the Korean War*. New York: Hyperion, 2007.

Hallion, Richard. *The Naval Air War in Korea*. New York, NY: Kensington, 1988.

Harris, Brayton, and Walter J. Boyne. *The Navy Times Book of Submarines: A Political and Military History*. New York: Berkley Books, 1997.

Hastings, Max, and Simon Jenkins. *The Battle for the Falklands*. New York: W. W. Norton, 1984.

Haynes, Richard F. *The Awesome Power: Harry S. Truman as Commander in Chief*. Baton Rouge, Louisiana: Louisiana State University Press. 1973.

Heinl, Robert Debs. *Victory at High Tide: The Inchon-Seoul Campaign*. Annapolis, Maryland: Nautical & Aviation Publishing Company of America, 1982.

Herrick, Robert Waring. *Soviet Naval Strategy: Fifty Years of Theory and Practice*. Annapolis, Maryland: U.S. Naval Institute Press, 1971.

Hess, Gary R. *Presidential Decisions for War: Korea, Vietnam, and the Persian Gulf*. Baltimore, Maryland: Johns Hopkins University Press, 2001.

Hickey, Michael. *The Korean War: The West Confronts Communism*. Woodstock, NY: Overlook Press, 2000.

Holloway, David. *Stalin and the Bomb: The Soviet Union and Atomic Energy, 1939-1956*. New Haven, Connecticut: Yale University Press, 1994.

Howarth, Stephen. *To Shining Sea A History of the United States Navy, 1775-1998*. Norman, Oklahoma: University of Oklahoma Press, 1999.

Hoyt, Edwin P. *The Pusan Perimeter*, New York: Stein and Day, 1984.

Isenberg, Michael T. *Shield of the Republic: The U.S. Navy in an Era of Cold War and Violent Peace, 1945-1962*. New York: St. Martin's Press, 1993.

BIBLIOGRAPHY

James, D. Clayton. *Refighting the Last War: Command and Crisis in Korea 1950-1953*. New York: The Free Press, 1993.

Johnson, Brian. *Fly Navy: The History of Maritime Aviation*. London: David & Charles, 1981.

Johnson, Paul. *Modern Times: The World from the Twenties to the Nineties, Revised Edition*. New York: Harper Collins, 2001.

Karig, Walter, Malcolm W. Cagle, and Frank A. Manson. *Battle Report: the War in Korea*. New York: Rinehart, 1952.

Keegan, John. *Intelligence in War: Knowledge of the Enemy from Napoleon to Al-Queda*. New York: Alfred A. Knopf, 2003.

Kiernan, John. *Information Please Almanac 1951*. New York: MacMillan, 1950.

King, R. W. *Naval Engineering and American Sea Power*. Baltimore, Maryland: Nautical & Aviation Publishing Co. of America, 1989.

Kissinger, Henry. *Nuclear Weapons and Foreign Policy*. New York: Published for the Council on Foreign Relations by Harper, 1957.

Knott, Richard C. *Attack from the Sky: Naval Air Operations in the Korean War*. Washington D.C.: National Historical Center, Department of the Navy, 2004.

Korea Institute of Military History. *The Korean War, Vol. 1*. Lincoln, Nebraska: University of Nebraska, 2000.

Kurzman, Dan. *Left to Die: The Tragedy of the USS Juneau*. New York: Pocket Books, 1994.

Lansdown, John R. P. *With the Carriers in Korea: The Fleet Air Arm Story 1950-1953*. Wilmslow, Cheshire: Crécy, 1997.

Leckie, Robert. *Conflict: The History of the Korean War, 1950-1953*. New York: G.P. Putnam's Sons, 1962.

Leffler, Melvyn P. *A Preponderance of Power: National Security, the Truman Administration, and the Cold War*. Stanford, California: Stanford University Press, 1994.

Lentin, H. T. *American Gunboats and Minesweepers, Series: World War 2 Fact File*. New York: Arco, 1974.

Levert, Lee J. *Fundamentals of Naval Warfare*. New York: MacMillan, 1947.

Love, Robert William. *The Chiefs of Naval Operations*. Annapolis, Maryland: Naval Institute Press, 1980.

MacArthur, Douglas. *Reminiscences*. New York: McGraw-Hill, 1964.

Maloney, Sean M. *Securing Command of the Sea: NATO Naval Planning 1948-1954*. Annapolis, Maryland: U.S. Naval Institute Press, 1995.

Manchester, William. *American Caesar: Douglas MacArthur 1880-1964*. Boston, MA: Little, Brown, and Company, 1978.

Maurstad, Raymond B. *SOS Korea 1950*. Edina, Minnesota: Beaver Pond Press, 2002.

McMurtrie, Francis E. and Raymond V. B. Blackman, editors, *Jane's Fighting Ships 1949-1950*, New York: McGraw Hill, 1949.

Meister, Jurg. *Soviet Warships of the Second World War*. New York: Arco, 1977.

Melia, Tamara Moser. *Damn the Torpedoes: A Short History of U.S. Naval Mine Countermeasures, 1777-1991*. Contributions to Naval History, No. 4. Washington D.C.: Naval Historical Center, Department of the Navy, 1991.

Middlebrook, Martin. *Operation Corporate: The Story of the Falklands War, 1982*. London: Viking, 1987.

------. *Argentine Fight for the Falklands*. Barnsley, South Yorkshire, 2003.

Mitchell, Donald W. *A History of Russian and Soviet Sea Power*. New York: MacMillan, 1974.

Morris, Eric. *The Russian Navy: Myth and Reality*. Briarcliff Manor, New York: Stein and Day, 1977.

Morison, Samuel E. *History of United States Naval Operations in World War II, Vol. 5: The Struggle for Guadalcanal August 1942-February 1943*. Urbana and Chicago, Illinois: University of Illinois, 2001.

------. *History of United States Naval Operations in World War II, Vol.12: Leyte, June 1944 - January 1945*. Urbana and Chicago, Illinois: University of Illinois Press, 2002.

Nash, Gary B. *The American People: Creating a Nation and a Society*. 6th ed. New York: Pearson Education, 2008.

Packard, Wyman H. *A Century of US Naval Intelligence*. Washington D.C.: Office of Naval Intelligence, 1996.

Paige, Glenn. *1950: Truman's Decision, the United States enters the Korean War*. New York: Chelsea House, 1970.

BIBLIOGRAPHY

Palmer, Michael A. *Origins of the Maritime Strategy: The Development of American Naval Strategy.* Annapolis, Maryland: U.S. Naval Institute Press, 1988.

Pearlman, Michael D. *Truman & MacArthur: Policy, Politics, and the Hunger for Honor and Renown.* Bloomington and Indianapolis, Indiana: Indiana University Press, 2008.

Perrett, Bryan. *Weapons of the Falklands Conflict.* Dorset, UK: Blanford, 1984.

Perrett, Geoffrey. *Commander in Chief: How Truman, Johnson, and Bush Turned a Presidential Power into a Threat to America's Future.* NY: Farrar, Straus, and Giroux, 2007.

Polmar, Norman. *Soviet Naval Power: Challenge for the 1970s, Revised Ed.* New York: Crane, Russack, 1974.

Polmar, Norman, and K. J. Moore. *Cold War Submarines: The Design and Construction of U.S. and Soviet Submarines.* Washington D.C.: Potomac Books, 2004.

Polmar, Norman, and Jurrien Noot. *Submarines of the Russian and Soviet Navies, 1718-1990.* Annapolis, Maryland: U.S. Naval Institute Press, 1991.

Poole, S. L. *A History of British Cruisers from 1889-1960.* London: Robert Hale, 1970.

Potter, E. B., and Chester W. Nimitz, editors. *Sea Power: A Naval History.* Englewood Cliffs, New Jersey: Prentice Hall, 1960.

Republic of Korea. *The History of the United Nations Forces in the Korean War, Vol. 1.* Seoul: Republic of Korea, Ministry of National Defense, 1972.

Roberts, Geoffrey. *Stalin's Wars: From World War to Cold War, 1939-1953.* New Haven, Connecticut: Yale University Press, 2006.

Rohwer, Jurgen, and Mikhail S. Monakov. *Stalin's Ocean-Going Fleet: Soviet Naval Strategy and Shipbuilding Programmes 1935-1953.* New York: Frank Cass, 2006.

Roland, Alex W., Jeffrey Bolster, and Alexander Keyssar. *The Way of the Ship: America's Maritime HIstory Re-envisioned 1600-2000.* Hoboken, New Jersey: John Wiley & Sons, 2008.

Roscoe, Theodore. *United States Destroyer Operations in World War II.* Annapolis, Maryland: United States Naval Institute Press, 1953.

Rose, Lisle A. *The Cold War Comes to Main Street: America in 1950.* Lawrence, Kansas: University Press of Kansas, 1999.

------. *Power at Sea: Vol. 3 A Violent Peace, 1946-2006.* Columbia, Missouri: University of Missouri Press, 2007.

Ross, Steven T. *American War Plans 1945-1950.* London: Frank Cass, 1996.

Rossiter, Mike. *Sink the Belgrano.* London: Transworld, 2007.

Rottman, Gordon L. *Korean War Order of Battle United States, United Nations, and Communist Ground, Naval, and Air Forces, 1950-1953.* Westport, Connecticut: Praeger, 2002.

Rottman, Gordon L., and Peter Dennis. Inch'on 1950: The Last Great Amphibious Assault. Oxford: Osprey, 2006.

Sandler, Sandy, editor. *The Korean War: An Encyclopedia.* New York: Garland, 1995.

Schratz, Paul R. *Submarine Commander: A Story of World War II and Korea.* Lexington, Kentucky: University Press of Kentucky, 1988.

Scheina, Robert L. *Latin American Wars Volume II: The Age of the Professional Soldier 1900-2001.* Dulles, Virginia: Potomac Books, 2003.

Schueler, Dave, Bill Madison, Chris Carlson, and Larry Bond. *Mighty Midgets: Scenarios & Rules for Small Craft in WWII, an Expansion Set for Command at Sea.* Phoenixville, Pennsylvania: Clash of Arms, 2002.

Service, Robert. *Stalin: A Biography.* Cambridge, Massachusetts: Harvard University Press, 2005.

Shrader, Charles R. *Communist Logistics in the Korean War.* Westport, Connecticut: Greenwood Press, 1995.

Schnabel, James F. *Policy and Direction: The First Year.* United States Army in the Korean War. Washington, DC: Center of Military History, United States Army, 1992.

Smith, Gordon. *Battle Atlas of the Falklands War 1982.* Penarth, UK: Naval-History.Net, 2006.

South Korea. *The History of the United Nations Forces in the Korean War,* Vol. 2. Seoul: Ministry of National Defense, Republic of Korea, 1972.

Spanier, John W. *The Truman - MacArthur Controversy and the Korean War.* Cambridge, Massachusetts: Belknap Press, 1959.

Spector, Ronald H. *At War at Sea: Sailors and Naval Combat in the Twentieth Century.* New York: Penguin Books, 2002.

Sumrall, Robert F. and Paul Bender. *Sumner Gearing Class Destroyers: Their Design, Weapons, and Equipment.* Annapolis, Maryland: U.S. Naval Institute Press, 1995.

Teller, Edward and Judith Schoolery. *Memoirs: a Twentieth Century Journey in Science and Politics.* Cambridge, Massachusetts: Persus, 2001.

Thornton, Richard C. *Odd Man Out: Truman, Stalin, and Mao and the Origins of the Korean War.* Washington D.C.: Brassey's, 2001.

Truman, Harry S. *Memoirs: Vol. 2, Years of Trial and Hope.* New York: Doubleday, 1956.

Tucker, Spencer C. editor. *Encyclopedia of the Korean War: A Political, Social, and Military History.* New York: Checkmark Books, 2002.

United States. *Ships of the American Merchant Marine.* Washington D.C.: U.S. Government Office, 1950.

Utz, Curtis A. *Assault from the Sea: The Amphibious Landing at Inchon.* Washington D.C.: Naval Historical Center, Department of the Navy, 1994.

Varble, Derek. *Essential Histories: The Suez Crisis 1956.* Oxford: Osprey Publishing, 2003.

Varhola, Michael J. *Fire and Ice: The Korean War, 1950-1953.* Mason City, Iowa: Savas, 2001.

Watson, Bruce W. and Peter M. Dunn, editors. *Military Lessons of the Falkland Islands War: Views from the United States.* Boulder, Colorado: Westview Press, 1984.

Weigley, Russell F. *The American Way of War: A History of United States Military Strategy and Policy.* Bloomington, Indiana: Indiana University Press, 1973.

Wettern, Desmond. *The Decline of British Seapower.* London: Jane's, 1982.

Whelan, Richard. *Drawing the Line: The Korean War, 1950-1953.* Boston: Little, Brown, 1990.

Winkler, David F. *Cold War at Sea: High-Seas Confrontation between the United States and the Soviet Union.* Annapolis, Maryland: U.S. Naval Institute Press, 2000.

Whitley, M. J. *Cruisers of World War 2: An International Encyclopedia.* London: Arms and Armour Press, 1996.

Worth, Richard. *Fleets of World War II.* Cambridge, Massachusetts: First Da Capo Press, 2001.

Yergin, Daniel. *Shattered Peace: The Origins of the Cold War and the National Security State.* Boston, Massachusetts: Houghton Mifflin, 1977.

Articles with Author Attribution

Addison Jr., Victor C. Captain USN and Commander David Dominy, RN. "Got Sea Control." 2010. U.S. Naval Institute, http://www.usni.org/ magazines/proceedings/2010-03/got-sea-control (accessed August 2011).

Bentley (Pseud). "HMS *Belfast* in Korea." *Naval Review* 38 no. 4. (November 1950) 372-381.

Bermudez, Joseph S. "Email to Korean-War-List Re: North Korean OOB," posted May 2002. hosted by the University of Kansas, http://www. korean-war.com/archives/ 2002/05/msg00353.html (accessed July 2008).

Bernstein, Marc D,. "The US Navy on the Eve of the Korean War." *Naval Aviation News* (1 May 2000), 10-17.

Cagle, Malcolm. "Sitting Ducks." USS Gurke.org, http://ussgurke.org/sducks.htm (accessed 26 February 2009).

------. "The Taking of Wolmi-do." Sea Classics, Vol. 33, No. 10, October 2000. USS DeHaven.org, http://ussdehaven.org/wolmi_do.htm (accessed 13 October 2011).

Carleton, A. "USS *Pledge*, Bulletin Board." post entry 22 May 2000, hosted by Korean War Project, https://www.koreanwar .org /html/units/ navy/uss_pledge.htm (accessed May 2009).

BIBLIOGRAPHY

Carrillo, Joe. "Desron Nine and the Oddysey of the Sitting Ducks." Welcome Aboard the USS *Collett* (DD-730), http://www.usscollett.com/ history.htm (Accessed 21 March 2012).

Cook, Preston. "Remembering those Astounding Atlanta-Class Anti-Aircraft Cruisers of WWII." *Sea Classics* Vol. 40, No. 4, (April 2007), 18-25.

Curtin, T. A. "The Galloping Ghost of the Korean Coast, A Memoir." USS Juneau.net http:// ussjuneau.net/ CLAA119/index.html (accessed 16 March 2008).

------. "USS *Juneau* (CLAA-119) In the Early Days of the Korean Conflict." An edited transcript of the diary of then ENS T. A. Curtin, USN. USS Juneau.net http://ussjuneau.net/CLAA119/ index.html (accessed 16 March 2008).

Digiulian, Tony. "Naval Weapon, Naval Technology, and Naval Reunions." NavWeaps.com, http://www.navweaps.com (accessed 31 January 2009).

Dingman, Roger. "Strategic Planning and the Policy Process: America Plans for War in East Asia, 1945-1950." *Naval War College Review* 32 (November-December 1979) 4-21.

Fielder, Wilson. "Last Train from Vladivostok." *Time Magazine* (24 July 1950).

Fincher, Lindsay. "North Korea: US Imperialists visit the Victorious Fatherland Liberation War Museum." At Home in the Wasteland, entry posted May 25, 2010, http://www.lindsayfincher.com/ 2010/05/north-korea-us-imperialists-visit-the-victorious-fatherland-liberation-war-museum-korean-war-museum-and-learn-how-the-korean-war-really-started.html; (accessed March 28, 2012).

GHS (Pseud.). "Naval Operations in Korea." *Naval Review* 38 no. 4 (November 1950) 382-386.

Grimsberg, Sharon. "Race for the Super Bomb." Television production, first aired 1999 *American Experience*. Public Broadcasting System.

Grygiel, Jakub J,. "The Dilemmas of US Maritime Supremacy in the Early Cold War." *Journal of Strategic Studies* 28, no. 2, (April 2005) 187-216.

Hall, Geoffrey. "A First Command - III." *Naval Review* 82. no. 1 (January 1994) 57-59.

Hamlin, C. F. "Diary 24 April 1950 - 4 October 1950." USS Juneau.net, http:// ussjuneau.net/ CLAA119/marines.html (accessed 16 March 2009).

Harper, Steven R. "Submarine Operations During the Falklands War." A paper submitted to the faculty of the Naval War College in partial satisfaction of the requirements of the Department of Operations. Naval War College, Newport, Rhode Island, 17 June 1994. The Defense Technical Information Center (DTIC), http://www.dtic.mil/cgi-bin/ GetTRDoc?Location= U2&doc=GetTRDoc.pdf&AD= ADA279554 (accessed 15 December 2011).

Hatch, David A., with Robert Louis Benson. "The Korean War: the SIGINT Background." National Security Agency, http://www.nsa.gov/about/cryptologic_heritage/center_ crypt_history/publications/koreanwar_sigint_bkg.shtml# 8 (accessed 14 April 2011).

Hauner, Milan L. "Stalin's Big-Fleet Program." *Naval War College Review.* Vol. LVII, no. 2 (Spring 2004) 87-120.

Hegarty, John. "HMS *Jamaica*: Korean War Service 1950." Britain's Small Wars. http://www. britains-smallwars.com/korea/jamaica2.htm (accessed 5 September 2007).

Hobbs, David. "British Commonwealth Carrier Operations in the Korean War." *Air & Space Power Journal.* Volume 18 no. 4 (Winter 2004) 62-71.

Hughes, Walter. "E-Boat Action off the Korean Coast: HMS *Jamaica*, 1950." Britain's Small Wars. http://www.britains-smallwars.com/korea/ walter/photos.htm (accessed 5 March 2009).

Ingram, M. D. "The United States Navy in Japan 1945-1950." United States Naval Institute *"Proceedings."* Vol. 78 (April 1952), 378-383.

BIBLIOGRAPHY

Lawson, Siri Holm. "Index of /singleships." Warsailors, http://warsailors. com/singleships (accessed 1 December 2008).

Kristiansen, Karl. "USS *Mansfield* DD-728 Mine Incident," Karl's Korner, USS *Mansfield* DD-728, Ship's History and Photos, http://web.meganet. net/kman/nfmine.htm (accessed 22 March 2012).

Manson, Frank A. "60th Anniversary of the Korean War." Part 1, Vol. 43 No. 6. *"Sea Classics.* June 2010.

------. "60th Anniversary of the Korean War." Part 2, Vol. 43 No. 7. *Sea Classics.* July 2010.

Marolda, Edward J. "The Sharp Edge of Containment." *Naval History.* (April 2006), 54-61.

------. "Vice Admiral C. Turner Joy, USN," Naval History & Heritage Command, http://www. history.navy.mil/wars/korea /joy.htm (accessed 12 August 2011).

Mason, Geoffrey B. "HMS *Triumph* - Colossus-class Light Fleet Aircraft Carrier." Naval-History.net. http://www.naval-history.net/xGM-Chrono-04CV-Triumph%20(ii).htm (accessed 11 January 2011).

Master Chief's Lair Blog. "Short Charge." The Master Chief's Lair Blog, http://www. silverfoxnavy.blogspot.com/ 2010/05/short-charge. html (accessed 3 June 2011).

McMullen, C. E. "USS *Pirate*; Report of Loss of USS *Pirate* (AM-275)." Ships History Branch, Naval Historical Center, Washington D.C., http:// www.history.navy.mil/faqs/faq103-3.html (accessed 19 February 2009).

Medynski, John. "Interview with John Medynski." John Medynski Collection (AFC/2001/001/1507). Veteran History Project. American Folklife Center. Library of Congress, 30 June 2002 (accessed 7 July 2010).

Min, Seow Hwye. "British Interests in the Korean War (1950-53)." *Pointer, Journal of the Singapore Armed Forces*. Volume 25, Number 3, July-September. 1999.

Moore, Don. "*Collett* in Tokyo Bay in 1945." USS *Collett*. http//www.uscollett.com/history/ d_moore/Don%20Moore%20 History.htm (accessed 15 February 2011).

BIBLIOGRAPHY

O'Toole, Tony. "The Forgotten Cruise: HMS *Triumph* and the 13th Carrier Air Group, The First Royal Navy Carrier Force in the Korean War, June-September 1950." Royal Navy Research Archive, http://www.royalnavyresearcharchive.org.uk (accessed 2 February 2011).

Ott, Thomas, Writer, Producer, Director. "Race for the Super Bomb." From the television series, American Experience. Public Broadcasting System (PBS). Originally aired 1999.

Paul, James and Martin Spirit. "Korea." Britain's Small Wars, http://www.britains-smallwars.com (accessed 9 September 2008).

Polmar, Norman. "The Navy's Frontline in Korea." *Naval History*. (April 2008) 14-15.

Rees, David. "Reckless War-Making; Review of Sergei N. Goncharov et al.'s Uncertain Partners: Stalin, Mao, and the Korean War." *National Interest*. (December, 1995).

Robinson, James. "Assault on the Canal: H.M.S. *Jamaica*." Britain's Small Wars. http://www.britains-smallwars.com/suez/Jamaica.html (accessed 25 November 2010).

Sauer, Bob. "Bob Sauer Remembers." USS De Haven Sailors Association, http://ussdehaven.org (accessed 23 August 2011).

Schindler, John R. "A Dangerous Business: The US Navy and National Reconnaissance During the Cold War." (Brochure) Fort George G. Meade, Maryland: Center for Cryptologic History, National Security Agency, No date, http://www.nsa.gov/about/_files/cryptologic_heritage/publications/coldwar/dangerous_business.pdf (accessed 15 December 2011).

Seow, Hwye Min, "British Interests in the Korean War (1950-53), *Pointer, Journal of the Singapore Armed Forces*, Volume 25, Number 3, (July-September 1999).

Shumer, Ed. "1949-1952: My Time On board USS *Collett*." March 2010. Welcome Aboard the USS *Collett* (DD-730), http://usscollett.com/history.htm (accessed 23 August 2011).

BIBLIOGRAPHY

Smith, Gordon. "HMS *Belfast*." Naval-History, http://www.naval-history. net/xGM-Chrono-06CL-*Belfast*.htm, (accessed 23 March 2009).

------. ""Battle of North Cape," Naval-History, http://www.naval-history. net/Cr03-56-00NorthCape.htm, (accessed 23 March 2009).

Smith, P. J. "History of USS *Juneau* CLAA-119." ussJuneau.net/CLAA119/jun2hist.html (accessed 7 June 2010).

Stephens, Michael. "The Galloping Ghost of the of the Korean Coast," Britain's Small Wars, http://www.britains-smallwars.com/korea/Jamaica.html (accessed 5 January 2011).

Thompson, Allyn. Email message to author. Former *USS Juneau* crew member. 28 February 2006.

Uhlig, Frank Jr. "The Threat of the Soviet Navy." *Foreign Affairs*. Vol. 30, no. 1 (October 1951) 444-454.

Weathersby, Kathryn. "Soviet Aims in Korea and the Origins of the Korean War, 1945-1950: New Evidence from Russian Archives." *Cold War International History Project*. Working Paper No. 8. Woodrow Wilson International Center for Scholars. Washington, D.C., November 1993.

Winkler, David F. "The Birth of the South Korean Navy." *Sea Power* (August 2000).

Wise, Robert M. and James Younger, Directors. "Wilhelm Gustloff." *Unsolved History*, Discovery Channel. 2003.

Yarnel, Paul R. "USS *Casinghead*." NavSource Naval History. http://navsource.org (accessed 16 March 2008).

------. "Remora (SS-487)." NavSource Naval History. http://navsource.org (accessed 16 March 2008).

Yegorova, Natalia I. "Stalin's Conception of Maritime Power: Revelations from the Russian Archives." *Journal of Strategic Studies*, Vol. 28 no. 2. (April 2005) 157-186.

Website Resources

British Imperial War Museum. http://hmsbelfast.iwm.org.uk.

CDR Salamander. http://cdrsalamander.blogspot.

BIBLIOGRAPHY

Cold War Files. http://legacy.wilsoncenter.org/coldwarfiles.

DANFS Online: The Dictionary of American Naval Fighting Ships. http://www.hazegray.org/danfs/

Destroyer History Foundation. http://destroyerhistory.org.

Global Security. http://www.globalsecurity.org.

Korean War Project. http://www.koreanwar.org

Maine Memory Network, Maine's Statewide Digital Museum. http://www.mainememory.net.

Miramar Ship Index. http://miramarshipindex.org.nz.

Naval History & Heritage Command. http://www.history.navy.mil.

Naval-History.net. http://www.naval-history.net

NavSource Naval History. http://www. navsource.org.

NOAA, National Weather Service. http://www.prh.noaa.gov.

The Ships List: Passengers, Ships, Shipwrecks. http://www.theshipslist.com.

U.S. National Weather Service, Central Pacific Hurricane Center. http://www.prh.noaa.gov/cphc

Welcome Aboard the USS *Collett*. http://www.usscollett.com/history.htm

WolframAlpha Computational Knowledge Engine. http://www.Wolframalpha.com.

IMAGE CREDITS

Cover Photo
Naval History and Heritage Command, [USS Juneau CLAA-119 anchored at Kagoshima, Japan], 1950, Source: U.S. Naval Historical Center Photograph #NH 52364, Public Domain*
http://www.history.navy.mil/photos/sh-usn/usnsh-j/cl119.htm

Outline Map of Korean Peninsula
F Blank Map, World Map, [Korea, Coastlines and Borders], All Free Map, English. Free map.jp,
http://english.freemap.jp/asia_e/korea.html

Pro-1 Sumner class Destroyer in Heavy Seas
Naval History and Heritage Command, [*Lyman K. Swenson* in Heavy Seas, 1945], 1945, Source: U.S. Naval Historical Center Photograph, Author: Photographed from USS Brush (DD-745), Courtesy of Robert O. Baumrucker, 1978, Public Domain*
http://www.history.navy.mil/photos/images/h89000/h89376.jpg

Pro-2 *Triumph* in Far East 1950
Naval History and Heritage Command, [HMS *Triumph* off Subic Bay, March 1950], 8 March 1950, Source/Author: Photo #: NH 97010, Official U.S. Navy Photograph, from the collections of the Naval Historical
Center, Public Domain*
http://www.history.navy.mil/photos/images/h97000/h97010.jpg

1-1 HMS *Belfast*
Wikimedia Commons, [British cruiser HMS *BELFAST* firing a salvo from her six inch guns against enemy troop concentrations on the west coast of Korea], March 1951, Source: This is photograph No. A 31890 from the Imperial War Museum collection No. 4700-01, Author: Royal Navy official photographer, Public Domain.
http://commons.wikimedia.org/wiki/File:HMS_Belfast_bombarding_Korea.jpg

1-2 HMS *Jamaica* in World War II Camouflage
Wikipedia, [British light cruiser HMS *JAMAICA* at anchor], 18 September 1943, Source: This is photograph No. FL 10556 from the Imperial War Museum collection No. 8308-29, Author: Royal Navy official photographer, Public Domain.
http://en.wikipedia.org/wiki/File:HMS_Jamaica_anchored.jpg

1-3 Altenfjord and North Cape
d-maps.com, [Scandinavia, coasts, states, white], 30 April 2012, License (Free), Terms and conditions of use: All the maps are protected by copyright. They are free for any use, even commercial, in the following conditions: The exact URL where the original map comes from must be mentioned and the number of used maps is limited to 10 for a publication (Web, DVD, book...).
http://d-maps.com/pays.php?lib=scandinavia_maps&num_pay=316&lang=en

1-4 German Battlecruiser SNS *Scharnhorst* in Action
Naval History & Heritage Command, [German battleship Scharnhorst firing her forward 283mm guns, during the engagement with the British aircraft carrier Glorious and her escorts], 8 June 1940, Source: U.S. Naval Historical Center Photograph #NH 83981, Author: Photographed from the battleship Gneisenau, Public Domain*
http://www.history.navy.mil/photos/sh-fornv/germany/gersh-s/scharn2.htm

1-5 HMS *Amethyst*
Wikipedia, British sloop HMS Amethyst], Source: This is photograph No. A 30156 from the Imperial War Museum's collections, Author: Royal Navy official photographer, Public Domain, http://en.wikipedia.org/wiki/File:HMS_Amethyst_WWII_IWM_A_30156.jpg

1-6 Outline Map of Japan
d-maps.com, [Japan, coasts, boundaries (white)], 30 April 2012, License (Free), Terms and conditions of use: All the maps are protected by copyright. They are free for any use, even commercial, in the following conditions: The exact URL where the original map comes from must be mentioned and the number of used maps is limited to 10 for a publication (Web, DVD, book...).
http://d-maps.com/carte.php?lib=japan_map&num_car=349&lang=en

2-1 Admirable Class Steel-Hulled Minesweeper
Wikimedia Commons, [National Archives Photo 19-N-55263], Unknown date, Source/Author: National Archives Photo 19-N-55263, Public Domain
http://commons.wikimedia.org/wiki/File:Notable_(AM_267).jpg

2-2 Essex Class Carrier Receiving Aircraft Later in the War Inner at Yokosuka with Mount Fuji in the Background
Wikimedia Commons, [The U.S. Navy aircraft carrier USS *Leyte* (CV-32) loading aircraft at Yokosuka, Japan, for transportation to the United States, at the end of her Korean War combat tour on 24 January 1951. Several decommissioned frigates (PF) are moored in groups across the harbour background and snow-capped Mount Fuji is visible in the left distance], 24 January 1951, Source: Official U.S. Navy Photograph NH 97295, from the collections of the Naval Historical Center, Author: U.S. Navy, Public Domain, http://commons.wikimedia.org/wiki/File:USS_Leyte_(CV32),_Yokosuka,_Japan,_1951.jpg

2-3 Wooden-Hulled Minesweeper USS *Mockingbird*
Wikipedia, [USS YMS-419], c. 1944/1945, Source:http://www.navsource.org/archives/11/ 05027.htm, Author: U.S. Navy photo NH-96909. Public Domain, http://en.wikipedia.org/wiki/USS_Mockingbird_(AMS-27)

2-4 USS *Remora*
Wikipedia, [Broadside view of Remora (SS-487) off Mare Island on 20 October 1947], 20 October 1947, Source: http://www.navsource.org/archives/08/08487.htm, Author: US Navy photo # 1919-10-47, courtesy of Darryl Baker, Public Domain,
http://en.wikipedia.org/wiki/USS_Remora_(SS-487)

2-5 Sumner Class Destroyer Refueling Underway
Naval History & Heritage Command, [USS *Platte* (AO-24) Refuels USS *Valley Forge* (CV-45) and USS *Lyman K. Swenson* (DD-729), while they were enroute from Pearl Harbor to San Diego during Operation "Miki", November 1949], November 1949, Source: Photo # NH70274, U.S. Naval Historical Center Photograph, Author: Photographed by Ted Huggins, Public Domain* http://www.history.navy.mil/photos/sh-usn/usnsh-v/cv45-k8.htm

3-1 USS *Juneau*
NavSource Naval History, [USS *Juneau* (CLAA 119) At the Mare Island Naval Shipyard, California, following overhaul, 26 January 1952], Source/Author: Official U.S. Navy Photograph, from the collections of the Naval Historical Center #NH 96893, Public Domain
http://www.navsource.org/archives/04/119/04119.htm

3-2 First *Juneau* CL-52 in Action at Battle of Santa Cruz 17 Days before Her Loss
NavSource Naval History, [USS *Juneau* (CL 52) Firing on attacking Japanese aircraft (marked by arrows), during the Battle of the Santa Cruz Islands], 26 October 1942, Source/Author: Official U.S. Navy Photograph #80-G-33331, Public Domain
http://www.navsource.org/archives/04/052/04052.htm

3-3 Sullivan Brothers on Board USS *Juneau*
Wikimedia Commons, [Sullivan brothers on USS Juneau (Joseph, Francis, Albert, Madison, and George (from left to right)], Date: 14 February 1942, Source: U.S. Naval Historical Center, Photo #NH 52362, Public Domain
http://en.wikipedia.org/wiki/File:Sullivanbrothers.jpg

3-4 USS *Juneau* at Anchor in Kagoshima Harbor with Mt. Sakurajima in Background
Naval History and Heritage Command, [USS Juneau CLAA-119 anchored at Kagoshima, Japan], 1950, Source: U.S. Naval Historical Center Photograph #NH 52364, Public Domain*
http://www.history.navy.mil/photos/sh-usn/usnsh-j/cl119.htm

4-1 Taebaek Mountain Range
F Blank Map, World Map, [Korea, Coastlines and Borders], All Free Map, English. Free map.jp,
http://english.freemap.jp/asia_e/korea.html

4-2 Pusan Harbor
Naval History & Heritage Command, [Pusan, South Korea, Aerial view of part of the city's waterfront], 4 April 1953, Source: Photo #: 80-G-479409 Official U.S. Navy Photograph, now in the collections of the National Archives, Author: Unknown, Public Domain*
http://www.history.navy.mil/photos/events/kowar/log-sup/kor51.htm

4-3 Chinhae, South Korea
Wikimedia Commons, [An aerial photo of the Republic of Korea naval base at Jinhae (Chinhae), South Korea]. Source: Retrieved from http://www.uscg.mil /history/ Korean_ War.html, Author: Unknown, Public Domain
http://commons.wikimedia.org/wiki/File:Korea_Jinhae_circa_1950.jpg

5-1 *Bak du San* Receiving Her New 3-inch Gun at Pearl Harbor March 1950
Naval History & Heritage Command, [Pak Tu San (Republic of Korea Patrol Craft, PC-701, formerly USS PC-823)], March 1950, Source: Official U.S. Navy Photograph # NH 97002 , from the collections of the Naval Historical Center, Author: Unknown, Public Domain*
http://www.history.navy.mil/photos/sh-fornv/rok/roksh-mr/paktusn.htm

5-2 YMS Minesweeper
Naval History & Heritage Command, [USS YMS-346 at the Norfolk Navy Yard, Portsmouth, Virginia], 14 November 1943, Source: Official U.S. Navy Photograph #: NH 98999, from the collections of the Naval Historical Center, Public Domain*
http://www.history.navy.mil/photos/sh-usn/usnsh-xz/yms346.htm

8-1 East Asia
d-maps.com, [East Asia], 30 April 2012, License (Free), Terms and conditions of use: All the maps are protected by copyright. They are free for any use, even commercial, in the following conditions: The exact URL where the original map comes from must be mentioned and the number of used maps is limited to 10 for a publication (Web, DVD, book...), http://d-maps.com/carte.php?lib=east_ asia_map&num_car=75&lang=en

9-1 German U-boat Type XXI
Wikipedia, [German submarine *U-3008* in Portsmouth Naval Shipyard, Kittery, Maine], Date: 30th August 1946, Source: Photograph from the Bureau of Ships Collection in the U.S. National Archives. Photo #: 19-N-95866, Author: Original uploader was John Tuttle at de.wikipedia, United States Public Domain,
http://en.wikipedia.org/wiki/File:German_submarine_U_3008.jpg

9-2 HMS *Black Swan*
Wikipedia, [Photograph of British sloop HMS *Black Swan*], 7 April 1945,
Source: This is photograph No. FL 2274 from the Imperial War Museum collection No. 8308-29, Author: Royal Navy official photographer, This artistic work created by the United Kingdom Government is in the public domain.
http://en.wikipedia.org/wiki/File:HMS_Black_Swan_1945_IWM_FL_2274.jpg

12-1 USS *Valley Forge* (late 1940s)
Naval History & Heritage Command, [USS *Valley Forge* (CV-45)], Photographed circa 1947-49, Source: Official U.S. Navy Photograph, Photo #: USN 1046225, Author: U.S. Navy, Public Domain*
http://www.history.navy.mil/photos/sh-usn/usnsh-v/cv45-b.htm

12-2 F9F-2 Panther Jet
Wikipedia, [A Grumman F9F-2 Panther (BuNo. 123494) of fighter squadron VF-21 Mach Busters on the aircraft carrier USS Midway (CVB-41) in 1952. VF-21 was assigned to Carrier Air Group Six (CVG-6) and deployed to the Mediterranean Sea from 9 Jan 1952 to 5 May 1952] 1952, Source: uss.midwaysailor.com, Author: USN, Public Domain
http://en.wikipedia.org/wiki/File:F9F-2_VF-21_CVA-41.jpeg

12-3 F4U Corsair
Wikipedia, [A U.S. Navy Vought F4U-4 Corsair of fighter squadron VF-1B, assigned to Carrier Air Group One (CVBG-1), aboard the aircraft carrier USS Midway (CVB-41). The Midway was on her first deployment from 29 October 1947 to 11 March 1948 to the Mediterranean Sea. VF-1B was re-designated VF-21 on 1 September 1948], 1947/48, Source: USS Midway website, Author: Charles J. Beggy, Jr., Electronics Technician Second Class, USN (ret.), Public Domain
http://en.wikipedia.org/wiki/File:F4U-4_VF-1B_CVB-41_1947-48.jpg

12-4 AD4 Skyraider
Wikipedia, [Three U.S. Navy Douglas AD-4 Skyraiders of attack squadron VA-115 Arabs get ready to launch from the aircraft carrier USS Philippine Sea (CV-47) in September 1950. The Philippine Sea with Carrier Air Group Eleven (CVG-11) embarked was deployed to Korea from 5 July 1950 to 26 March 1951. Behind the AD-4s are Vought F4U-4Bs of fighter squadron VF-114 Executioners, two F4U-5Ns (with the white radar housing on the right wing) of composite squadron VC-3 Det.3 Blue Nemesis, and Grumman F9F-2 Panther jets of VF-111 Sundowners and VF-112 Fighting Twelve.], September 1950, Source: Official U.S. Navy "Dictionary of American Naval Aviation Squadrons Volume 1 The History of VA, VAH, VAK, VAL, VAP and VFA Squadrons", Author: U.S. Navy, Public Domain
http://en.wikipedia.org/wiki/File:AD-4s_VA-115_CV-47_Sep1950.jpg

12-5 Supermarine Seafire 47
Wikimedia Commons, [Two Supermarine Seafire F.47's of 1833 Squadron RNVR dis-playing at the Wolverhampton air show] 16 May 1953, Source: Own work. Author: RuthAS, License: Attribution 3.0 Unported (CC BY 3.0) http://creative commons.org/ licenses/by/3.0/deed.en
http://commons.wikimedia.org/wiki/File:Supermarine_Seafire_47_VP487.474_18 33_Sqn_WVTN_16.05.53_edited-2.jpg

12-6 Fairey Firefly Mk. 1
Wikimedia Commons, [Fairey Firefly], unknown date, Source/Author: unknown source/author most likely a WW2-era publicity shot from Royal Navy, This artistic work created by the United Kingdom Government is in the public domain
http://commons.wikimedia.org/wiki/File:Firefly.jpg

12-7 Pyongyang Airstrike
Naval History & Heritage Command, [First Korean War Carrier Air Strikes, 3-4 July 1950], Source: Official U.S. Navy Photograph, now in the collections of the National Archives, Photo #: 80-G-417148, Author: U.S. Navy, Public Domain*
http://www.history.navy.mil/photos/images/g410000/g417148.jpg

14-1 British Fighter with Special Black and White Striping
Naval History & Heritage Command, [Hawker "Sea Fury" Fighter], circa June 1951, Source: Official Royal Navy Photograph, from the "All Hands" collection at the Naval Historical Center, Photo #: NH 97044, Author: U.S. Navy, Public Domain*
http://www.history.navy.mil/photos/images/h97000/h97044.jpg

15-1 Heavy Cruiser *Toledo* and Light Cruiser *Juneau* (note the difference in size)
Naval History & Heritage Command, USS *Toledo* (CA 133) and USS *Juneau* (CLAA 119) moored at Naval Operating Base, Yokosuka, Japan, following Korean War operations, Photographed during July-October 1950, Source: Official U.S. Navy Photograph, now in the collections of the National Archives #80-G-424598, Author: U.S. Navy, Public Domain*
http://www.history.navy.mil/photos/images/g420000/g424598.jpg

15-2 *Juneau* Moored in Foreground with *Valley Forge* nearest to Her at Sasebo, Japan (late 1950)
Wikimedia Commons, [United Nations ships assigned to support military operations in Korea pictured at anchor in Sasebo, Japan, during a break in the action. Pictured from front to back HMS Unicorn (I72), USS *Juneau* (CLAA-119), USS *Valley Forge* (CV-45), USS *Leyte* (CV-32), USS Hector (AR-7), and USS Jason (ARH-1)], circa 1950-1951, Source: U.S. Navy National Museum of Naval Aviation photo No. 1999.272.030, Author: U.S. Navy, Public Domain
http://commons.wikimedia.org/wiki/File:Aircraft_carriers_at_Sasebo_Japan_195.jpg

15-3 USS *Lyman K. Swenson* off Wolmi-do during Pre-Invasion Bombardment 13 September 1950 (40-mm guns in foreground)
Wikipedia, [Wolmi-Do island under bombardment on 13 September 1950, two days before the landings at Inchon], 13 September 1950, Source: http://www.history. navy.mil/photos/ events/kowar/50-unof/inch-2.htm, Author: U.S. Navy, Public Domain
http://en.wikipedia.org/wiki/File:Pre-invasion_bombardment_at_Inchon.jpg

15-4 Inchon Landing 15 September 1950 (*De Haven* in foreground)
Naval History & Heritage Command, [Inchon Invasion, September 1950, First and second waves of landing craft move toward Red Beach at Inchon at 0700Z. USS De Haven (DD-727) is in the foreground, Source: U.S. Naval Historical Center, Photo #: NH 42351, Author: Courtesy of Colonel Robert D. Heinl, USMC, June 1966, Public Domain*
http://www.history.navy.mil/photos/images/h42000/h42351.jpg

15-5 *Collett*, *Lyman K. Swenson*, *Mansfield*, and *De Haven*
Naval History & Heritage Command, "Teamwork, Courage, and Skill", 18 December 1951, Source: From the "All Hands" collection at the Naval Historical Center, Photo #: NH 97090, Author: U.S. Navy, Public Domain*
http://www.history.navy.mil/photos/images/h97000/h97090.jpg

16-1 Direct Channel (lower) and Russian Channel Leading to Wonsan, North Korea
Wikipedia, [Wonsan Harbor during the Korea War, 1950.jpg, The Clearance of Wonsan Harbor map, a United Nations naval operation to clear sea mine fields off

Wonsan, North Korea in 1950 during the korean War], 27 November 2010, Source: http://www.usnavy.mil, Author: U.S. Navy, Public Domain
http://en.wikipedia.org/wiki/File:Wonsan_Harbor_during_the_Korea_War_1950.jpg

16-2 *Pirate* (far right) in Her Final Moments before Sinking
Wikipedia, [The final moments of USS *Pirate*, just before fully submerging, 12 October 1950 as viewed from USS Endicott], 12 November 2010, Source: http://www.usnavy.mil,Author: G.D. Carpenter, United States Navy, Public Domain http://en.wikipedia.org/wiki/file:uss_pirate_sinking_5.jpg

16-3 South Korean Minesweeper Blowing up in Harbor at Wonsan
Naval History & Heritage Command, [Opening of Wonsan, October 1950], October 1950, Source: Official U.S. Navy Photograph, now in the collections of the National Archives, Photo #: 80-G-423625, Author: U.S. Navy, Public Domain*
http://www.history.navy.mil/photos/images/g420000/g423625.jpg

Epi-1 USS *Juneau* w/Crew in Summer Whites on Deck 1951
Wikimedia Commons, [The U.S. Navy anti-aircraft cruiser USS Juneau (CLAA-119) underway with her crew on deck in "Whites", 1 July 1951], Date: 1 July 1951, Source: Official U.S. Navy Photo, from the collection of the Naval Historical Center, Photo # NH 96890, Author: USN, Public Domain
http://commons.wikimedia.org/wiki/File:USS_Juneau_(CLAA-119).jpg

Post-1 G5 in Pyongyang
Wikipedia, [Torpedo Boat No.21, a "meritorious boat", which, according to North Korean propaganda, sunk USS *Baltimore* in 1950], Source: KoreanWar NK TB2.JPG, Author: Kalligan, Public Domain
http://en.wikipedia.org/wiki/Battle_of_Chumonchin_Chan.

Post-2 HMS *Belfast* in the Pool of London on the Thames River
Wikipedia, [HMS *Belfast* at her London berth, with Tower Bridge behind, 16 December 2005. Brightened, cropped and straightened version], 2010-10-20 19:46 (UTC), Source: HMS_Belfast_(C35),_London,_England-16Dec2005.jpg, Author: Raymond McCrae from Glasgow, UK, derivative work: IxK85 (talk), This is a retouched picture, which means that it has been digitally altered from its original version. The original can be viewed here: HMS_Belfast_(C35),_London,_England-16Dec2005.jpg. Modifications made by IxK85, Reuse: Attribution 2.0 Generic (CC BY 2.0) http://creativecommons.org/licenses/ by/2.0/deed.en, http://commons.wikimedia.org/wiki/File:HMS_Belfast_(C35),_London,_England-16Dec2005_cropped.jpg

*All images from the **Naval History and Heritage Command** website are used based on the website's Privacy Policy statement referenced on their Home Page. *"#2 All information on this site is in the **public domain** and may be distributed or copied unless otherwise specified. Use of appropriate byline/photo/ image credits is requested.*

Index of Ships

A

Alacrity, **26**, **120**, **140**
Amethyst, **22-24**, **268**
Anchises, **24**
Atlanta, **50**

B

Bak du San, **68-75**, **231**, **270**
Baltimore, **243**
Bataan, **150**
Belfast, **13-17**, **19-21**, **26-27**, **110**, **131-132**, **150**, **152**, **161**, **164-166**, **173-174**, **226**, **244-245**, **259**, **264**, **267**, **273**
Black Swan, **23-24**, **26**, **120**, **121**, **140**, **144**, **147**, **165-167**, **224**, **244**, **247**, **270**
Boxer, **108**
Brush, **108**, **267**

C

Cabezon, **108**, **150**
Casinghead, **37**, **264**
Catfish, **108**, **150**, **230-231**, **233**
Chatterer, **37**, **185**, **212**
Cockade, **26**
Collett, **36-40**, **42**, **126**, **139**, **140**, **185**, **189**, **193-199**, **202**, **211**, **213**, **230**, **233**, **237**, **241**, **248-249**, **260**, **262-263**, **265**, **272**
Comus, **26**
Conqueror, **239-241**
Consort, **22**, **26**, **131**, **150**, **165**
Cossack, **5**, **26**, **131**, **150**, **165**

D

Daegu, **132**
De Haven, **1-5**, **10**, **36**, **38**, **42**, **79-81**, **85**, **126**, **132-140**, **173**, **193-195**, **199**, **201**, **202**, **230**, **249**, **263**, **272**
Decoy, **227**
Diamond, **227**
Duchess, **227**
Duke of York, **17**, **20**
Dumangang, **133**
Dunedin, **120**

E

Espora, **241**
Eversole, **108**, **150**

F

Fletcher, **108**, **150**
Flying Clipper, **78**
Fort Charlotte, **182**

G

General Belgrano, **237-241**
Goseong, **71**
Green Ranger, **182**
Gurke, **193-194**, **196**, **199**, **259**
Guwolsan, **71**

H

Harry S. Truman, **220**
Hart, **26**, **167**
Henderson, **193-194**
Hipolito Bouchard, **237-238**, **240**

Hull, 3

I

Inchon, **230**
Incredible, **37**, **208**, **212**, 214-216, **225**

J

Jamaica, **13-17**, **20**, **21**, **24**, **26**, **48**, **131-132**, **139-146**, **165-169**, **227-229**, **244**, **247**, **261**, **263-264**, **267**
Jesse Lykes, **67**, **87**, **223**
Juneau, **v**, **36**, **42**, **45-56**, **107**, **114**, **123**, **125-128**, **130**, **132-149**, **164-168**, **170-171**, **173-175**, **184**, **188-190**, **225-226**, **244**, **248**, **253**, **260-264**, **267**, **269**, **272-273**

K

Katsonis, **231**
Kite, **37**, **185**, **214**

L

Leyte, **214**
London, **23**
Lusitania, **113**
Lyman K. Swenson, **36-38**, **42**, **126**, **128-129**, **158**, **167-169**, **173**, **193-194**, **196**, **199**, **202**, **209**, **230**, **249**, **267**, **269**, **272**

M

Maddox, **108**, **150**
Magpie, **24**
Mainstay, **37**, **42-43**, **208**

Mansfield, **36**, **38**, **42**, **79-80**, **81**, **85**, **126**, **128-129**, **140**, **158**, **170-173**, **193-194**, **202**, **209-210**, **230**, **233**, **237**, **249**, **262**, **271**
Marine Snapper, **85**
Missouri, **40**, **101**
Mocking Bird, **37**, **185**, **212**
Monaghan, 3
MTB #21, **125**, **144**, 243
MTB #22, **125**, **143**
MTB#23, **125**, **144**
MTB #24, **125**, **143**
MTB #25, **125**

N

Navasota, **149**
Nissho Maru #32, **55**
Norelg, **82**, **224**
Norfolk, **17**, **19-20**

O

Orbital, **46**
Osprey, **37**, **185**, **212**
Ozungzu, **133**

P

Partridge, **37**, **185**, **212**
PC-823, **68-70**, **74**, **270**
Philippine Sea, **215**, **272**
Piedra Buena, **233**, **237-241**
Pioneer Dale, **67**, **77-79**, **87**, **224**
Pirate, **37**, **42**, **207-208**, **212-217**, **225**, **262**, **273**
Pledge, **29-30**, **37**, **42-43**, **208**, **212-217**, **259**
President Hoover, **223**

R

Radford, **108, 150**
Redhead, 37, **185, 214**
Reinholt, **82-85, 224**
Remora, **36-38, 230-231, 264, 268**
Resolute, **77**
Rochester, **108, 149-150, 189**

S

S-13, **113-115**
Samuel L. Moore, **108**
Santa Fe, **233-237**
Scharnhorst, **18-20, 250, 268**
Segundo, **108, 150**
Sheffield, **17**
Shelton, **108, 150**
Spence, **3**
Steuben, **113**
Stone Crop, **120**

T

Takaghisani Maru, **46**
Tausig, **108**
Titanic, **113**

Toledo, **189, 196, 199, 271**
Triumph, 5, **24, 26, 27, 28, 111, 131, 132, 150, 151, 154, 155, 156, 158, 182-183, 226, 229-230, 260, 262-263, 267**

U

Unicorn, **24, 26, 272**
Unita, **129**

V

Valley Forge, **105-106, 108, 149-154, 156, 158, 160-161, 182-183, 189-190, 226, 229-230, 249, 269-270, 272**

W

Wilhelm Gustloff, **113-115, 264**
Worcester, **213**

Y

YMS-512, **70**
YMS-518, **70**

Printed in Great Britain
by Amazon